The Art of Jihad

The Art of Jihad

Realism in Islamic Political Thought

MALIK MUFTI

Cover art: iStock by Getty Images.

Published by State University of New York Press, Albany

© 2019 State University of New York

All rights reserved

No part of this book may be used or reproduced in any manner whatsoever without written permission. No part of this book may be stored in a retrieval system or transmitted in any form or by any means including electronic, electrostatic, magnetic tape, mechanical, photocopying, recording, or otherwise without the prior permission in writing of the publisher.

For information, contact State University of New York Press, Albany, NY
www.sunypress.edu

Library of Congress Cataloging-in-Publication Data

Names: Mufti, Malik, author.
Title: The art of jihad : realism in Islamic political thought / Malik Mufti.
Description: Albany : State University of New York Press, Albany, 2019. | Includes bibliographical references and index.
Identifiers: LCCN 2018052662 | ISBN 9781438476377 (hardcover) | ISBN 9781438476360 (pbk.) | ISBN 9781438476384 (ebook)
Subjects: LCSH: Islam and politics. | Political realism. | Jihad.
Classification: LCC BP173.7 .M77 2019 | DDC 320.55/7—dc23
LC record available at https://lccn.loc.gov/2018052662

10 9 8 7 6 5 4 3 2 1

For my beloved parents, Özcan and Zuhayr

Contents

Acknowledgments		ix
Transliteration Note		xi
Introduction		xiii
Chapter 1	Competing Visions of Jihad	1
Chapter 2	Imperial Foundations	23
Chapter 3	The Political Turn in Islamic Philosophy	57
Chapter 4	Ibn Khaldun's Synthesis	89
Chapter 5	Contemporary Echoes	123
Notes		141
Bibliography		185
Index		209

Acknowledgments

I wish to thank Rob Devigne, Leila Fawaz, Ioannis Evrigenis, Kenneth Garden, Louise Marlowe, Tony Smith, Riccardo Strobino, and Vickie Sullivan for their generous help in various aspects of this book's preparation. Some sections of chapter 2 and chapter 4 are derived from two of my articles that appeared in *History of Political Thought* (published by Imprint Academic) in 2007 and 2009, respectively, while the section entitled "A Rushdian Revival?" in chapter 5 summarizes parts of my article that appeared in the *Journal of Islamic and Muslim Studies* (published by Indiana University Press) in 2017. I am grateful to both journals and their publishers for allowing me to draw on those articles. I would also like to thank the two anonymous reviewers for SUNY Press for their helpful comments, as well as my editors there, Michael Rinella and Diane Ganeles, for seeing this project through to completion. Above all, I am, as always, deeply grateful for the loving support of my wife Karen and daughter Setenay.

Transliteration Note

In transliterating Arabic and Turkish words, I have followed the transliteration guidelines of the International Journal of Middle East Studies (https://ijmes.chass.ncsu.edu/ijmes_translation_and_transliteration_guide.htm).

Introduction

A few months after the September 11, 2001 attacks, I had a conversation in Washington with a mid-level government official who belonged to the "neoconservative" circles pushing for a radically different American approach to the Near East. At one point he said that his office was interested in ways of "changing Islam"—not, he explained, in the sense of promoting one "moderate" interpretation or current over others, but of coming up with an entirely "new religion." A year later the RAND Corporation published a monograph by Cheryl Benard (wife of Zalmay Khalilzad, subsequently appointed ambassador by President George W. Bush first to Afghanistan and then to Iraq) which began by considering the same question: "It is no easy matter to transform a major world religion. If 'nation-building' is a daunting task, 'religion-building' is immeasurably more perilous and complex."[1] Benard, however, concluded that the United States "needs to avoid the impression" that it is "opposed to Islam," and relayed an exchange in which her interlocutor "conceded that a frontal critique of Islam was not realistic at this time, and that efforts to promote a kinder, gentler, 'defanged' Islam were likely to achieve better results."[2] She therefore advocated U.S. backing for those Muslim elements—designated as "modernists" and "Sufis"—who distance religion from politics, rejecting any notion of an Islamic state and understanding jihad as a purely "symbolic term referring to personal spiritual development."[3] It is these apolitical elements, she argued, which "should be cultivated and publicly presented as the face of contemporary Islam."[4]

Many Muslims naturally take exception to outsiders seeking to "defang" their religion, as is further discussed in chapter 1. In reality, however, the far more formidable challenge comes not from the transformative ambitions of some U.S. government agency or think-tank denizens, or their counterparts in academia, but from structural transformations—culminating in democratization—that arise primarily from internal dynamics and that will compel Islamic societies, as they have compelled other societies, to reconsider long-held verities. In the face of such transformations, the only alternatives need not be reactionary obstinacy and abject capitulation to alien values. The purpose of this book is to identify a third alternative for Islamic polities—a realist political tradition, as indigenous as can be, that can help them navigate through the current upheaval because it has already anticipated some of the most critical challenges of the emergent culture.

In order to delineate the contours of this realist tradition, and also in the process to clarify the character of the challenges looming ahead, it will be helpful to begin with a brief review of the trajectory taken by its Western counterpart. Like all realisms, the Western tradition sets out from a naturalistic grounding; specifically, from the conviction that a proclivity toward evil inheres in human nature. Left to their own devices, without any restraining influence, human beings are disposed to selfishness and aggression, so that power becomes the primary currency, and conflict the ubiquitous feature, of human affairs. Political communities therefore require the repression or sublimation of such natural drives. Law is the primary mechanism for dealing with this problem, but it does not suffice because the aggressive energies cannot simply be extinguished. Hence the other age-old solution: redirecting them against a common external enemy. United by fear and hostility toward this enemy, the community is better able to sustain the more positive bonds that make decent political life possible.

It is evident that such a solution entails a cooptation, rather than outright rejection, of natural impulses such as ambition, belligerence, and deceit. They are disciplined and redeployed, but not eliminated. They become components—subordinate but nonetheless indispensable—of a greater good. An effective statecraft must therefore be prepared to venture into those gray areas where necessity compels the recruitment of lesser evils against greater ones. Such a solution, moreover, can never be final or definitive, because circumstances never stay the same and the calculus of necessary accommodations constantly changes. Sometimes, for example, a more aggressive temper among the populace is called for; sometimes a more pacific one. Determining what is most needful at any given time, and being able to bring it about, are the chief requirements of realist statecraft.

Until recently, the main counterpart to realism has been what may be called idealism, according to which it is in fact possible to perfect human nature. This is accomplished by introducing into human affairs a code of principles and standards that do not derive from nature, but from an external source—such as divine providence or some other sort of transcendent right or law—capable of eliminating the aggressive and dominating aspects of the human character, and thereby establishing, here on earth, a permanently harmonious and peaceful order in both domestic and international politics. This transcendent conception of idealism sometimes takes an activist, even militant, form, in line with its conviction that utopia on earth is within reach so long as no accommodations or compromises are made. When confronted by a social environment impervious to its call, however, it can also lead its adherents to retreat from the world into an expectant monasticism.

In the West, realism gained a decisive upper hand over idealism with the advent of the modern secular era, and assumed a primary manifestation congruent with the spirit of the new age: Machiavellianism, an uninhibited embrace of the impulses and appetites of the now fully liberated self; concerned as Machiavelli himself put it with the *is* rather than the *ought*, and accordingly focused on the "value-free" techniques, the science, of pursuing one's own goals. In contrast to premodern realists such as Thucydides who sought to preserve the distinction between noble and base ends, Machiavelli valorized strife—between factions balanced within a polity, between polities in a multipolar international arena—as well as the qualities of character that strife elicits, for the sake of a notion of "greatness" that seems, to say the least, unmoored from moral concerns. Life thus becomes a war of all against all devoid of restraint.

It takes a very exceptional type of personality to sustain such a steely conception, however, and most twentieth-century realists ultimately shied away from it. Although his entire understanding of international politics rested on "the ubiquity of the desire for power" which "constitutes the ubiquity of evil in human action," Hans Morgenthau, for example—scorched by the horrors of European militarism, and driven perhaps also by fear of nuclear Armageddon—ended up arguing that "as there can be no permanent peace without a world state," and as current circumstances preclude such a world state, "[f]oreign policy should be conducted" in order "to create the conditions" that will make it possible and thereby "make peace permanent" as well.[5]

Morgenthau's American students, lending his tortured European realism their native optimism, went on to formulate its latest articulation, "neorealism." Here the scientific element becomes more prominent. In the interests of scientific parsimony, for example, the decisive human impulses are boiled down to a preoccupation with maximizing power, whether for security or gain. Still, the neorealists start out retaining their predecessors' resignation about the inevitability of conflict, and consequently aspire at first only to understand—not reform—the dynamics of the international system. The most they will allow is that such understanding enables one to make better informed and therefore more prudent decisions. An actor seeking maximum power, for instance, may benefit from the information, gleaned from the historical record, that the pursuit of hegemony tends to generate successful counter-coalitions. And if an appreciation for balances of power induces moderation, according to the neorealists' leading light Kenneth Waltz, all the more so in the case of the most robust of such balances, the bipolar system: "In a world in which two states united in their mutual antagonism far overshadow any other, the incentives to a calculated response stand out most clearly, and the sanctions against irresponsible behavior achieve their greatest force."[6]

And yet it is not at all clear that such information suffices to deter would-be hegemons, because as another prominent neorealist, Robert Gilpin, points out after reviewing the same historical record: "The conclusion of one hegemonic war is the beginning of another cycle of growth, expansion, and eventual decline. . . . Disequilibrium replaces equilibrium, and the world moves toward a new round of hegemonic conflict. It has always been thus and always will be, until men either destroy themselves or learn to develop an effective mechanism of peaceful change."[7] Already in his final clause, however, Gilpin's nerve seems to crack. The old pessimism gives way to a new—to the American character, much more congenial—hope; even a new "faith": "Through the advancement of knowledge, humanity can learn to master the blind forces of change and to construct a science of peace. . . . Political realism is, of course, the very embodiment of this faith in reason and science."[8] In this way neorealism moves farther from its Machiavellian origins (to say nothing of the still older tradition exemplified by Thucydides), and closer to an alternative, altogether new perspective. Within the context of contemporary international relations theory it identifies itself as "neoliberalism" and, in a crafty tactical maneuver, presents itself as merely, in the words of one of its leading practitioners, an "adaptation" or "modification" of realism—one that believes its premises "need to be supplemented . . . not replaced."[9]

While neoliberal theorists, seeking to avoid the charge of naïve idealism leveled at earlier articulations of the liberal outlook, deny that they rely on any super-natural moral code, however, their claim to naturalism differs from realism in that it is grounded neither in the hierarchy of values pointing toward more elevated human ends characterizing the premodern realists, nor in the acceptance of aggressive and dominating impulses characterizing the modern Machiavellians. Instead, they look to a distinctive and even more prosaic set of human drives—primarily the desires for security and prosperity—as the foundations of a permanently pacific and cooperative political order. To the extent that contemporary neorealists embrace those same drives in search of "a more just and more peaceful world," therefore, they allow themselves to be absorbed into the great liberal conception that has come to dominate modern political thought.[10]

Now the new challenger emerges into view. For the promise of ever more security and ever more prosperity, liberalism exacts only the price of renouncing the preoccupation with nobility in favor of an appreciation for equality, of subsuming compelling communal commitments under an overarching valorization of the liberated and autonomous self, and of replacing the lust for power with much tamer appetites. Some in the West have viewed the advent of the liberal age with trepidation, fearing that its valorization of the self will generate a hedonism and nihilism that will pave the way either for the emergence of some new kind of tyranny from within, or for enervation and defeat at the hands of more vigorous enemies from without. Even those critics, however, acknowledge the humane, mild, altogether extraordinarily attractive character of the bargain liberalism offers. One of them asks, "[W]hat apocalypse has ever been so kindly?"[11] Others see no credible alternative arising from any quarter, and so confine their concerns to an "end of history" devoid of idealism and heroism.[12] But the most prevalent response by far has been to embrace liberalism whole-heartedly. Even where religion, say, does survive—as in America—it has adapted itself to the new conditions by taking on a more individualistic emphasis on personal spirituality and self-fulfillment.[13]

It is this phenomenon that is now bursting—perhaps most visibly in its political manifestation, democracy—upon the Muslim world.[14] Abdolkarim Soroush, the Iranian dissident who is one of the most discerning Muslim thinkers of our time, assured his listeners at a 1995 seminar in Tehran on "cultural development" that they have little to fear: "Those who speak with agitation about development do so because they do not have a clear view of science and cannot separate the issue of knowledge from the other components of Western civilization . . . Science is not like the customs, morality, art, and habits of the infidels and Westerners."[15] Soroush acknowledges that the Western variant of modernizing development rested on a "recognition of the base, lowly and afflicted aspects of human existence, and their employment in building the new world," and acknowledges also that this led to dire consequences: "From this point on private vices become public virtues. . . . Thus a new morality was gradually born. . . . Low and vile values came to power, were upheld, played their part proudly in building the new livelihood, and came to be held in esteem. . . . A revolution has truly taken over that brought high things down to a low level."[16] But he insists that the baser aspects of secular liberalism are not universally "inevitable prerequisites and values for development."[17] It is possible to isolate them from the "cornucopia of blessings" otherwise offered: "tolerance and lenience, . . . beautiful arts, . . . [the] essential unity of religions, . . . ecumenism, a flourishing of science, . . . women's rights, . . . democracy."[18] By shielding it from any taint of "debauchery and corruption," by defending it against various forms of anti-rationalism as well as an unhealthy "Sufi-like morality based on asceticism,"[19] and by arraying it instead in its most appealing features, Soroush seeks to give the newcomer—modern science and its bounty of material, cultural, and social liberation—as fine an introduction as possible: "no human being seeking the truth today can fail to feel kindness, pleasure, and sensitivity toward this plump guest in the family of humanity."[20]

Soroush's assurances that the various aspects of this modernizing transformation can be so easily disaggregated remain open to question.[21] Nevertheless, he makes a compelling case that must be taken seriously, all the more so as it is in turn grounded in a serious reading of both Western and Islamic political thought. The same cannot be said of others who embrace the revolution without a clue as to what they are giving up and what they are getting in return. Among these are some of the cruder Turkish Westernizers, such as Hüseyin Cahit, who wrote in 1898 that "Ibn Khaldun's philosophy of history belongs to the infantile age of the science of history. Since then, the child has grown. . . . The modern science of history is to come from Europe, not from the Arabs."[22] Or the former Education Minister Hamdullah Suphi Tanrıöver, who proclaimed with satisfaction in 1928 that the "old literature is doomed to moulder away."²³ Perhaps more surprisingly, however, a similar disdain for one's own intellectual heritage is sometimes heard among Islamist circles as well. The Tunisian Rashid Ghannoushi, for example, whose Nahda Party won the first free elections following the revolution of 2011, once asked many years earlier: "I wonder how our students feel studying 'Islamic philosophy' when it offers them only a bunch of dead issues having nothing to do with the problems of today."²⁴ The realist tradition in Islamic political thought which this book seeks to explicate is perhaps the most unduly neglected strand of this altogether too hastily dismissed heritage, and the objective here will be to show that it does in fact offer insights relevant to the problems and challenges of today.

Chapter 1 sets the stage through the contemporary debate on jihad, or justified warfare in Islam; a debate that is emblematic of the broader impasse in modern Islamic political thought. Its main protagonists are often designated in the relevant literature as "militants" who advocate uncompromising offensive jihad on the one side, and "modernists" who assert full compatibility between Islam's teachings and contemporary norms of international relations, including the imperative of striving for permanent peace, on the other. While both clearly proceed from an idealist outlook, this chapter will argue that even as the modernists increasingly dominate today's discourse, pointed criticisms by the militants are pushing them more and more in a comprehensively liberal direction. There is accordingly a lacuna in contemporary Islamic political thought occupied by realism in other cultures. It is this absence of a realist perspective in Islamic writings on war, peace, and statecraft, an absence surprisingly neglected in the relevant scholarship, which the present study seeks to address.

Chapters 2 through 4 trace the evolution of just such a realist tradition in the premodern Islamic world. The thinkers reviewed lived in such different times and places, however, and pursued such diverse intellectual agendas, that it may be asked whether one can even speak of a "tradition" encompassing them all. These chapters proceed from the premise that to the extent they alerted the best and brightest of their times to the full range of political pathologies—including some of the vulnerabilities which modern critics ascribe to liberalism—in order to rally them to a flexible type of engagement that recognizes the ubiquity of evil and strife in this world, they can indeed be grouped together coherently. Acknowledging that great intellects resist neat or comprehensive categorization, then, this study seeks only to outline the contours of an Islamic realism along the same lines that one can speak (as any number of university course syllabi attest) of a Western realist tradition encompassing figures as varied as Thucydides, Machiavelli, Hobbes, and Morgenthau, as well as his American offspring. At the same time, no claim to exhaustiveness is made here. There are no doubt other thinkers worthy of inclusion in a less preliminary overview of medieval Islamic realism, but whose contributions to it will need to be elaborated on elsewhere.

Chapter 2 begins by outlining three primary responses—revolutionary idealism, ascetic idealism, and Islamic realism—to the establishment of an imperial Islamic state after 661 CE, then goes on to identify systematically some key features of the emerging realist current as reflected in the writings of figures such as Ibn al-Muqaffaʿ, al-Jahiz, and the anonymous author of a ninth-century military manual. These include not only features shared with realist traditions everywhere—a this-worldly focus on prudent statecraft, for example, or a recognition of the ubiquity of conflict in worldly affairs—but also those where the Islamic tradition is distinctive: in its insistence on the political centrality of religion, in its rejection of scientific certainty, in its valorization of hierarchy as opposed to equality, and in its adherence to empire as the optimal framework for virtuous action.

The central figure in chapter 3, the philosopher Ibn Rushd (d. 1198), is shown to articulate a philosophical expression of the emerging realist tradition outlined in the previous chapter. His project, carried out in large part through a highly critical reading of his predecessor Ibn Sina, entailed affirming the philosopher's obligation to attend to the well-being of the political community by engaging actively in political reform; delineating a clear division of labor between rational and religious inquiry rooted in his understanding of the diversity of human types; and eschewing both theoretical certitude and legal dogmatism in favor of an artful and flexible imperial statecraft. The pursuit of such an agenda, according to Ibn Rushd, constitutes a practical (political and moral) counterpart and complement to the theoretical pursuit of the Good. This focus on Ibn Rushd's realism is accordingly informed by but also departs from influential alternative perspectives rejecting the notion that *political* philosophy occupied any significant place in medieval Islamic philosophy,[25] or privileging more mystical or gnostic currents as the true representatives of Islamic philosophical thought, or reading Ibn Rushd and other Muslim philosophers as advocates of private contemplation rather than political engagement.

Chapter 4 presents Ibn Khaldun (d. 1406) as the synthesizer of the insights of his predecessors into a comprehensive realist vision; a vision with a normative goal (a civilization in which human creativity can flourish to its maximum potential) that shapes a practical agenda: establishing a polity of sufficient magnitude, complexity, and duration—in short, an empire—capable of sustaining advanced culture. Ibn Khaldun's realism emerges in his account of how political communities, as well as the normative ties of solidarity that bind them together (ʿaṣabiyya), grow through conflict and conquest from primordial origins to ever more complex polities; and how internal contradictions can then set in that begin a process of enervation and decline. Contrary to the prevailing interpretation, however, it is argued here that this is far from a fatalistic vision. The purpose of his historical account is to draw instructive lessons from the past that can help future statesmen counter the engines of social and political decay. This analysis of Ibn Khaldun as a systematic synthesizer of the realist elements formulated by earlier writers stands in contrast to influential scholarly views of him either as an orthodox thinker who reasserted the legal authority of religious scholars over political rulers, or alternatively as so unique as to be a "solitary genius" without predecessors and successors in the history of Islamic political thought.[26]

With the core elements of the Islamic realist tradition having now been outlined, chapter 5 opens by briefly discussing an efflorescence of Ibn Khaldunism during the waning years of the Ottoman Empire, exemplified in the writings of the scholar Kâtip Çelebi, in order to show the persistence of this tradition beyond Ibn Khaldun. It then leaps ahead to today, interpreting the current upheavals besetting the post-Ottoman political order in the Near East as a region-wide "ʿaṣabiyya crisis" of identity and legitimacy, and reviewing the range of responses this crisis is eliciting, from the revolutionary militant to the proto-democratic. The chapter ends by considering the recent revival of interest in Ibn Rushd among Arab intellectuals, with a view to determining the extent to which the long-forgotten realist tradition may yet prove relevant in the context of the democratizing and liberalizing flood tide looming on the horizon of the Muslim world.

CHAPTER 1

Competing Visions of Jihad

The scholarship on contemporary debates about jihad typically differentiates between two main approaches: a "fundamentalist" or "militant" approach which advocates offensive warfare for the propagation of Islam, and a "modernist" approach which argues that Islam's teachings are fully compatible with the liberal norms of international relations prevailing globally today, including the imperative of striving for permanent peace.[1] Despite the recent prominence of the militants, moreover, much of this scholarship recognizes that the latter, more pacific approach has for some time now been growing increasingly hegemonic in contemporary Islamic thought.[2]

Rather than trying to ascertain which of the two contending approaches is better grounded in authoritative religious texts, the central argument here will be that the increasingly trenchant criticisms of their militant antagonists are forcing the modernists step by step toward a more thoroughgoing liberalism, one that encompasses domestic politics and governance as well. At the same time, such an assessment of the dynamic between the two approaches will delineate the empty space, currently unclaimed, occupied by realist theories in other cultural traditions, which in turn will justify the investigation, undertaken in subsequent chapters, into what a much earlier set of Muslim thinkers had to say on the subjects of war, peace, and statecraft.

Modernist Evolution

The modernist argument that Islamic law is compatible with contemporary norms of international law—indeed that in many respects it anticipated them—rests on a number of core premises: that Islam may not be imposed coercively, that offensive or aggressive war is therefore prohibited, and that peace is consequently the norm between Muslim and non-Muslim polities. Citing the Qurʾanic prohibition on coercion in religion (2:256), the modernists unite behind the judgment of the Egyptian scholar Mahmud Shaltut (1893–1963) that "lack of faith is not a [legitimate] cause for war."[3] His compatriot and fellow leader in the vanguard of the modernist movement, Muhammad Abu Zahra (1898–1974), agrees: "war is not justified . . . to impose Islam as a religion."[4] Scripture apparently suggesting otherwise only seems that way because the context is ignored: a Qurʾanic verse (9.29) that calls for fighting non-Muslim "people of the Book" (such as Christians and Jews) until they are forced to submit, for example, is said to refer only to those who had previously provided a *casus belli* by violating treaties or repressing the practice of Islam.[5]

One of the most striking features of the modernist argument is the insistence of many of its proponents on distinguishing their approach from a "classical doctrine" of war and peace said to have been developed by Muslim jurists during the eighth and ninth centuries, and rooted in the exigencies of that imperial period. The Egyptian modernist Mohammad Talaat al-Ghunaimi, for example, ascribes to "the classical Muslim doctrine" which encompassed the generality of "the earliest Muslim jurist-theologians, broadly speaking," the conviction that "the 'raison d'être' of the Islamic state is to achieve the universal rule of Islam" through "a holy war of aggression under the doctrine of the jihad . . . a theory that is generally irreconcilable with the modern standards of international law."[6] Likewise, the American modernist Sherman A. Jackson cites the "majority" of "classical jurists" as approving "aggressive jihad" as a "communal requirement to be carried out at least once every year."[7] There was of course a range of opinion on jihad among the medieval jurists, and even the proposition that a majority sanctioned offensive jihad has been disputed.[8] Whatever the historical truth of the matter, the salient point here is that so many modernists oppose themselves to a putative classical doctrine because the more pacific interpretation of Islamic international law they seek to advance rests on a distinction between the medieval and modern contexts.

Thus, Muhammad Abu Zahra describes the classical judgment that war is the fundamental principle or basis of relations between Muslims and non-Muslims as temporally contingent (*ḥukm zamānī*);

a reflection of the fact that the jurists of Islam's "monarchical" era lived in an age of continuous warfare, so that many of them could not conceive of peaceful relations beyond a tactical and temporary truce.[9] In reality, Islam "considers war to be one of Satan's incitements"; an "odious" disruption of normal life to be avoided whenever possible.[10] Similarly, the division, with various modifications and refinements by individual jurists, of the world into an "abode of Islam" (*dār al-Islām*) and an "abode of war" (*dār al-ḥarb*) is one modernists such as the Syrian Wahba al-Zuhayli reject as having "no textual support, for no provision is made for it either in the Qurʾan or in the Hadith,"[11] and as deriving instead solely, in the Lebanese Sobhi Mahmassani's words, "from the reasoning of the jurists based on the actual practice" of their time.[12]

A holistic and therefore correct reading of Islamic scripture will show, the modernists claim, that there is neither contradiction between, nor abrogation of, various Islamic rulings; they can all be shown to affirm the same rationale and objective—to wit, that the true basis of international relations in Islam is peace.[13] What then does justify the waging of war in Islam? The modernist answer focuses overwhelmingly on defense. As Mahmud Shaltut puts it, just cause for war "is limited to repelling aggression as well as safeguarding the [Islamic] mission and freedom of religion."[14] This means not only resisting enemy attacks on Muslim lands, but also intervening in foreign countries if the authorities there attempt to persecute their Muslim minorities or repress the dissemination of the Islamic message. Most modernists, moreover, extend such defensive considerations to a further justification for war: to combat injustice and cruel tyranny more generally. They could hardly do otherwise, given the Islamic imperative to do good and oppose evil. As a result, Shaltut and his colleagues are also led to sanction warfare "for the sake of rescuing the weak . . . for the sake of resistance against tyranny and despotism."[15] Wahba al-Zuhayli describes interventions on behalf of the victims of injustice as corrective war (*ḥarb taʾdībiyya*).[16] Since the imperatives of securing freedom of religion and of preventing tyranny and oppression are not restricted to Muslim victims, such wars may also be waged on behalf of "a friendly or allied nation even if it is not Islamic."[17]

In both its reactive (self-defense) and proactive (humanitarian intervention) dimensions, this modernist conception of legitimate war parallels its Western counterpart extending from medieval Christian idealists to the secular liberal tradition of more recent times. In line with the shared premise that war is an evil to be avoided, furthermore, the parallels extend to the conduct of warfare as well. Thus most modernists agree that responsibility for determining when there is just cause, and for initiating and prosecuting the war to its conclusion, lies exclusively with the existing political authority (*walī al-amr*).[18] They also agree in limiting the scope of war as much as possible, here as well departing from the classical doctrine on the grounds of its obsolescence. Classical doctrine, for example, reflecting the norms of its time, understood war as a conflict between the entire peoples—rather than just the formal armed forces—of the polities involved. The majority of medieval jurists therefore sanctioned engaging and killing all enemy able-bodied adult males, even as they exempted other categories of people so long as they did not participate in combat, such as children, women, the elderly, and the physically or mentally infirm. Likewise, they did not differentiate between public and private property when ruling on what goods may be seized in conquered enemy lands. Such rulings were "correct when war in the past was considered a struggle between the peoples of two states. But today, when war has been restricted to organized armies, it is necessary to restrict the effects of war to them as well, not to the rest of the population, and within the limits of what concerns governments only."[19]

If one steps back from the narrowly legalistic disputations about which categories of people are specifically cited in the religious texts as being exempted from harm, in other words, or about how war booty is to be collected and distributed, and one focuses instead on the overall spirit of those texts, it becomes possible according to the modernists to formulate rulings that are more appropriate to the conditions and norms of our own time. Since the civilian-military distinction is much sharper today, the general principle protecting "those who do not fight and have no say in war" can be extended to include able-bodied adult males as well, in line with contemporary international law.[20] Wahba al-Zuhayli, for example, extends the exemption from harm to enemy war reporters and chaplains, and argues that military medical personnel—who do after all contribute to the enemy war effort by healing soldiers—should also be detained as prisoners of war rather than killed.[21] Similarly, private property in conquered lands can now be left alone, and enemy civilians may even be compensated for damage done to their property by Muslim forces.[22] The same logic applies to Muslim armies, which have been transformed into clearly defined professional organizations: the share of legitimately seized enemy public property that used to be distributed as booty among individual Muslim warriors is now to be assigned to the Islamic state's formal military budget instead.[23]

Other issues differentiating the classical doctrine and modernist approaches include the treatment of prisoners of war, with some of the earlier jurists allowing Muslim commanders a choice only between killing or enslaving them, and others—on the principle of serving the public interest (*maṣlaḥa*)—giving commanders more discretion to ransom prisoners (for example, in exchange for Muslim prisoners or for money) or even to release them unconditionally. Seizing on this principle of public interest, and pointing to the obsolescence of practices such as slavery, virtually all modernists by contrast narrow the options to those sanctioned by contemporary international norms: releasing prisoners upon the cessation of hostilities either unconditionally or as part of reciprocal exchanges.[24]

A similar contrast between the two approaches relates to the *dhimma* contract with non-Muslims who come to live under Islamic rule. In the classical doctrine, it entailed paying a poll-tax called the *jizya*, along with various legal and social restrictions such as having to wear distinctive attire, in return for being permitted to observe one's religious practices individually and communally. The earlier jurists generally agreed on the subordinate character of *dhimma* status, but differed on its eligibility, with some restricting it to monotheistic "people of the Book," and others extending it to all except Arab pagans (who could only choose between conversion and death). The modernists, however, in addition to tending toward the most inclusive eligibility interpretation, insist that *dhimmīs* "are not a second class below the Muslims."[25] They are citizens (*muwāṭinūn*) and not subjects (*raʿāya*), and the *jizya* they pay is not a punishment but a tax in lieu of the *zakāt* tax which Muslims must pay and also in lieu of the military service from which non-Muslims are exempt. Indeed, if non-Muslims elect to serve in the armed forces voluntarily, they are exempted from the *jizya* as well.[26] The influential contemporary Egyptian scholar Yusuf al-Qaradawi, who shares modernist views on many key points, adds that since the true intent of Islamic rulings is not to insult or punish non-Muslims, and since the words *dhimmī* and *jizya* have apparently acquired offensive connotations for non-Muslims over the years, there is no objection to replacing them with other, more neutral, terms.[27] As for demeaning provisions on clothing, travel, building, and so on, these are dismissed by the modernists as later innovations reflecting the conditions and mores of the ʿAbbasid age, and as being no longer applicable. According to Sobhi Mahmassani for example, most of these "restrictions and obligations do not appear in the scriptural texts, but were imposed by practice and custom and habit, and were mandated by treaties and covenants for practical political reasons, and were at any rate temporary."[28] The modernists thus seek to accord all non-believers living in Islamic states today fully equal status.

When it comes to peaceful relations with non-Muslims living beyond the rule of Islam, finally, the classical doctrine generally envisioned only a tactical truce (*hudna*). Given the over-arching principle of permanent war until the triumph of Islam, such truces were products of necessity (*ḍarūra*)—when the enemy proved too strong to defeat, or when achieving victory entailed too high a cost—and by definition temporary, though some jurists granted Muslim authorities the discretion to extend them repeatedly in accordance with the public interest. In reality, the modernists point out, the imperatives of geopolitics often induced Muslim leaders to conclude treaties that went well beyond tactical ceasefires, with stipulations that varied according to relative capabilities and that occasionally even entailed the Muslims having to pay tribute or cede territory to the other side. Such imperatives in turn led the Shafiʿis, for example, to elaborate a third "abode" of international relations—the "abode of treaty" (*dār al-ʿahd*) which provided local autonomy in return for the payment of tribute—and likewise to sanction neutrality as a legitimate option alongside war and peace.[29] Their legalistic scruples, moreover, led those jurists to insist on the binding character of such treaties, barring Muslims from breaking them even if the other side engaged in oppression of its Muslim subjects.[30] Generally more pragmatic jurists such as the Hanafis, however, rejected the concept of binding treaties, preferring the flexibility afforded by renewable—but also suspendable—temporary ceasefires.

Literally making a virtue out of necessity, the modernists by contrast invoke what they see as the general spirit of Islamic scripture to affirm the validity, and indeed desirability, of permanent peace treaties. They describe the primarily ʿAbbasid jurists who could conceive only of temporary ceasefires as having misconstrued the continuous warfare of their (in fact) historically contingent circumstances as an immutable reality.[31] At the same time, however, many modernists in this instance take strong issue with the Hanafis who appealed to the public interest to argue that treaties may be broken under emergency conditions—a pragmatic argument with serious implications for the integrity of religious and international law alike—and insist instead on absolute fidelity to treaty commitments.[32] As long as Muslims are allowed to practice and propagate their faith freely, then, the modernists favor the conclusion of permanent and binding peace treaties on a fully equal status with all non-Muslim states. Since the United Nations Charter accords with this requirement, modernists such as Muhammad Abu Zahra and Wahba al-Zuhayli are ready to assert that every compliant member state should be considered as belonging to a permanent global "abode of treaty."[33]

Perhaps the most distinctive feature of the modernists' progressive approach, then, is their rejection of the assertion made by "some of the ancient and modern writers" that war is a permanent condition of international relations.[34] It is this conclusion—that war can and should be eliminated altogether—that above all differentiates these modernist idealists not only from the classical doctrine jurists, but also from those "ancient and modern writers" who proceed from the premise expressed by Ibn Khaldun when he wrote that war "is something natural among human beings." Wahba al-Zuhayli, for example, cites and rejects Ibn Khaldun's thesis, arguing instead that war is not a natural but "a social phenomenon that can be terminated."[35] It is also this conclusion that reveals most tellingly the affinity between Islamic modernist doctrine and the Western liberal tradition in international relations theory.

In both Islamic modernism and Western liberalism, the legal imperatives that apply in the domestic sphere have equally binding counterparts in the international sphere. As the Moroccan modernist ʿAbd al-Khaliq al-Nawawi puts it, states are governed in their interactions by the same ethical code as individuals are in theirs, so international treaties are as morally and legally binding as private contracts.[36] In both approaches, therefore, international commitments—expressed in bilateral and multilateral treaties—can finally effect the establishment of a universal and permanent peace analogous to domestic civil order: "Beginning with the Covenant of the League of Nations after WWI and culminating in the signing of the United Nations Charter after WWII," argues the modernist Sherman Jackson, "the territorial integrity of every nation on earth has been rendered inviolable. In effect, this development dismantled the general 'state of war' and established peace as the assumed and normal relationship between all nations. . . . [U]nder a 'state of peace,' there is no obligation to wage aggressive jihad."[37] In both approaches, only violations of such a peace can justify—indeed oblige—individual or collective military action, whether in the form of self-defense against aggression or humanitarian intervention against religious and other kinds of oppression. And in both approaches, finally, police actions necessary for the restoration of universal peace must themselves conform to regulations that set strict limits on their conduct and scope in order to minimize the harm done to combatants and non-combatants alike.

The modernists, in short, adopt a progressive view of history according to which conditions, as well as the norms corresponding to them, have evolved radically beyond those that underlie the classical doctrine, so that chauvinism and hostility have gradually given way to tolerance and positive cooperation. They seek therefore to distance themselves from what Yusuf al-Qaradawi describes as "dogmatic and narrow opinions that cling to the letter of what is found in books that were written at a time other than ours, and for a society other than ours, and under conditions other than ours. Such opinions do not bind us . . . [because] everything in our lives has changed quantitatively and qualitatively from what it was in the days of those jurists."[38] The alternative approach the modernists seek to articulate, which they claim better conforms both to modern conditions and to the true spirit of Islam, rests then on what is said to be a more holistic methodology that analyzes and relates all the authoritative injunctions (in the Qur'an and Hadith) on a specific subject together, instead of selectively choosing passages without adequately taking their contexts into account. Such an approach, they argue, can successfully explain away apparently contrary evidence, whether textual or historical.

Thus, a Prophetic Tradition on fighting until the unbelievers embrace Islam is said to have referred only to the hostile Arab polytheists of Muhammad's time, and even so to have constituted a "temporary" injunction necessary for the initial establishment of Islam and so is no longer in effect.[39] The "wars of apostasy," waged under Caliph Abu Bakr after the Prophet's death to bring rebellious Arab tribes back into the fold of Islam, are likewise depicted as directed against political sedition rather than "freedom of conscience and belief."[40] The Qur'anic injunction to fight non-Muslim monotheists until they submit and pay the *jizya* is explained, as has already been noted, as referring specifically to those who had already aggressed against the Muslims and thereby given justification for war. So too, the Qur'anic verse (5.51) against befriending Christians and Jews is described as a specific warning against divulging secrets to "the warriors and people of aggression among them," and contrasted with other verses and traditions encouraging friendly relations with non-hostile Christians and Jews.[41]

Historical examples of practices incompatible with modernist standards are explained in the same way: either as products of a contextually specific necessity that is no longer applicable, or as indefensible deviations that should be repudiated altogether. When discussing the killing of enemy prisoners during the early years of Islam, Wahba al-Zuhayli for example describes such incidents as rare "individual instances for specific conditions" necessary for the establishment of the Islamic state.[42] One much cited episode is the execution in Medina of almost all adult males of the Jewish Banu Qurayza tribe, which broke its alliance with the Muslims and colluded with their Qurayshi enemies. While acknowledging that some of those executed belonged to protected categories (such as the elderly) even by the standards of many classical doctrine jurists, ʿAbd al-Khaliq al-Nawawi points to the critical implications for the survival of the new religion of an alliance between Banu Qurayza and Quraysh to argue that the Medina incident was a "special case" under "extreme circumstances" that was not an application of the normal Islamic rules of war but an "exception;" a "particular ruling" for an "exceptional situation."[43] Such actions, in short, are viewed by the modernists as arising from imperatives specific to the founding of the Islamic polity, and consequently as becoming illegitimate thereafter. Thus, any practices in the period following the Prophet and his immediate successors that did not conform to modernist standards of just cause and legitimate rules of war are described as "deviations"—arising from personal or cultural pathologies—that cannot be ascribed to Islam.[44]

To conclude, then, according to this progressive historicist reading it is only in the modern context, when international relations have evolved to the point where universal norms against aggression and persecution have begun to take hold—eliminating the only valid justifications for jihad—that the true and fundamentally peaceful spirit of Islam can finally manifest itself in full clarity.

Militant Revolution

Militant writers denounce the modernists as defeatists—apologists seeking to appease the Western Orientalists under whose thrall they have fallen by proving how peaceful and inoffensive their religion is.

The consequent alleged distortion of the Islamic ideal is then explicated through a point-by-point refutation of the modernist approach to international relations. The starting point of this critique is the Islamic imperative to do good and combat evil, which the modernists deploy in order to justify humanitarian intervention against gross acts of tyranny and oppression. According to the leading figure in the vanguard of the modern militant movement, Egypt's Sayyid Qutb (1906–1966), however, the "greatest servitude in the view of Islam is the submission of human beings to laws legislated for them by other human beings."[45] Any political, legal, cultural, economic, or social system that delegates ultimate decision-making authority to mere mortals constitutes a "deification of human beings," setting up some of them as lords and masters over others and thereby usurping the sovereignty of God. This is the true tyranny, and the prime Islamic imperative must therefore be understood as "the destruction of the kingdom of man in order to establish the kingdom of God on earth."[46]

Now, says Qutb, the fundamental error of the modernists becomes apparent: they conflate Islam as a faith—in which, it is true, there can be no coercion—with Islam as a regime, which mandates action to eliminate all "institutional and governmental" obstacles to the worship of God alone and obedience to His Law.[47] Once those obstacles are removed and Islam as a regime is established, people can then choose in "true freedom" whether to embrace Islam as a faith as well, or whether to remain as *dhimmī*s under the Islamic regime. What they cannot freely choose to do is revert to a regime of human sovereignty and man-made laws.[48] Moreover, since Islam aims at liberating all of humanity from human subservience, the Islamic regime must be established throughout the world, so that "truth and falsehood do not coexist on this earth."[49] And since, finally, the oppressors and usurpers of God's sovereignty will not "surrender their power merely in response to instruction and explanation," it is necessary to coerce them into doing so.[50] Hence the core rationale for jihad.

Contrary to the modernists, then, war *is* waged for the universal imposition of Islam—as a regime if not as a faith—and such war must be offensive as well as defensive. Whereas the modernists adopt a holistic reading of the Qurʾan and Hadith to conclude that injunctions to fight unbelievers reflect a transient stage of history, for Qutb and his successors it is not the scriptural injunctions to war but the scriptural injunctions to pacifism that reflect a temporary and transient reality: the particular exigencies of the Prophet's initial Meccan and early Medinan periods.⁵¹ According to Qutb, the correct progression in Islam is one in which fighting went from being forbidden, to being permitted, to being obligatory only against those who first initiate hostilities, to being obligatory against all unbelievers.⁵² In its final and true articulation, Islam mandates "taking the initiative." Even if the unbelievers choose to desist from attacking Islam in return for being allowed "to continue the subservience of man to man within their own territorial borders," in other words, "Islam will not countenance such a truce."⁵³ Contrary to the modernists, accordingly, there can be no question of permanent peace with non-Islamic political regimes. Islam rejects that "cheap peace which consists merely of securing the particular patch of land whose inhabitants embrace the Islamic faith." War is "the permanent condition, not the transient case" in the militant understanding of Islamic international relations.⁵⁴

Most subsequent militant writings on war and peace constitute mere elaborations of Qutb's ideas. One example is ʿAbd al-Malik al-Barrak's 1997 *Responses to Obfuscations and Falsehoods about Jihad*, which begins with a general denunciation of those "who live their lives in a spirit of abject defeatism and feelings of inadequacy" toward the West, reflected in their assertion that Islam sanctions jihad only as defense against aggression. Among the many such "links in the chain of lies" named are Mahmud Shaltut, Muhammad Abu Zahra, ʿAbd al-Khaliq al-Nawawi, and Wahba al-Zuhayli.⁵⁵ Al-Barrak's primary target, however, is Muhammad Saʿid Ramadan al-Buti, a prominent Syrian religious scholar until his assassination in 2013 (see below), whose book on jihad echoed most of the modernist themes and concluded that "permanent peace" (*ṣulḥ dāʾim*) is possible with non-Muslims.⁵⁶ Al-Barrak buttresses his counter-argument that the true justification for war is indeed unbelief by describing some of the earliest Islamic campaigns, during and after the Prophet's life, as purely "offensive" (*hujūmī*).⁵⁷ In the case of the Persian Empire, for example, "the Muslims were the initiators of the invasion, not the Persians. In fact the Persians did not want to fight, and indeed sought and requested a peace."⁵⁸ He also affirms that the division of the world into two hostile abodes is not "an innovation . . . of the jurists, as some would have it," but rather a correct reflection of the permanent conflict between polities submitting to a divinely ordained Islamic ideal and polities governed by man-made laws.⁵⁹

Al-Barrak fleshes out the implications of his approach when discussing the rules of war and conquest. If just cause for war is provided by unbelief rather than aggression, modernist attempts to maximize the sphere of immunity from harm lose their grounding. The point is illustrated by the execution of the Jewish Banu Qurayza adult males, at least some of whom, al-Barrak writes, could not have contributed in any way to the hostile actions of their tribe. It is also illustrated by the fate of Jaʿd ibn Dirham in the eighth century, who was rightly put to death even though he expressed his heretical views discreetly in a treatise esoteric to most people.[60] Having asserted the legitimacy of killing unbelievers for their unbelief, al-Barrak is then able to define as legitimate targets all those *capable* of contributing to enemy operations, whether they actually participate in combat or not. It is only on this basis that women, children, and the elderly may potentially be considered immune from attack.[61] Even though such innocents may not be deliberately targeted, however, they may of course fall victim to collateral damage: often, for example, it is impossible to reach well-protected tyrants "without sacrificing some people."[62] Here the distinction with the modernists lies not so much in formal principle—there can be no reasonable notion of justified war that does not accommodate collateral damage in some manner—as in underlying temperamental drive, or the extent of impatience with humanitarian niceties in the face of a greater good. "Significant casualties," writes al-Barrak, "are inevitable in the establishment of God's religion and law on His earth, and the road is not strewn with roses." One should not, therefore, "value temporal life more than it is worth."[63]

A similar animus characterizes militant views on relations between Muslims and non-Muslims after the conclusion of war. The modernists are said to err once again when they interpret texts such as verse 60.8 of the Qurʾan as encouraging friendly relations with non-hostile unbelievers. In fact, says al-Barrak, that verse refers only to those non-Muslims who are incapable of contributing to the enemy's campaigns, such as women, children, the elderly, and monks who have retreated into spiritual seclusion. Even then, he adds, citing a twelfth-century commentator, the rationale is not amity but self-interest: facilitating the enslavement of their women, and encouraging their men to follow the example of monks by abandoning fighting and all other worldly pursuits, so that the martial spirit of the unbelievers is weakened and they become easier to subjugate.[64] More generally, the correct treatment of subject non-Muslims who are allowed to maintain their religion—as reflected according to al-Barrak by the words and actions directed at them by the Prophet and his successors, and by the humiliating restrictions subsequently imposed on them—is one in which "the degradation and ignominy are as clear as the sun."[65] Though other militants may not go so far, most would agree that *dhimmī*s cannot be considered "citizens" on a fully equal footing with Muslims.[66]

Finally, and again following Qutb, the definition of "abode of war" as including any polity governed by man-made laws means that "all the countries of the world today are lands of unbelief and apostasy" and accordingly constitute legitimate targets of offensive jihad.[67] Such a definition shifts the militants' focus from the "far enemy" (non-Muslim polities) to the "near enemy" (the leaderships of nominally Muslim polities)—a shift that assumes center stage in revolutionary tracts such as *The Neglected Imperative* by Muhammad ʿAbd al-Salam Faraj, the ideologue of the Egyptian Islamic Jihad organization who was executed in 1982 along with the assassins of President Anwar Sadat.[68] A crucial corollary to this shift in focus is the negation of the conventional requirement that only rulers have authority to declare and conduct war. Since the current rulers are all illegitimate, and since jihad always remains an imperative, that authority devolves to any private groupings or even individuals who are obliged to take up the banner of jihad.

Faraj's treatise exhibits several characteristic features of the militant mindset, most notably a resistance to getting bogged down in idle theoretical disputation: the prescriptions of jihad "can easily and simply be studied, and in a very, very short time. . . . [For] knowledge is available to all."[69] One need only begin fighting, and God will surely intervene—even to the extent of reversing the "laws of nature"—to bring about a victory that will leave "everything . . . in the hands of the Muslims" and usher in the final reign of truth and justice.[70] This is not to say that militant thinkers ignore the scholarly tradition altogether. Many of them, like many of their modernist opponents, are ready to buttress their arguments by turning to authoritative jurisprudential sources whenever opportune.[71] But, as is to be expected in a revolutionary movement, their clear overall inclination is in favor of action over scholarly deliberation. It is this combination of individual activism and utopian triumphalism, so succinctly expressed by Faraj, that explains much of the appeal that the militant vision holds for Muslims who find the prevailing political and social conditions of their lands intolerable.

At the same time, however, certain equally characteristic difficulties arise when a more permissive attitude on violence is coupled with an anarchic structure in which there is no recognized authority to determine what is excused by necessity and the general interest. Some of those difficulties are illustrated by the career of Abu Muhammad al-Maqdisi (b. 1959), a Palestinian writer who has emerged, in one apt assessment, as "the key contemporary ideologue in the Jihadi intellectual universe," second in influence only to Sayyid Qutb himself.[72] A one-time mentor of Abu Musʿab al-Zarqawi, the late leader of al-Qaʿida in Iraq, al-Maqdisi like his fellow militants advocates a proactive war against all unbelievers until the imposition of a universal Islamic regime in which people are no longer subservient to other people but to God alone.[73] While insisting that "I do not wish to extinguish the firebrand of fervor in the breasts" of militant youths, however, and while continuing to defend the 9/11 attacks on New York and Washington and to praise their perpetrators as "heroes," he has grown increasingly concerned about the "harmful and destructive" effects of many recent militant actions.[74]

Al-Maqdisi's critique centers on the twin imperatives of acting in accordance with the dictates of Law (*al-sharīʿa*), and acting in accordance with the dictates of reality (*al-wāqiʿ*).[75] The Law forbids certain actions (such as deliberately targeting non-Muslim women, children, and others who have no part in fighting), and allows others (such as killing adult male prisoners or retaliating against aggressors). It is not sufficient, however, for an action to be allowed by Law—it must also make sense in terms of Islamic interests. And the greatest interest or "fruit" of jihad is the establishment of an actual Islamic state on some piece of ground.[76] Only such a state can serve as a haven in which Muslim warriors can take refuge and from which they can venture forth. Only such a state can generate the military might necessary for victory. Only such a state, crucially, can house a political leadership with the vision to act in accordance with the dictates of both law and reality, and with the authority to rally the Muslim masses around it.[77] Without such a state and such a leadership, militant action can only remain undisciplined and disjointed, lacking any overall strategic vision.

It is on the basis of both legal and practical considerations, then, that al-Maqdisi takes issue with some militant behavior. On the legal level, there are lines that cannot be crossed: "the ends do not justify the means, for we are not Machiavellians, and the means must be as legitimate as the ends."[78] Illegitimate means include the killing, whether motivated by excessive zeal or a mercenary coveting of the victims' property, of people whose moral transgressions (selling alcohol, for example) do not suffice to warrant capital punishment. Al-Maqdisi underscores the dangers of this slippery slope by affirming—in language that evokes Marxist critiques of "lumpen" criminals—that he himself while in prison came across youths who justified such "theft" and "usurpation" as jihad.[79] Likewise, al-Maqdisi condemns the deliberate targeting of non-Muslim non-combatants, such as the bombing of the International Committee of the Red Cross offices in Baghdad in 2003 and the execution of the relief worker Margaret Hassan there in 2004, as acts that could only be perpetrated by "highwaymen" and "criminals."[80] Also illegal, when better alternatives are available, is the collateral killing in indiscriminate bomb attacks of non-Muslim non-combatants and, even worse, of Muslim innocents.[81]

It is only when better alternatives are not available, and the interest involved is "absolutely necessary" (*maṣlaḥa ḍarūriyya qaṭ'iyya*), that the collateral—but not deliberate—killing of innocents and non-combatants is allowed.[82] Even then, however, a calculation must be made on the practical level as well: does the benefit of the proposed action outweigh its harm? Executing and decapitating a male American civilian and then posting the deed on the Internet, for example, may be legally permitted strictly speaking, he writes, but "I do not support it nor do I like it." The reason is that at a time when war is being waged not just on the battlefield but in the media as well, it distorts and harms the reputation of jihad.[83] Similarly the 9/11 attacks, laudable as they were in many ways, remained a retaliatory action that did not advance the prime imperative of establishing a territorial state, and indeed diverted many enthusiastic young Muslims from more constructive pursuits.[84]

Such concerns impelled al-Maqdisi to take issue with his former protégé Abu Mus'ab al-Zarqawi publicly. In a 2005 interview on Al-Jazeera television during a brief interlude between prison terms, for example, al-Maqdisi began by praising al-Zarqawi and insisting that he "will not accept that what I may have in terms of reservations or suggestions be exploited in order to malign this blessed personality." Then he criticized both the tactics attributed to al-Zarqawi—"When did we ever advocate killing women and children? When did we ever advocate killing the generality of the Shi'a?"—and the overall strategy adopted by him and by al-Qa'ida:

> I do not disagree with Abu Mus'ab or with others on fighting the enemy occupying Muslim lands in Palestine and

Afghanistan and Iraq. I do not disagree with them but I have my own priorities. . . . Every stage has its priorities, and in this stage I do not want Iraq or some other place to become a crematorium for the sons of this movement. . . . I mean, I want to achieve a result.[85]

For al-Maqdisi, the prime imperative of consolidating an authoritative Islamic state on some piece of territory takes precedence over skirmishes here and there with the Americans or their proxies—skirmishes that are unlikely to yield positive results precisely because they lack a centralized leadership capable of maintaining the proper balance between what is legally binding and what is realistically necessary, and of judging which actions advance the cause and which actions retard it.[86]

This brings al-Maqdisi to a crucial question: where is such leadership to be found? He insists vehemently that the answer does not lie in the ballot box. First, following Sayyid Qutb, democracy is a "religion" inimical to Islam because it usurps God's sovereignty by delegating law-making authority to mere human beings.[87] Second, it relies on the judgment not of the best human beings, but of a "deviant majority" likely to be motivated by the basest motives.[88] Third, it reflects a liberal desire to "extinguish the flame of jihad": the United States seeks to impose democracy because it wants to "invent a domesticated 'modern' Islam . . . with neither claws nor fangs, stripped of swords and ammunition."[89] True Islam consequently mandates jihad against representative assemblies ("the palaces of polytheism and fortresses of paganism") and all who participate in them, whether as elected representatives or as those who elect them.[90] Instead, al-Maqdisi asserts—without going into further detail—the desired leadership should somehow emerge from the ranks of the warriors themselves. Having demonstrated their worth by repelling "the Russians and Serbs and others in Afghanistan and Chechnya and Bosnia . . . are they not the most devoted, clean, and trustworthy people for governance?"[91]

Yet, as al-Maqdisi acknowledges, time after time in practice that has not happened—"for reasons that those who undertake jihad should study and contemplate and review"—and leadership has passed instead to elements who fail to maintain the correct balance in pursuit of the correct ends.[92] The vagueness of his solution to the leadership question, therefore, only serves to accentuate the concerns he raises. In the context of a war that considers all existing political structures, as well as the individuals who sustain them, legitimate targets of violence, who is to decide which actions are "absolutely necessary" and whether better alternatives are or are not available? Al-Maqdisi's objections to the tactics used in Iraq, for example, prompted "our brothers in the field" to reply that he did not understand the exigencies of their situation.[93] More recently, in an even more vivid illustration of the authority problem for militant idealists, al-Maqdisi has denounced the leaders of the "Islamic State" in Iraq and Syria—despite their having established the territorial state he had long been calling for—as being even "worse than the Kharijis" because of their "ignorance" and "stupidity," as well as their readiness to spill the blood not only of Muslims with whom they disagreed (including al-Maqdisi himself), but also of the many misguided youth who came to join their cause.[94]

The Authority Problem

At the same time, of course, the identical problem applies to the modernists as well. Indeed, it lies at the core of what is perhaps the most telling criticism of them by the militants. The modernists' reluctance to sanction prosecution of jihad by any actor other than the established political leaderships of Muslim states means—because so many of those leaderships today are so manifestly lacking in legitimacy, so evidently driven by despotic motivations rather than virtue or the general interest—that the jihadi imperative to do good and combat evil is effectively suspended. To insist on allocating a monopoly on the use of force to such leaderships is therefore to partake in their illegitimacy, and to advocate acquiescence in an indefensible status quo.

An instructive illustration is provided by the Syrian religious scholar Muhammad al-Buti, who affirmed that no one may wage jihad "except the leader of the Muslims, whether he is called caliph or imam or king or president." Rather than justice, moreover, the decisive criterion for leadership is the power (*shawka*) to enforce decisions: the injustice of the ruler possessing such power has no disqualifying effect, while by contrast no amount of piety or justice displayed by private individuals and groups can compensate for the compelling power commanded by political leaders.[95] Obedience to the ruler is therefore "obligatory" as long as he does not explicitly command his subjects to do what Islam considers sinful.[96] Al-Buti emphasized the point: "it is not permitted in Islamic law to rebel against the leader or head of the Muslims, no matter what injustice or immorality he exhibits."[97] Such a stance is evidently vulnerable to charges of hypocrisy and collusion with tyrants, as in al-Barrak's withering attack. Al-Buti himself revealed the perils of his position when he exempted Egypt's Islamist militants from his denunciation of rebellion—because of Anwar Sadat's peace agreement with Israel (opposed by the Syrian regime at the time)—while confirming the illegality of similar uprisings in Syria and its ally Algeria.[98] The untenability of al-Buti's stance became painfully clear when the Arab uprisings hit Syria in early 2011. After criticizing the demonstrators in a televised interview, he was videotaped fleeing his mosque in order to avoid getting caught up in another anti-regime protest and, two years later, was himself assassinated.[99]

Al-Buti's predicament suggests that the attempt to formulate a theory of jihad compatible with liberal principles of international law becomes problematic without a parallel approach in domestic politics. It is a predicament illustrated also by ʿAli Jumʿa, Egypt's Grand Mufti until 2013, who has been featured as another leading modernist alongside al-Buti.[100] Jumʿa backed the military coup which ousted Egypt's first democratically elected government on July 3, 2013, as well as the violent repression of dissidents that followed it.[101] For the probable majority of modernists who will recoil from such authoritarianism, the most appealing path left open will likely be the one leading to a much more comprehensive embrace of political liberalism. The apprehensions of al-Maqdisi and other militants about the democratizing and liberalizing tendencies of the modernist approach to war would therefore seem to be warranted.

Such apprehensions will be further heightened by consideration of the parallel trajectory taken by the Christian just war tradition. According to one review of that trajectory, following Augustine (354–429), "who decisively arrested the apolitical or even antipolitical tendencies of early Christian thought," Thomas Aquinas (1225–1274) emerged as a main proponent of reconciling church doctrine with the worldly rationales of imperial rule.[102] Thomas required that war be waged on the authority of a political leader; that it arise from an intention "that aims at either the promotion of good or the avoidance of evil"; and that it target unbelievers—"not indeed for the purpose of forcing them to believe but to compel them not to hinder the faith of Christ"—as well as apostates, who by contrast are obliged to recant.[103] Thomas's successor Francisco de Vitoria (ca. 1485–1546) further elaborated on the acceptable justifications for war, including not only ensuring the right "to preach and announce the Gospel" unhindered, but more proactively defending foreign subjects from exceptionally inhumane treatment at the hands of their rulers.[104] The parallelisms with Islam extend to the laws of war as well. The Thomistic conviction that international relations is regulated by a transcendent legal order led Vitoria to specify who may or may not be targeted. While otherwise innocent civilians may not be killed except as unintended collateral damage, they "may be plundered or (unless they are also Christians) enslaved." Not only combatants, on the other hand, but "all the adult men in an enemy city are to be thought of as enemies . . . and therefore they may all be killed."[105]

In this account, however, a compelling logic drives the evolution of the Western just war tradition away from its legalistic origins. The application of Christian morality to political practice during and after the Roman Empire appeared to reveal a growing incongruence between the dictates of Christian law and the dictates of realpolitik. If Thomistic legalism strictly specifies the kinds of transgressions that warrant a just declaration of war, the authors of this review ask, "how far back in historical time may and ought one go to right old injustices?"[106] Likewise, what about prudent acts of necessity such as Britain's breaking of international covenants when it violated Norwegian neutrality during the war against Nazi Germany, or preemptive war more generally against an emerging but still potential threat?[107] Over time, such practical difficulties in ascertaining where justice truly lies, and how it is to be reconciled with the imperatives of necessity, contributed to an inexorable and decisive shift toward a conception of international relations marked by the greater "prominence of self-defence and self-concern, rather than concern for others or for society as such."[108]

It is easy to see how this gradual depreciation of morality, and the concomitant appreciation of self-help in international relations, left standing as the main alternatives in the Western tradition—at least in the eyes of many contemporary Muslim observers—a realpolitik devoid of restraints on the one hand, and a liberal theory of permanent peace grounded primarily in selfish concern for security and prosperity on the other. Hence Abu Muhammad al-Maqdisi's denunciations of both Machiavellianism and liberalism. More specifically, hence also the vehemence of his attacks on the democratic inclinations of more and more modernists, in which it is possible to discern a profound anxiety that the compelling logic of liberalism's relentless advance in the West—along with its enervating consequences for martial élan—will be replicated in the Muslim world as well.

∽

This is not the place for a comprehensive review of the challenges peculiar to militant idealism, or of the difficulties in sustaining a state of permanent revolution and permanent war until the elimination of all injustice. Ever since the passing of the "rightly-guided caliphs" in the seventh century, at any rate, political outcomes in the Muslim world have almost never been of the kind to satisfy the school of Qutb and al-Maqdisi. During the past two or three decades, moreover, it has become increasingly clear that the global wave of liberalization execrated by the militants is approaching the shores of Islam as well. Populist Islamist movements such as Turkey's AK Party and the various Arab Muslim Brotherhoods have undergone a consequential shift from opposing democratic norms and practices to embracing them—a shift that has led to bitter polemics between them and their militant critics. A growing body of polling data has been revealing the dissemination of such norms to the populace as a whole across the Muslim world.[109] At the same time, the intensification of terrorist attacks close to home appears to have also begun shifting public opinion, just as al-Maqdisi warned it would, against the militant approach to jihad.[110] Even as the ramifications of the Arab uprisings that broke out in 2010–2011 continue to unfold, then, already visible through the fire and haze are signs suggesting that the Muslim world may be preparing to welcome Abdolkarim Soroush's amiable "plump guest in the family of humanity." A central conclusion of this chapter is that such developments are likely to further the convergence between international relations modernists and the democratizing bandwagon—precisely because the modernist requirement that just war may only be taken up by legitimately constituted authorities is bumping up against the increasingly hegemonic norm that only democratically elected political authorities are legitimate.

But the challenges posed by the dictates of realpolitik to Muslim theorists of legally justified war, as to their counterparts in other traditions, will not disappear merely because leaders are chosen democratically. How, for example, is one to ascertain the spirit of the law in situations not explicitly anticipated by the binding texts? Or to select the best course of action even when the law does leave a range of acceptable options to the discretion of the ruler? Most fundamentally, even as an unduly flexible approach to the law's moral underpinnings can lead to a utilitarianism in which self-interest ends up sweeping aside all considerations of nobility and virtue, so too an excessively inflexible application of the law, grounded in an unwarranted faith in human perfectibility, can lead the modernists to a new variant of idealism—as unrealistic as that of the militants—in which the permissibility of peaceful relations with non-Muslims transmogrifies into an insistence on enforcing permanent universal peace. Thus:

> The world order that Islam seeks is one from which war is banished once and for all. . . . For any people to enter the new order, it is necessary for them to disband their army, destroy their weapons, or surrender them to the world government, except those necessary for maintenance of public order or for the enforcement of the verdicts of the courts of law. The covenant of peace under which no dispute or claim may be settled except through adjudication, arbitration or negotiation, must be offered to all peoples. Every people is entitled to it, as well as obliged to join it.[111]

How then to reconcile the requirements of virtue with the exigencies of the real world? The question itself suggests a useful definition of statecraft, the crucial mediating principle. The historian Fred M. Donner, lamenting the fact that the "precolonial Islamic tradition of statecraft has simply been allowed to die," has argued that the "recovery and reconstruction of the full Islamic tradition of statecraft and war should be a desideratum for all historians of the Islamic lands."[112] As the preceding discussion seeks to demonstrate, such a recovery would benefit more than just historians. The Muslim modernists, whose approach seems more consonant with the emerging spirit of our age than that of their militant rivals, and who seem to be blithely following in the footsteps of their Western counterparts, may therefore want to reconsider their hasty dismissal of "those ancient writers" and their investigations into virtuous and effective statecraft.

CHAPTER 2

Imperial Foundations

Controversy over core political issues such as the relationship between religion and government, the legitimacy of rule, and the justification for war emerged almost as soon as the Muslim community became an Islamic polity. The major fault lines on such questions began to crystallize with the civil war over succession that broke out—after the assassination of the third caliph ʿUthman in 656—between the supporters of ʿAli ibn Abi Talib (cousin and son-in-law of the Prophet) and Muʿawiya ibn Abi Sufyan (scion of a powerful Meccan clan that had initially opposed Muhammad's message). Unable to secure a decisive outcome on the battlefield, the two sides agreed to refer their dispute to arbitration. This led some of ʿAli's more zealous supporters to recoil on the grounds that one could not "arbitrate" between good and evil; that "judgment belongs to God alone." ʿAli's acquiescence (however reluctant) to arbitration meant he was conceding the absolute rightness of his position, and therefore forfeiting his claim to leadership. ʿAli reportedly replied that rejecting human judgment, however fallible, amounted to anarchism: "you are saying that there should be no government, whereas the people cannot but have a ruler, whether righteous or wicked."[1] The dissidents, who came to be known as Kharijis, nevertheless took up arms against ʿAli and eventually assassinated him.

Kharijism appears to have originated as a reaction of some Arab elements to the emergence of an increasingly centralized, ultimately imperial, state. In what follows, "state" denotes the institutions of governance through which rulers aspire (with variable success) to consolidate control over policy formulation and execution—a minimalist definition meant to sidestep questions of the applicability to an

Islamic context of European conceptions of the state as an abstract or impersonal entity with particular attributes of sovereignty, representation, and judicial autonomy.[2] According to Patricia Crone, Kharijism "marks a transition from a tribal to a complex conception of society" occasioned by the Islamic conquests and the emergence of a diverse empire: "This was more than the Kharijites could accept. By expelling all dissenters as infidels . . . they hoped to create a Muslim society as uniform as the tribal one from which they hailed."[3] Their ranks later swelled by marginalized non-Arab converts attracted by their radical egalitarianism, the Kharijis became, at least in their most prominent manifestations, the permanent revolutionaries of the Islamic realm, ever ready to employ violence not only against the political authorities, but against any Muslim who did not adopt their views.

These Kharijis, then, combined an embrace of activism with a rejection of expediency. Their revolutionary idealism became a chronic and destructive feature of political life in the Muslim world, but, like most such utopian movements, they remained for the most part a marginal force. Far more consequential was the tension between two other sets of responses to the emergence of the imperial state that began when Mu'awiya ascended to the caliphate and founded the hereditary Umayyad dynasty in Damascus in 661, and continued after the 'Abbasid revolution of 750 moved the empire's capital to Baghdad: one set of responses which shared the idealistic Khariji yearning for certitude and perfection but did not believe they could be found in the political realm, and one which shared the Khariji commitment to political action but realistically accepted the uncertain accommodations such a commitment must entail. It is this dichotomy—between an apolitical, even ascetic, idealism on the one hand, and an engaged worldly realism on the other—that constitutes the central concern of this chapter.

The next section begins by questioning an influential scholarly perspective on this central dichotomy, then outlines some salient characteristics of the ascetic idealist current as articulated by its leading representatives. The remaining three sections of this chapter seek to identify the main features of the emerging realist counter-current: the drive to combine and concentrate political and religious/legal authority in the hands of the imperial state (with Ibn al-Muqaffa' as a leading exemplar), the effort to reconcile equality and hierarchy as necessary but potentially conflicting elements for the well-being of a vast and diverse empire (with al-Jahiz as a leading exemplar), and the advocacy of artful and pragmatic statecraft—including, inevitably, warcraft—against dogmatic certitude and inflexibility of any kind (with the anonymous author of an early 'Abbasid military manual as a leading exemplar).

Self and State in Islam

In his influential reading of the transition to a more complex Islamic polity, the Orientalist Hamilton Gibb argued that a decisive turning point came around the middle of the eighth century when a group of Umayyad court secretaries and translators—themselves for the most part of non-Arab origin—introduced Greek and especially Persian traditions of imperial statecraft that constituted an alien "discordant element" in "the general fabric of Islamic culture." These efforts intensified with the early 'Abbasids, culminating in the famous "inquisition" (*miḥna*) imposed by Caliph al-Ma'mun (r. 813–833) to bring the religious establishment under state control. Even though the *miḥna* failed, the continuing "influence of the secretarial class" ensured, according to Gibb, that a tradition of realpolitik would henceforth remain in permanent tension with religious orthodoxy. This "kernel of derangement" in Islamic political thought would be exacerbated by the absence of a wall of separation (such as the one that arose in the West) between the temporal and spiritual spheres.[4] As a result, both sets of concerns suffered. The religious establishment found itself forced to accommodate political necessity and expediency in a way that progressively undermined the integrity of religious law (*sharī'a*); a trajectory Gibb traced from al-Ash'ari (d. 936) to al-Mawardi (d. 1058) to Ibn Jama'a (d. 1333).[5] At the same time, the ultimate subordination of political authority to *sharī'a* as interpreted by the religious establishment—a subordination affirmed, according to Gibb, by the likes of Ibn Khaldun (d. 1406) and al-Dawwani (d. 1502)—produced a system of government, culminating with the Ottomans and Mughals, that failed in the end to keep up with the innovativeness and dynamism of its secular Western counterparts.[6]

In another variant of the Gibb thesis, Patricia Crone and Martin Hinds reject the notion of a foreign imperial model, arguing instead that the caliph's all-encompassing primacy was an indigenous and original feature of Islam: "the caliphate clearly did fuse religion and politics from the start, whereas they were only twins on the other side. Neither the Persian nor the Byzantine emperor was on a par with the *khalīfa*, who was intrinsic to the acquisition of worldly prosperity and heavenly bliss alike."[7] When the court secretary Ibn al-Muqaffa' suggested a codification of religious law around 755, therefore, or when Caliph al-Ma'mun inaugurated his inquisition in 833, they were engaged according to Crone and Hinds in attempts to *restore* caliphal authority over the law.[8] The abolition of the *miḥna* in 848 thus represented the successful culmination of a decades-long campaign of "usurpation" by the religious scholars (*'ulamā'*) of the caliph's authority.[9] "[T]he textbook view of the nature of the caliphate is substantially correct from this point onwards," continue Crone and Hinds, and they highlight al-Mawardi and Ibn Khaldun as leading affirmers of *'ulamā'* primacy in the sphere of law.[10] Finally, and again now in line with Gibb, they conclude that "the victory of the [religious] scholars" had "profound" and ultimately negative consequences for Islamic political thought and practice:

> The historically significant point is that a ruler who has no say at all in the definition of the law by which his subjects have chosen to live cannot rule those subjects in any but a purely military sense. . . . The state was thus something which sat on top of society, not something which was rooted in it; and given that there was minimal interaction between the two, there was also minimal political development: dynasties came and went, but it was only the dynasties that changed.[11]

Both the Gibb thesis and its Crone and Hinds variant, then, posit a fundamental conflict between political and religious authority to which is ascribed the subsequent history of Islamic authoritarianism and stagnation. More recently several aspects of this "textbook view" have come under criticism. According to Muhammad Qasim Zaman, for example, the notion of a zero-sum conflict between the royal court and religious scholars (many of whom were, after all, appointed officials) cannot be sustained: leading *'ulamā'* such as Abu Yusuf, Malik, Ibn Hanbal, and al-Mawardi all recognized the caliph's share in religious authority; at the same time, there is "little evidence" that "with the exception of al-Ma'mun" any early 'Abbasid caliphs claimed exclusive religious authority for themselves.[12] Other scholars go even further, arguing that if anything the autonomy of the religious scholars allowed them to "limit the monopoly of the state" and serve as an "effective check on the ruler" in ways that tempered arbitrary rule while at the same time endowing government with legitimacy, and thus altogether enhanced political order and stability.[13]

Still, such historically more nuanced readings do not go as far as denying any tension whatsoever between the political and religious establishments. Zaman himself, for example, acknowledges the limits of overlap between the two spheres,[14] and recognizes the distance between a scholar such as Sufyan al-Thawri who described the temptation to collaborate with rulers even for a righteous cause as "the deceit of the devil," and a court secretary such as Ibn al-Muqaffaʿ who—some eighty years before the *mihna*—veered "rather blatantly in the direction of making the caliph the source of religious authority" and viewed religious scholars "essentially as functionaries of the caliph, co-opted into the state apparatus."[15] The distance separating these two contemporaries reflects the fateful gap between political withdrawal and engagement that emerged in early Islamic thought.

In order to illustrate the magnitude of the chasm that opened up here, it may be best to begin with Sufyan's predecessor, al-Hasan al-Basri (642–728), who has been described as the "greatest religious genius of the period."[16] Al-Hasan was born into servitude, according to Ihsan ʿAbbas's insightful biography, to Persian parents who were then manumitted into the status of *mawālī*, or non-Arab converts to Islam. His father worked at farming and his mother was a servant.[17] Not surprisingly, given this background, he found himself drawn at an early age to the figure of Abu Dharr, a companion of the Prophet noted for articulating the resentments of the downtrodden.[18] Al-Hasan participated in the eastern military campaigns as a young man, but because the *mawālī* were denied the glory afforded ethnic Arabs, ʿAbbas writes, he grew further embittered and came to the conclusion that whereas "the *mawālī* in war do not accomplish anything that makes them immortal, they are capable of achieving something memorable in the arts of peace."[19] He accordingly returned to Basra and soon gained recognition as a religious scholar.

Sadness at humanity's sinful state and fear of divine punishment emerged as the central features of both his public teaching and his private demeanor—to the point of "sickness," as ʿAbbas puts it; to the point that he was said not to have laughed in thirty years.[20] A contemporary described him so: "When you saw him, it was as if he had just buried his mother. When he sat, it was as a prisoner sits who is about to have his head struck off. When he talked, he talked the talk of a man who has been condemned to the Fire."[21] In terms of politics, al-Hasan affirmed the primacy of the religious scholars as ultimate authorities on God's law, and did not shy from denouncing government officials if he believed they violated that law.[22] He was also said to have criticized ʿAli for submitting to arbitration with Muʿawiya, since he had right on his side—a rejection of political necessity that seemed to bring him close to the Kharijis. But there is a crucial difference: whereas the Kharijis went to war for their beliefs, al-Hasan preached renunciation of worldly pursuits and patience in the face of injustice and oppression. He stood by during Ibn al-Zubayr's revolt even though he admired him, opposed subsequent uprisings by Ibn al-Ashʿath and Ibn al-Muhallab, and more generally urged his followers not to take sides in civil conflicts but to focus on personal reform instead.[23]

Al-Hasan al-Basri's apolitical asceticism proved enduringly influential. The afore-mentioned Sufyan al-Thawri (716–778), for example, opposed the ʿAbbasid revolution in 750 and spent the rest of his life evading the authorities.[24] So intense was his focus on the private cultivation of spirituality that he is reported to have said it is better to recite the Qurʾan than to go on military campaigns against the unbelievers,[25] and to have argued—contrary to prevailing opinion among religious scholars of his time—that jihad is obligatory only in defense.[26] Sufyan's protégé, Abu Ishaq al-Fazari (ca. 730–802), marked a new stage in the relationship between this current in religious scholarship and the imperial state. A traditionist more comfortable transmitting received opinion than engaging in personal reasoning and offering juristic interpretations of his own, al-Fazari's scholarship was later criticized by the likes of Ibn Qutayba and Ibn al-Nadim, and his book on warfare has been described aptly as "quite anodyne."[27] Nevertheless, he emerged as "the leading figure" among the first generation of "warrior scholars" who "began to congregate in large numbers along the Arab-Byzantine frontier."[28] This new-found interest in warfare did not reflect a turn to worldly pursuits—the warrior scholars continued to practice and preach personal asceticism and remained aloof from court politics.[29] Rather, jihad had now become the latest arena of competition between the ascetic idealists and the imperial state.

Around 780, the ʿAbbasid caliphs began assuming direct command over combat operations and deploying imperial troops recruited from different parts of the realm (notably Khurasan) in order to reclaim the mantle of jihad from the ascetic volunteers, and perhaps also to neutralize "incipient military aristocracies" along the Byzantine frontier.[30] The ascension to the caliphate in 786 of Harun al-Rashid—backed by his advisors from the Barmakid family of noble Persian *mawālī* who dominated court politics for several decades—further consolidated the concentration of power in the imperial capital. Al-Fazari's significance lies in his opposition to caliphal jihad and his assertion of the primacy of "scholar-ascetics" as authorities in this arena as well.[31] His followers fought as unpaid irregulars who viewed combat as a form of personal devotion aimed at the afterlife rather than as a tool of statecraft, in many cases actively sought martyrdom, and accordingly evinced a certain "disregard for the actual outcome of war"—often to the frustration of official commanders trying to organize disciplined campaigns.[32] Al-Fazari himself maintained a distinctly cool stance toward the state, reportedly banning from his lectures in Damascus anyone who "had dealings with the government (*man ya'tī al-sulṭān*)."[33]

Al-Fazari's colleague ʿAbdallah ibn al-Mubarak (736–797) wrote a book on jihad that epitomizes the spirit of the apolitical ascetic idealists. In it, he "shows even less interest than Fazari in the general theme of obedience to the imam [leader], or in the issue of who may grant permission to wage war. Instead, the *Kitab al-Jihad* exhorts people to take the obligation upon themselves, to volunteer."[34] Ibn al-Mubarak writes that whenever Muslims engage in jihad, angels descend to record their intentions: only those who fight for the sake of God alone will enter paradise, as opposed to those seeking worldly ends such as dominion or glory or profit.[35] The book is suffused with yearning for martyrdom, and recounts story after story along the same lines: the Muslim at Qadisiyya who prayed to exchange his repulsive wife for a heavenly houri; the warrior who asked God to make his wife a widow and his son an orphan; the religious scholar who donned a white robe before battle while marveling at how fine blood looks on a white background.[36] "The Islamic state and its goals," Michael Bonner observes, "have little to do with all this."[37] More than any legal differences about the scope and conduct of combat, it is this focus on personal salvation and martyrdom, and disregard for political ends, that distinguishes the tradition extending from al-Hasan al-Basri through Sufyan al-Thawri, al-Fazari and Ibn al-Mubarak from the more mainstream religious scholarship exemplified by al-Shaybani (d. 805), who helped shaped both the Hanafi and later Maliki doctrines on war.[38]

Centralization

No one could be farther removed from this ascetic idealist tradition than ʿAbdallah ibn al-Muqaffaʿ (ca. 720–756). Born into Persian nobility and a convert to Islam, Ibn al-Muqaffaʿ grew wealthy as an Umayyad official, survived the ʿAbbasid revolution, and for a time remained active in the urbane intellectual circles of Kufa and Basra. He was associated in particular with the cadre of translators built up by the Umayyad secretary Salim Abu al-ʿAlaʾ, known primarily for sponsoring the transmission of the Greek "mirror for princes" literature, adapted in the form of a purported correspondence between Aristotle and Alexander the Great.[39] Ibn al-Muqaffaʿ himself translated a large quantity of material from Persian into Arabic, including the *Kalila wa Dimna* fables of ultimately Indian origin, as well as several works of Persian imperial history and administrative practice. He also wrote treatises of his own, such as the *Kitab al-Adab al-Kabir*, which offers practical and moral advice to princes as well as courtiers and other figures of standing. In stark contrast to Sufyan al-Thawri, who urged that all books in Greek be burned because of their possibly blasphemous content,[40] Ibn al-Muqaffaʿ expresses his appreciation for the Persian—and also Greek[41]—influences reflected in this treatise by opening it with a description of "the people before us" as in every way superior, and more proficient in religious and worldly matters alike.[42]

The most important of Ibn al-Muqaffaʿ's own surviving works is the "Epistle on the Companions," apparently addressed to the second ʿAbbasid caliph al-Mansur (r. 754–775). Written only about five years after the ʿAbbasid revolution, it displays a preoccupation with political legitimacy and imperial order—and hence with the close tie between state and religion. As one of the key translated Persian texts, *The Testament of Ardashir*, had put it: "Beware of taking lightly those who seek leadership by exhibiting asceticism (*zuhd*) and irascibility (*ghaḍab*) on behalf of religion, for no sooner do people congregate around a religious leader than he wrests authority from the king's hands."[43] Ibn al-Muqaffaʿ's epistle accordingly begins by warning the caliph in vivid terms of the unorthodox and extreme views prevalent among his crack Khurasani troops: one who sets out with such a force is like a man riding a lion—a terrifying sight for all to see, but most terrifying for the rider himself.[44] He urges the caliph to issue an authoritative statement of religious doctrine through which he can impose "ideological control" over the troops.[45] More generally, he points to the multiplicity of norms and rules across the realm that often contradict each other and lead their adherents to "spill blood unjustifiably" on behalf of their diverse understandings of what constitutes right usage and precedent. He therefore recommends that the various accounts of legal tradition and reasoning be codified in an exhaustive compendium so that the caliph can review them, formulate a divinely-inspired opinion (*alladhi yulhimuhu Allah*) appropriate to each case, and thereby resolve the mishmash of true and false opinions into "one correct judgment"—and so that his successors can do likewise as changing circumstances warrant.[46] Ibn al-Muqaffaʿ emphasizes the need for flexibility in religious-legal analogical reasoning (*qiyās*) by insisting that public welfare must always guide legal judgment, giving as an example the prohibition against lying: should one not lie to someone pursuing a man in order to kill him unjustly?[47]

The caliph's judgment, then, is circumscribed only by rulings unambiguously specified in scripture, so that he may not "prohibit prayer, fasting or pilgrimage, nor prevent the implementation of mandatory punishments, nor permit what God forbids."[48] "All other matters" requiring personal reasoning, by contrast—the adjudication of legal differences discussed above as well as other political questions relating to advance and retreat in war, collection and distribution of resources, employment and dismissal of personnel, and so on—are the governing authority's exclusive prerogative.[49] In this manner Ibn al-Muqaffaʿ carves out an autonomous sphere for political action, with distinct standards and ends of its own. He accordingly goes on to propose the professionalization of the army through a series of reforms including removing from it responsibility for tax collection (a practice that had fostered corruption), and establishing comprehensive personnel registers so that troops could receive salaries accurately and on a regular basis.[50] As for civilian religious scholars (*ahl al-fiqh wa-l-sunna wa-l-siyar wa-l-naṣīḥa*), they are to be incorporated into the state bureaucracy as well, tasked with monitoring the populace at large and helping to suppress "innovation" and "sedition."[51]

Beyond legal and administrative centralization, finally, Ibn al-Muqaffaʿ "seems to have been one of the first" to advocate the blending (*ikhtilāṭ*) of people from different ethnicities and regions into a broader, more cosmopolitan imperial Islamic identity.[52] What emerges as a result is a conception of an integrated and hierarchically organized polity far removed from both the individualism and the leveling egalitarianism of the ascetic idealists. Ibn al-Muqaffaʿ, who is also "one of the first authors" in Islam "to employ the categories of *khāṣṣa* [elite] and *ʿāmma* [commonalty],"[53] emphasizes the indispensability of a well-ordered political framework for human well-being by quoting the poet al-Afwah al-Awdi:[54]

> The people will not prosper if there is no distinction between
>   them and no head over them;
> And they will have no head so long as their ignorant
>   ones prevail.

Ibn al-Muqaffaʿ therefore ends his epistle by highlighting the importance of statecraft because, he says, just as the multitudes need elites to take care for and guide them, so too the elites need a leadership capable of uniting and protecting them.[55]

It is in this regard for the worldly needs of elites and multitudes alike, as well as for the distinctions between them; in his insistence on rational statecraft having ultimate legal authority and overseeing professionalized governing institutions so that political order is secured and "ignoramuses" (*juhhal*) do not prevail; and in his quest for an imperial structure that is both cosmopolitan and centralized enough to sustain such an order, that Ibn al-Muqaffaʿ stands as a pioneering exponent of an alternative, realist, approach within Islamic political thought. Ibn al-Muqaffaʿ himself met a cruel death at the hands of his enemies at the age of 36, and while it remains unclear how much of an actual impact if any this epistle had on Caliph al-Mansur, he epitomizes in his writings better than anyone else the logic of the unfolding transition to empire characterizing his time.

Similar themes can be found in the works of Ibn al-Muqaffaʿ's colleague and friend ʿAbd al-Hamid al-Katib (ca. 688–750). Also from a family of *mawālī*, probably of Persian origin, ʿAbd al-Hamid became a secretary in the circle of Salim Abu al-ʿAlaʾ (whose sister or daughter he married), ended up in the employ of the Umayyad prince Marwan ibn Muhammad in 732, and continued to serve him loyally from the time the latter became caliph in 745 until the ʿAbbasid revolution claimed the lives of both men.[56] Like Ibn al-Muqaffaʿ, ʿAbd al-Hamid's focus is on the imperatives of practical statecraft, so he too grants rulers absolute authority in the application of Islamic law, and warns against those who seek to disrupt the political order through religious appeals.[57] While using the same term as Ibn al-Muqaffaʿ— "inspiration" (*ilhām*)—to describe the divine basis of the ruler's judgment,⁵⁸ moreover, he too urges his addressees to couple reliance on God with the pursuit of wisdom as well as human machination and planning.⁵⁹ ʿAbd al-Hamid's worldly realism is particularly evident in his "Letter to the Crown Prince," composed on behalf of Caliph Marwan to his son ʿAbdallah who is about to set off on a military campaign against the Kharijis. Here he observes that evil "inheres in people as fire inheres in a [flint]stone,"⁶⁰ and offers practical advice such as letting one's underlings mete out punishment while reserving forgiveness—and the gratitude it engenders—for one's self.⁶¹

The longest section of the epistle, constituting some two-thirds of the total, deals with military matters—not so much combat tactics per se, as the deployment or disposition of troops. Here too, his focus is primarily secular, as suggested by the greater frequency of the word "war" (ḥarb) as opposed to "jihad." And here too there is evident reliance on Greek and Persian motifs, not least in the repeated stress on "caution" (ḥadhar) and the preference for stratagem and subterfuge over brute force.⁶² According to Ihsan ʿAbbas, ʿAbd al-Hamid's contribution lies precisely in his amalgamation of Greek wisdom with some elements of a distinctively "Islamic ethics" to create "the most important military document not only in the Umayyad age, but for a long time after as well"—as evidenced by the (attributed and unattributed) traces of it found in treatises extending up to the fifteenth century at least.⁶³ Wadad al-Qadi expands on the Islamic elements in the epistle, noting the "strictly religious counsel" abounding "especially" in its military section. Injunctions to pious behavior, warnings to obey God's law, and exhortations to seek "salvation in the next world" and not just "a good reputation in this one" all add up, according to al-Qadi, to a conception of "God as the sole guarantor of victory."⁶⁴ Moreover, she adds, ʿAbd al-Hamid's epistle can be understood in the context of a broader Umayyad ideology stressing obedience to the caliph as God's will, and consequently "denying human initiative in human affairs" and affirming that the Umayyads "will surely have the upper hand in all their battles on the basis that granting victory to Islam and the Muslims is part of God's primordial plan for mankind."⁶⁵

ʿAbbas and al-Qadi are certainly right in viewing ʿAbd al-Hamid's work as a milestone in the synthesis of older imperial lore with an Islamic ethic. There is, of course, nothing forced or artificial about such a synthesis, because profound sociopolitical dynamics that were in fact transforming the Islamic polity into an empire also generated a need for a conceptual or normative accommodation of that fact—just as they generated counter-conceptions in the form of Kharijism and apolitical ascetic idealism that were no less, but also no more, indigenous or "authentic." As pioneers in the formulation of this imperial conception, however, Ibn al-Muqaffaʿ and ʿAbd al-Hamid al-Katib were concerned more with establishing the primacy of *raison d'état*, and of the political rationality required for its pursuit, than with foregrounding the outlines of the Islamic ethics component of the posited synthesis. ʿAbd al-Hamid's conventionally pious exhortations—to recite "the Qurʾan every day," for example, or to invoke "God with particular invocations when the battle approaches"[66]—do not reveal very much. Nor is there much in his epistle to suggest a triumphalism based on confidence in divine rather than human agency. ʿAbd al-Hamid consistently depicts war as a frightful evil, at one point describing experienced soldiers as having "tasted the vagaries of war, and drunk from the bitterness of its cups, and swallowed choking torments from its teats."[67] Elsewhere he urges the prince as far as possible to avoid plunging his troops into the fire of combat, because that is sure to bring "hateful calamities . . . and pain" and also because "you cannot know to which of the two sides victory will come." It is far "nobler" and "more beneficial" to attain victory by relying on skillful planning and stratagem—for example by offering inducements or deterrents, or sowing discord among the enemy. This will better ensure the "well-being of your troops and your subjects and the people of your community."[68] All this is a far cry from the reveling in blood, yearning for martyrdom, and altogether personal focus characterizing, for example, Ibn al-Mubarak's book on jihad, but by contrast still very much in line with the spirit of the Greek and Persian literatures so familiar to ʿAbd al-Hamid. A sharper expression of the distinctively Islamic aspect of the emerging synthesis would come some decades later.

Equality and Hierarchy

The growing self-confidence of Muslim intellectuals vis-à-vis their Greek and Persian predecessors was already in evidence by the time Caliph al-Maʾmun came to power in 813 after prevailing over his brother in a sharp civil war. Well-versed in the "ancient books" he had, according to the historian al-Masʿudi, "worked hard at reading," al-Ma'mun devoted himself to implementing their insights by centralizing imperial rule, particularly in the legal, fiscal, and military fields.[69] His reforms included strengthening the office of chief judge (*qāḍi al-quḍāt*), first established by his father, in order to consolidate top-down ideological control and preempt religious rabble-rousers, in line with the ancient Persian admonitions conveyed by the likes of Ibn al-Muqaffaʿ.[70] He adopted the title "God's Caliph" in 816–817, backed theological approaches that privileged reasoning in legal judgments, and instituted his famous inquisition (*miḥna*) against the independent traditionist jurists in 833.

A similar rationale seems to have driven al-Ma'mun's foreign policy, where his main initiative was to launch a war against the Byzantine Empire that went well beyond the limited seasonal campaigns waged by his immediate predecessors, aspiring instead to renew the dramatic territorial expansion and colonization of Islam's earlier years. As Dimitri Gutas notes, this "total war" had a new "ideological component" as well: "The Byzantines were portrayed as deserving of Muslim attacks not only because they were infidels . . . but because they were also culturally benighted and inferior not only to Muslims, but to their own ancestors, the ancient Greeks. . . . [T]he Byzantines turned their backs on ancient science because of Christianity, while the Muslims had welcomed it because of Islam." Thus, "the Islamic polity . . . is the true heir to ancient Greece and all the human sciences. Byzantium . . . is culturally defunct; there now only remains to eliminate it politically as well."[71]

Al-Ma'mun's pursuit of a greater and more dynamic empire—including his sponsorship of the arts and sciences, centered in the Baghdad translation institute, library, and research academy known as the House of Wisdom (*Bayt al-Ḥikma*)—brought about a peak in Islamic civilization; one of those moments of extraordinary intellectual and creative efflorescence that occur all too rarely in human history. Just as the House of Wisdom went beyond translation to produce original scholarship, moreover, the intellectuals of al-Ma'mun's time had, as Gutas's observation indicates, by now gained the confidence not only to learn from their ancient and foreign predecessors, but also to assert their superiority over them.

A case in point is the belletrist and polemicist Abu ʿUthman ʿAmr ibn Bahr al-Fuqaymi al-Basri (ca. 776–869), known as al-Jahiz ("ogle-eyed") due to a malformation of his eyes, who was born in Basra in the third decade of the ʿAbbasid caliphate to a family of non-Arab converts to Islam "probably of Abyssinian origin."[72] Apparently an auto-didact, he started out acquiring a name for himself in the related fields of theology and politics. In theology, his rationalist inclinations led him toward the Muʿtazili school, which affirmed free will and ethical reasoning—though his openness to intuition and doubt as opposed to dogmatic certainty seem to have made him a nonconformist within this circle as well.[73] In politics, his works on the imamate, or Islamic leadership, secured the approval of Caliph al-Maʾmun, and drew him increasingly to Baghdad. While he does not appear to have held official positions there for any length of time, devoting himself primarily to the literary pursuits for which he was to become most famous, as a court favorite he did receive occasional remuneration in the form of stipends or rewards for the dedications of his books, and consorted with powerful officials and patrons of the arts such as the chief judge Ahmad ibn Abi Duʾad and the court secretary al-Fath ibn Khaqan.[74]

Al-Jahiz's vigorous support of the *mihna* launched by al-Maʾmun against the scholars of Prophetic Traditions (*ahl al-hadīth*) has been widely noted. In the first place, of course, this was due to differences on specific doctrinal issues—such as the traditionists' insistence on God's corporeality; on His not being subject to human moral categories of good and evil; on denying the createdness of the Qurʾan; and on predestination rather than free will in human action—as well as to a broader dispute about the utility of dialectical argumentation and reasoning (*kalām*), affirmed by the Muʿtazilis and denied by the traditionist jurists, in textual exegesis. Several commentators have further noted that al-Jahiz casts this theological dispute in the framework of a sociopolitical distinction between the elite (*al-khāṣṣa*) and the commonalty (*al-ʿāmma*), describing the traditionist jurists as upstarts or "weeds" (*nawābit*) who draw strength from the vulgar dregs of society, and expressing his fear that should they succeed, "hope will disappear, truth will die, and the one who stands for truth will be killed."[75] What is relevant for our purposes, however, and what has not received sufficient attention to date, is al-Jahiz's characterization of the psychological motivations of this formidable challenge, and their political consequences.

The most important psychological motivations are made evident right at the start of al-Jahiz's essay on "The Distinction between Enmity and Envy": "Envy induced the false pretenders to knowledge to slander the true scholars, and to malign and defame them. . . . They hoped thereby . . . to consolidate their leadership over the riffraff and rabble. . . . No era has ever been free of this class, nor ever will be. Love of power has been the cause of the ruin of nations in the past, as it will continue to be until the end of time."[76] Envy and love of power, then, are the twin driving forces behind the challenge of the populist traditionists to the rationalist theologians and their state patrons.

Al-Jahiz's main point here is that envy—a massive central theme in all his writings—is a far more fundamental and pathological drive than enmity. Whereas enmity normally arises from a particular offense, is guided by intellect, and can end in reconciliation or acceptance when that offense is removed, envy is irrational and never wears out, "whether denied or gratified." It does not cease until the object of envy itself is destroyed. Envy therefore reflects a true "corruption of nature . . . and disorder of character," al-Jahiz concludes; envy is an essential substance, enmity an incidental acquisition.[77] The reason is that envy originates in real, objective differences between the envious and the envied. The envious in this case—the ignorant pseudo-scholars who "imitate" true scholars in hopes of attaining their status[78]—in fact lack both the intellectual attributes and consequently the political influence of their targets. Their only hope for satisfaction, al-Jahiz indicates, lies in destroying the objects of their envy, even if that means whipping up the likewise marginalized and disgruntled rabble, and overthrowing a political order that exhibits its virtue by rewarding excellence with one that panders to the resentments of the mediocre and lowly.

Several disastrous consequences would then follow. On a cultural level, the valorization of ignoramuses at the expense of intelligence portends a dark age in intellectual inquiry, further exacerbated by an atmosphere of ascetic dourness fatal to the exuberant inquisitiveness so characteristic of al-Jahiz himself.[79] On a political level, the most immediate result is an erosion in centralized caliphal authority—a dire prospect for a thinker whose experience of the bitter civil war between al-Ma'mun and his brother led him to write repeatedly of the dangers of anarchism.[80] Erosion of power at the top, in turn, threatens to generate a broader collapse in social and political hierarchy, creating a situation in which "the elite have no power over the commonalty, and the noble (*al-'ilya*) have no power over the base (*al-arādhil*)."[81] This constitutes perhaps the greatest danger of all, in al-Jahiz's eyes: a leveling of distinctions and differences that are, he insists in treatise after treatise, necessary for the flourishing of any healthy polity. Had

God not differentiated between the "natures of people" (*ṭabāʾiʿ al-nās*), he writes elsewhere, they would all pursue the same ends, the division of tasks essential to communal livelihood would fail to occur, and perdition and ruin would ensue.[82]

In another book dedicated primarily to defending the legitimacy of the first three caliphs, al-Jahiz clarifies his conception of natural inequality by contrasting it to the pre-Islamic Persian caste structure, which "did not allow a craftsman to move into the secretarial profession, or the secretary to move into leadership, or allow their sons anything but what their fathers did."[83] Instead, he once again emphasizes differences in "nature," manifested in characteristics such as "miserliness and generosity, stupidity and cleverness, treachery and faithfulness, cowardice and intrepidity, anxiety and patience, inconstancy and forbearance, magnanimity and neglect, recollection and forgetfulness, inarticulateness and eloquence."[84] It is such qualities that rightfully determine an individual's place in society and distinguish true elites from commoners. Since the complexities of religious interpretation and political governance lie beyond the ken of common people, who are inclined instead to "sway with every wind" and to "prefer those who are false over those who are true," their primary role should be to serve the elite as "tools" for the conduct of necessary mundane affairs such as commerce and defense of the realm: "The well-being of the world and the attainment of prosperity rest on the administration of the elite and the obedience of the commonalty."[85] Upsetting this relationship, overturning natural hierarchy, brings disorder and divisive conflict, and paves the way for internal collapse or external attack.

For al-Jahiz, therefore, it is critically important to uphold an understanding of Islam that transcends ascriptive distinctions as much as possible, while still affirming natural ones, so as to counteract the leveling and ultimately enervating effects of envy. His denunciations of the Byzantines—deployed on behalf of al-Maʾmun's broader ideological campaign against them—accordingly focus not on their Greek ethnicity but on their Christian religion.[86] While even the ancient Greeks could be criticized for being "thinkers, not doers,"[87] he argues, still in their pagan rationalism they towered over their descendants with their emasculating Christian asceticism and pacifism—the first pathology as described in al-Jahiz's "Response to the Christians," where he goes so far as to accuse them of practicing castration,[88] and the latter in another treatise: "We know that before the Byzantines adopted Christianity they used to hold their own against the kings of Persia, and gave as good as they got in the wars between them. But when they came no longer to believe in killing and fighting, or retaliation and reprisal, they were afflicted by cowardice and battle became burdensome to them. When this religion pervaded their characters and permeated their flesh and blood, it overcame their natures and they went from victory to defeat."[89] Similarly, when the Toquz Oghuz Turks converted to a heretical religion that was "even worse than Christianity in its restraint and pacifism, their courage diminished and their vigor evaporated."[90] Most Turks, who converted to Islam, by contrast continued to distinguish themselves "in war as the Greeks did in philosophy and the people of China in art . . . and the Sasanians in rule and leadership."[91] One senses from these instructive examples that al-Jahiz's advocacy of an understanding of Islam that celebrates distinction in virtues such as intelligence, spiritedness, or magnanimity is directed not only against other religions, but also and perhaps primarily against enervating ascetic tendencies within the Islamic political community itself.

There is an obvious self-serving dimension to al-Jahiz's conflation of a natural aristocracy of virtue with the dominance of his own faction. His attempt to hitch his particular political and theological interests to these more general themes, at any rate, suffered a defeat with the end of the *miḥna* under Caliph al-Mutawakkil (r. 847–861), who recognized the religious authority of the traditionist jurists and thus ensured their ascendancy over the dialectical theologians. Now it was the traditionists who could lay claim to being the moral and intellectual elite. More enduring, therefore, may have been al-Jahiz's attack on another dimension of the destructive envy and resentment manifested by marginalized but ambitious groupings, this one expressed in ethnic terms: the *shuʿūbiyya*. A movement that peaked between Islam's third and fifth centuries, during the transition period between early Arab predominance and a more truly cosmopolitan Islamic community, *shuʿūbiyya* entailed the assertion of indigenous cultural traditions by non-Arab converts—most notably, though not exclusively, Iranians—against what they viewed as their less refined Arab conquerors. Al-Jahiz's treatment of *shuʿūbiyya* recapitulates in all essential respects his treatment of the *nābita*. Indeed, he repeatedly draws an explicit connection between ethnic and religious discord:

> The bulk of those who are skeptics in regard to Islam, at the outset, were inspired by the ideas of the *Shuʿūbiyyah*.

> Protracted argument leads to fighting. If a man hates a thing then he hates him who possesses it, or is associated with it. If he hates [the Arabic] language then he hates the [Arabian] peninsula, and if he hates that peninsula then he loves those who hate it. Thus matters go from bad to worse with him until he forsakes Islam itself, because it is the Arabs who brought it; it is they who provided the venerable forebears and the example worthy of imitation.[92]

Al-Jahiz also highlights the interrelationships between the two kinds of resentment in his essay on the *nābita*, where he identifies those theological "weeds" or upstarts as non-Arab converts (*mawālī*) who are the latest to manifest the kind of zealous chauvinism that has "left no religion uncorrupted and no world undestroyed."[93]

Once again, then, al-Jahiz's starting point is psychological: like the theological *nābita*, these proponents of *shu'ūbiyya* have "envy" (*ḥasad*) lurking "in their livers."[94] He illustrates the point in a biting dissection of the affectations of the (mostly Persian) court secretaries and scribes, frustrated by the disjunction between their vanity and their total subordination to their masters, who seek validation by mocking the ways of the Arabs and by taking every opportunity to recall the excellence of pre-Islamic Persian governance.[95] Once again, such psychological pathologies have serious political consequences. Ethnic resentments erode the normative bonds that hold the caliphate together, as indicated by al-Jahiz's point about dislike of Arabs leading to alienation from Islam, and as he reiterates when he alleges that "no secretary has ever been seen to take the Qur'an as his reading companion . . . and if one of them happens to be found speaking of (religious) matters, he does so without eloquence or grace."[96] Perhaps most dangerous of all, however, is ethnic factionalism within the military, a phenomenon that impelled al-Jahiz to write a treatise on the "Merits of the Turks"—in part to defend an ethnic group rapidly on the ascendance in the caliphal army against its detractors, but more generally in an attempt to foster the military concord and efficacy so vital for the well-being of any political order.[97]

Al-Jahiz has often been criticized for his apparent contradictions—denouncing the *shu'ūbī* secretaries' partiality toward Sasanian political traditions, for example, while elsewhere praising the governance of "the House of Sasan, of Anushirwan and all the descendants of Ardashir son of Babak;"[98] or decrying ethnic chauvinism while asserting the superior virtues of the Arabs in works ranging from his *Book of Misers* to the "Kitab al-ʿAsaʾ" section of *Al-Bayan wa-l-Tabyin*, and penning epistles such as "The Vaunting of the Blacks over the Whites." With regard to similar apparent contradictions in his treatment of contending theological sects, it has been suggested that al-Jahiz's intention was to present al-Maʾmun with a comprehensive overview of the strengths and weaknesses in the doctrines of each sect so that the caliph could formulate objective policies.[99] Certainly in his discussions of ethnicity and *shuʿūbiyya* as well, it is clear that al-Jahiz is concerned not with upholding any specific group over others, but with highlighting the merits of each in order to demonstrate their potential contributions to the Islamic caliphate. Despite its title, his treatise on "The Vaunting of the Blacks over the Whites," for example, which concludes with a section extolling Indian culture as well, explicitly rejects any notion of inherent ethnic superiority or inferiority: "Blackness and whiteness are due to the disposition of the environment, and the properties imparted by God on its water and soil, and to the proximity of the sun and the intensity of its heat. They cannot be ascribed to malformation or punishment, disfigurement or inferiority."[100]

Instead, al-Jahiz once again celebrates distinction. Just as differences in human nature generate love for the various pursuits and professions that allow a complex society to flourish, so too, he argues in his essay on the merits of the Turks, the characteristic excellences of different nations in various fields—such as the Chinese in arts and crafts, the Greeks in philosophy and literature, the Persians in governance, and the Turks in warfare—are indispensable for the well-being of imperial civilization.[101] At the same time, however, he shies away from equating cultural differences among nations with character differences among individuals. In the first and decisive place, soon after outlining the talents prevalent among various nations, he takes care to add that such cultural generalizations cannot be extrapolated to the individual level.[102] Beyond that, he argues, relying on a rather murky analysis of patron-client conventions, that all the ethnic groupings in the caliphal army are "one" and on an equal footing in terms of lineage (*nasab*), so that the distinctions and honors accruing to one group come to reflect on all.[103] Here once again al-Jahiz treads a fine line between notions of difference and hierarchy that are merely ascriptive and politically corrosive on the one hand, and those that are natural—based on "knowledge" (*ʿilm*) and "constitution" (*bunya*)[104]—as well as politically salutary on the other.

Recent scholarship has questioned al-Jahiz's characterization of the proponents of *shuʿūbiyya* as "egalitarians" or "levelers" (*man yataḥalla bi-ism al-taswiya*[105]), pointing out that many of their leading figures were well-born, highly educated converts who occupied prominent positions in the political or cultural realms, and who themselves upheld notions of hierarchy.[106] If one keeps in mind the psychological and sociological starting points of his argument, however, the difficulty is resolved. For al-Jahiz, the weeds themselves—the leaders of discord and rebellion—are distinct from the soil in which they sprout. The traditionist religious scholars, in his view, are ambitious upstarts of insufficient learning and erroneous opinions, but they are not the illiterate rabble from whom they draw strength and on the backs of whom they hope to ride to power. Like the *nābita*, the *shuʿūbī* leaders too can claim a more elevated social status while at the same time pursuing their frustrated ambitions by stoking the fires of populist—in this case, ethnic—resentment, and in doing so posing a mortal threat both to the imperial order and to the religion that holds it together.

Al-Jahiz lived a long life, reportedly dying in his nineties under a collapsed pile of the books he loved, but the reversal of the *miḥna* and the triumph of his theological adversaries rendered him a political outsider in his later years. In a letter to a friend apparently penned during this period, he writes of "the grotesque situation now prevailing, the ruination of our time, with the empire taken over by riffraff. . . . I observe that intelligence leads to unhappiness in the same measure that ignorance and stupidity produce happiness. . . . Grief has lasted too long, unhappiness drags on, the darkness deepens, the candle gutters, and solace is long in coming."[107] Even as al-Jahiz's flame guttered, however, a new leading light in the world of letters was emerging from among the ranks of his enemies.

Abu Muhammad ibn Qutayba al-Dinawari (828–889) is thought to have been born in Kufa to a family of Iranian converts from Khurasan. He gained prominence as a scholar both of religion and *adab*—the urbane humanistic arts which include literature, history, and social manners, of which Ibn al-Muqaffaʿ was a founder and al-Jahiz one of the most celebrated practitioners. In the introduction to his *ʿUyun al-Akhbar*, a major compendium of epigrams, anecdotes, and poetic verses on traditional *adab* subjects, Ibn Qutayba affirms that there are many paths to God and that he wrote it for those focused on worldly affairs as much as for those focused on the afterlife. At the same time, however, he aligns himself with the traditionalists who upheld the Prophet's transmitted words and deeds against those theologians, such as the Muʿtazilis, who sought to interpret religious texts through the exercise of reason.[108] So much so, that that paragon of orthodoxy, Ibn Taymiyya, himself contrasted Ibn Qutayba with al-Jahiz as representative spokesmen for the two opposing camps.[109] As al-Jahiz's political fortunes declined following the end of the *mihna*, accordingly, Ibn Qutayba's flourished, and the younger man was unsparing in his criticisms of his predecessor, describing him as "among the most mendacious" of people and alleging that "he had no religion."[110]

Nevertheless, it is striking that the two men held nearly identical views on the psychological origins and political consequences of *shuʿūbiyya*. Ibn Qutayba's primary work on the subject is a treatise called "Book of the Arabs," alternatively titled "Response to the *Shuʿūbiyya*" and, in some designations, "Censure of Envy."[111] Indeed, it opens by identifying envy as the underlying driver of anti-Arab chauvinism, and warning that left unchecked it ultimately erodes belief in Islam itself. Ibn Qutayba later quotes the Prophet as telling a Persian companion: "Do not despise the Arabs, for you will despise me."[112] He elaborates on al-Jahiz's psychological insight, moreover, by arguing that this envy is rooted not among the nobility of the non-Arabs, who are already satisfied with their social status, but among their commoners, who seek to enhance their prestige by claiming superiority for their ethnic group as a whole.[113]

Ibn Qutayba's refutation unfolds on several levels. He begins by denying that non-Arab commoners can in fact partake of the past glories of their noble elites—they were rabble then, and they remain rabble now.[114] Then he denies that Arab culture in general is inferior, pointing to admirable Arab characteristics such as forbearance, modesty, hospitality, and courage in warfare. He observes in this connection that while both the Arabs and Persians have ruled empires, "the Arabs are superior in that the basis of their rule is prophecy (*nubuwwa*)"—a basis that evidently makes for greater political success: "the Arabs are superior in that their rule extended to the furthest lands on the horizons of the earth, whereas Persian rule was but a sliver of it."[115] Ibn Qutayba is just as concerned as al-Jahiz to defend this imperial advantage bestowed by Islam against the divisive resentments of the *shuʿūbiyya*.

Finally, having established a hierarchical distinction between elites and masses that cuts across ethnic lines, and thereby prepared the groundwork for a new pan-Islamic solidarity of elites, Ibn Qutayba gradually transforms the basis of the hierarchy itself. He does so first by piously observing that when all people return to dust in the end, all "lineages are severed" and the only relevant distinction remaining is devotion to God; and then by making the more worldly point that it is possible to have a distinguished lineage without occupying a high rank of honor: "This means that the primary thing about a person is quality of soul . . . if his soul is base and his ancestors eminent, it avails him nothing."[116] Here, then, is the point on which Ibn Qutayba unites with his political and theological opponent al-Jahiz: the critical importance of safeguarding a conception of hierarchy that preserves the distinction between noble and base, and reconciling it with the ethnic egalitarianism and universalism that any successfully diverse empire must exhibit.

Statecraft

Ibn Qutayba's ʿUyun al-Akhbar contains an entire "Book on War" citing Islamic and non-Islamic (especially Persian, Greek, and Indian) sources, several passages of which closely parallel an older treatise on military affairs entitled *Mukhtasar Siyasat al-Hurub* (Epitome or Summary of the Management of Wars).[117] In the most complete of its five surviving manuscripts the title is followed by an attribution to "al-Harthami, companion of al-Maʾmun." A Khalil ibn al-Haytham al-Hartami is mentioned by the historian al-Masʿudi (d. 956) as the author of a treatise entitled "Stratagems and Ruses in War."[118] Similarly, Ibn al-Nadim (d. 990) lists several texts on warfare in his authoritative compendium of Arabic scholarly and literary works, but whereas most are cited only by name and author, one—"Stratagems"—is described at length as a substantial tome written by Harthami (or Khalil al-Harthami in some editions) al-Shaʿrani for the Caliph al-Maʾmun (d. 833).[119] Whether the relatively short *Mukhtasar* was also written by this same Harthami or not, internal evidence, such as its use of a phrase (*shākiriyya*, denoting a type of military unit) that fell out of use by the late 800s, reinforces the dating of the treatise to sometime during the early to mid-decades of the ninth century.[120] And whatever the extent of its fidelity to an ostensible original text, it stands as a fascinating and illuminating work in its own right, worthy of being celebrated as a masterpiece of Islamic military literature.

The *Mukhtasar*'s chief interest lies in the way it both recapitulates and goes beyond the Greek and Persian military thinking relayed more or less faithfully by the likes of ʿAbd al-Hamid al-Katib, in the process articulating some of the most distinctive features of the realist political perspective under investigation here. Thus, it further contributes to the valorization of reason by emphasizing the centrality of deliberation in warfare—but it does so without losing sight of either (a) the inevitable uncertainties of the battlefield which militate against replacing faith in supernatural intervention with an equally unwarranted faith in science, or (b) the necessary existence of evil in the world, which renders war an eternal imperative and precludes any hope of perpetual peace. This is in stark contrast to the anxious faith in craft and technique articulated by the Greek Aelian in the second century when he boasted that the "degree of mathematical information" he possessed would yield "such tactical precepts as will ensure the safety of those who observe them, and will bring destruction on their enemies," or by the Byzantine Emperor Maurice (d. 602) who insisted: "Long and careful deliberation promises great safety in war."[121]

The anxiety underlying such faith in science is reflected in two characteristic features of Byzantine military literature. One, noted by Walter Kaegi, is that "the need for the general ideally to possess the coup d'oeil, the ability to discern at a glance the principal strategic features of a situation or piece of land . . . is missing."[122] Intuitive genius is far too contingent a quality on which to rest one's hopes. What is required instead is a much more accessible craft, within reach of any reasonably competent general willing to train hard. The other characteristic feature, shared also by their Sasanian counterparts in Iran, is described by John Haldon as a preference "to use craft, intelligence, wiles, bribery, ideological blackmail and countless other devices rather than commit themselves to set battles or even warlike confrontations of any sort. Even in warfare, the predominant tendency is for armies to proceed with the utmost caution."[123] Thus, the mindset of Maurice's *Strategikon* emerges as resolutely defensive. Even when discussing the actual "Day of Battle," it is striking that his instructions on what to do "After a Defeat" precede—and are twice in length as—his instructions on what to do "After a Victory." Other examples of this defensive outlook include his discussion of espionage, which focuses almost entirely on detecting enemy spies while saying almost nothing about deploying them oneself; his instruction to commanders to set up fortified camps even in friendly territory; and his discussion of laying siege (shorter than his discussion on withstanding sieges) which itself begins by warning against counterattacks by the besieged.[124] Almost every passage of Maurice's text, in short, is colored by presentiments of defeat and doom. And almost every passage accordingly reveals that Maurice's deepest yearning is not for victory, not for conquest, certainly not for "empty glory"[125]—but for the safety of peace. It is for this purpose that one prepares for war, and it is for this reason that "the general ought to be ready, even after victory, to listen to proposals of the enemy for peace on advantageous terms."[126]

For the *Mukhtasar*'s author, by contrast, neither scientific certainty nor secure peace are within reach. He begins his very brief preface with an injunction: "Know that the affairs and accidents of wars are more numerous and more subtle than can be encompassed by books or grasped by imagination." Then he describes his treatise as an "effort to draw attention and alert" based on "concepts that have come to us from the books of the ancient ones (*al-awāʾil*)." Although he will try faithfully to relay those concepts—much of which deal with "deployments and engagements and such"—in hopes that they will prove of some use, he emphasizes a second time that "the variations and accidents of wars are too numerous for planning to take into account." Right from the start, then, the author sets up a central dichotomy underlying his entire work: between the presentation of tactical knowledge accumulated through the ages on the one hand, and his own interventions concerning the limited utility of such knowledge on the other.

The presentation of ancient expertise—usually denoted by preceding a discussion with "they said" or "they preferred" or by citing "those who have knowledge of war"—constitutes the bulk of the text. The author's own commentary is signified either by omitting such formulations or occasionally by replacing them with "we said." Only the preface and the concluding chapters 39 and 40 lack an opening "they said" in the two most complete manuscripts. Chapters 1, 5, and 38 also lack an opening "they said" in one of these manuscripts, although the phrase does appear in the other. All other chapters in all five manuscripts open with "they said." It seems reasonable to conclude, therefore, that the *Mukhtasar*'s author concentrates his own interventions in introductory and concluding chapters that bracket the more conventional arguments of the core text.

After the preface and list of forty chapter titles comes an opening chapter which, in line with conventional practice, emphasizes the importance of piety and justice. It starts by urging the "master of war" to rely on God and act in obedience to Him, because victory comes from Him alone and "not from cleverness or artifice, nor from capability or numbers." God in turn blesses those who are just, defined here as those who care for the welfare of their subjects. Then, however, comes the awkward observation that we often see evildoers and infidels triumphing over the just and the faithful. That happens because God's intentions are obscure—perhaps it is part of some divine test—and should not dissuade readers from applying what is found "in this our book or in others except in a manner that pleases God." The chapter's pious tone is reinforced by a Prophetic saying (one of only two in the entire treatise) to the effect that oppression in this world will yield suffering in the next. Still, the crucial point has been made: in this world at least God does *not* always favor the just.

The discussion then turns to military matters proper—again, in organization and content very much in line with its Greek and Persian models. It begins with a section of eight chapters devoted to what might be called the politics of military command: the management of lieutenants, soldiers, advisers and spies, including knowledge of the qualities and virtues to be sought in each category of personnel. Indeed knowledge—acquiring it by one's own insights or those of reliable advisers, stealing it from the enemy by espionage, protecting it by keeping secrets—emerges as a central motif here. In contrast to the apparent fatalism of the opening chapter, the author asserts that labor informed by knowledge is in fact the "cause of success." The introduction of knowledge or reason, in turn, necessitates attention to some further imperatives. One is a certain openness of mind, or ability to transcend parochial biases: urging commanders to seek knowledgeable advice wherever it is found, for example, chapter 6 points out that even Persian bondmaids may have something useful to say.

Another corollary of reason is a motif that "they" (his unnamed predecessors) especially emphasized: prudence. Chapter 4 accordingly discusses the importance of hiding one's weaknesses while striving to discover those of the enemy, and the advisability of erring on the side of over-estimating enemy strength as one considers battle. Chapter 5 ("On Deliberateness and Gentleness") introduces a third corollary of reason, temperance, by highlighting the "hateful things" entailed even when victory is won on the battlefield. Since seeking the enemy's submission "whenever possible" through artifice or persuasion better promotes the "welfare of your companions and your subjects," writes the author echoing ʿAbd al-Hamid al-Katib, the truly "notable victory" is one characterized by avoidance of bloodshed. Indeed, here the author seems generally content to paraphrase others: Caliph ʿUmar ibn al-Khattab's warning that unreliable spies can become "eyes against you, not for you"; ʿAbd al-Hamid's advice to over-estimate one's enemy, and to isolate one's spies from one's soldiers lest the latter "point them out with their fingers"—all are found in identical or near-identical words in chapters 4 and 9 of the *Mukhtasar*.[127]

Next comes a central section of twenty-six chapters on military field tactics: from the organization and deployment of one's forces on the march, at camp, and on the battlefield, to the treatment of auxiliary activities such as scouting missions, ambushes, night raids, and sieges. Here again the conventional character of the subject matter is highlighted by references to earlier works. Here again the same motifs—knowledge and caution—are prominently in evidence. Yet there are also ambiguities that seem to subvert some of the more pedantic discussions.

Knowledge of warfare seems to begin with a naming of parts. Chapter 11 names the three principal parts of deployment (center, right flank, left flank) then lists thirty types of units such as the vanguard and rearguard, specialized parties of scouts and spies, and various categories of cavalry. The next chapter names military formations by size, from 40-man platoons to grand armies of more than 12,000. Chapter 21 names the ranks of personnel and where they should be positioned in a battle array. Knowledge also means familiarity with one's surroundings, so the master of war is urged to send out scouts in order to discover what lies ahead during a march (chapter 13), to organize his camp so that everything's location is known at all times (chapter 15), to survey the battlefield in order to position oneself optimally for battle (chapters 16 and 24), and to know every point of weakness and strength in various kinds of fortifications whether mounting or withstanding a siege (chapters 34 and 35). Here too there is much that is familiar in older Greek and Persian sources.[128]

Most critical, perhaps, is knowledge of the qualities and capabilities of one's own forces. Chapter 31 cites "the people of knowledge in war" urging commanders to learn everything they can about their soldiers, including especially the exact nature of their courage or cowardice, and what motives (shame, pride, desire, etc.) drive each of them to fight.[129] Such knowledge will then allow commanders to implement recommendations such as those in chapter 20 to position one's most powerful men in the front lines of the center, one's most agile men at the front of the right flank, and one's wiliest men at the rear of the center.[130] The science of deployment relates not just to individuals but to entire units of various sizes as well, but this subject—which occupies pride of place in most Roman and Byzantine military manuals—receives scant and derivative attention here in a handful of chapters clustered around the middle of the text. Chapter 17 ("On the Types of Battle Lines in an Engagement"), for example, consists of just over 100 words and concludes with the terse observation that "they liked" to deploy their troops in close order and straight line formations. Providing practical information on tactics is clearly not of paramount concern in the *Mukhtasar*.

Instead, its author seems far more interested in the parameters of precision and uncertainty more generally. He has already raised this issue in his preface, and will confront it directly in his concluding chapters, but here in the central section it is addressed more subtly, in the form of several apparently unsuccessful efforts to replicate the fussy—or as Aelian says, "mathematical"—precision of his predecessors. Thus, while it is possible that the error in chapter 32 (in which the author claims to list twelve qualities desirable in one's lieutenants while actually listing eleven) is the result of a transcribing mistake, the same cannot be said of other occasions in which his explications of venerable teachings succeed only in undermining them. In chapter 18, for example, he takes up the conventional penchant for playing with configurations of different numbers of men, and winds up with what Hugh Kennedy describes as a "bizarre" discussion of how to deploy units consisting of just one individual.[131] In chapter 24 he takes the straightforward injunction (variously attributed to the Persian King Anushirwan and to the Prophet Muhammad) to delay combat until the end of the day whenever possible, and all but nullifies it by adding: "unless you see an opportunity before then, in which case seize it."[132] And whereas Maurice and others suggested knowing as much as possible about one's troops, in chapter 31 we encounter—notably in a text otherwise almost devoid of references to historical figures or events—an actual (albeit unnamed) commander who is alleged to have known not only the names, lineages, geographical origins, and demeanors of his 4,000 men, but also the types and capabilities of the weapons, steeds, and attendants each one possessed.

Having raised at least as many questions as it answers about certainty, the *Mukhtasar* turns in this long central section to the second theme of reliance on caution. Once again the initial impression is one of fidelity to older traditions. Commanders are urged to deploy defensively when marching, and to fortify and post guards scrupulously when camping.[133] On the battlefield itself, one should hold back if the enemy appears in good order, and otherwise avoid advancing more than a third of the distance between oneself and the enemy. One should at all times beware of ambushes and tricks—such as a feigned retreat—and under no circumstances engage in plunder before being certain of victory. If victory is achieved, one should pursue very carefully and never stand in the path of the fleeing enemy or block his access to water, lest desperation reinvigorate him. Even when besieging the enemy's fortifications, it is best to win by trickery—luring his forces out and then ambushing them—while remaining on guard against counter-ruses.[134] Once again, however, old tropes are often elaborated to the point of parody. It is one thing for Polyaenus to observe that Iphicrates used to erect palisades even in friendly territory. It is another to describe, in chapter 10 of the *Mukhtasar Siyasat al-Hurub*, a general "they mentioned" who, setting out from Syria to wage war in India, ordered trenches dug around his camp every night from the very first night until he reached his destination.[135] Here as well, then, the *Mukhtasar*'s author seems to gently mock too ready an acceptance of conventional expertise.

The last four chapters of this central section begin to move the focus away from tactics and back to broader questions of governance, with discussions of military crimes and punishments (chapter 33), the importance of rhetorical skills (chapter 34), and the maintenance of discipline while besieged (chapter 35). Chapter 36 ("On Sundry Matters in War") opens with a reiteration of the importance of not denying a desperate enemy water, and ends with an elaboration of the one-man army motif—citing "some people knowledgeable in war" mentioned by "them" who derived the tripartite battle array from a warrior's right eye, ear and limbs performing the functions of the right flank; his left eye, ear and limbs performing the functions of the left flank; and his mouth, breast and heart performing the functions of "preparation and deliverance" specific to the center. The notion that military organization might have political and even psychological parallels is reinforced by the apparently disconnected sentences between the beginning and end of this complex chapter. These contain advice about when to allow one's beasts of burden to graze and when not to hunt wild creatures for sport, about employing brave champions to serve as rallying points for their comrades but preventing their desire to show off in duels from undermining discipline, about discrediting tribal leaders (*ashrāf*) while maintaining one's own credibility, and about knowing when to ease up on one's troops and how to intervene against incipient mutinies.

A short chapter on the military characteristics of various peoples comes next. It does not describe those characteristics, restricting itself to the observation that "war is not one thing" because the motivations of different peoples (Turks, Persians, Byzantines, Indians, Kurds, Arabs, Kharijis, and brigands are mentioned) vary so widely, ranging from raiding for booty to conquering the world. One's preparations, therefore, must depend on the nature and motivations of each particular adversary—some enemies should elicit wariness, for example, while others can be approached more boldly. Unlike similar chapters in earlier texts that claimed to summarize the fighting styles of various potential enemies (such as Book 11 of Maurice's *Strategikon*), here readers are once again simply alerted to the great range—indeed elusiveness—of the knowledge required. As with field tactics and governance earlier in this long central section, then, the discussion of enemy characteristics highlights the importance of understanding while at the same time pointing to the inadequacy of relying on technical blueprints or blanket injunctions to caution.

Finally we reach the three concluding chapters in which the author again speaks more explicitly in his own voice. He starts in chapter 38 by considering various factors in military planning: courage and cowardice, dexterity and its lack, numerical superiority and inferiority, favorable terrain and its absence, foresight and blindness, knowledge and its lack, reason and ignorance. It is the gap between oneself and the enemy along each of these dimensions that determines warcraft. But, the author then adds, the "master of war" must understand that possessing any of these "desirable tools"—with one exception—may sometimes result in the "greatest harm" to him, just as the presence of any of their undesirable opposites may sometimes yield the "greatest benefit." The singular exception is reason, which is beneficial "in all circumstances." Reason is thus neither quickness nor the mere possession of information, but something subtler: a type of "discernment" (*tamyīz*) in military affairs—and, it is stressed, in "other" human affairs as well—akin to the Clausewitzian *coup d'oeil*.

This concern with the limitations of technical or scientific expertise is further explored in the penultimate chapter, enigmatically entitled "The Third Chapter Drawing Attention to the Resemblance and Difference Between Error and Truth."[136] Here the author points out that what is correct and incorrect in matters of war may be arrived at through either planning or chance. Fortune thus makes its first explicit appearance, though it has lurked in the shadows of the text from the very beginning. Error and truth, at any rate, may be evident or hidden or mistaken for each other, both by oneself and by the enemy, and both as they relate to one's own military disposition and that of the enemy. In matters of war, then—and, the author does not fail to emphasize yet again, in matters other than war as well—one's best bet remains to pursue truth in all its complexity, while trusting in God regardless of the uncertain outcome.

Chapter 40 is entitled "On Apologizing for Falling Short of Achieving the Agreement of All." Though we have tried our best, the author begins, is it really possible to reach a consensus on military matters when people have such different sentiments, characters, values, doctrines, and customs, so that "what is true for one is false for the other? If only it were. But it is an impossibility." Some critics demand pithy summaries. If pressed to provide one, "we would say that what the commander needs in war can be summarized in two points: good governance of his companions, and careful planning for war. But would our stating this conclusion suffice for one who has no knowledge of good governance of companions or planning for war?" Others say that military tactics must be precisely "calculated" so that the young can learn them from the old without any need for extensive experience. But again, the *Mukhtasar's* author insists, no technical short cut can lead to an adequate comprehension of military matters in all their variability and complexity.

Having dismissed the possibility of a science of war, our author turns to a second group of critics. These argue that the cunning required for victory cannot be taught, or that necessity and desperation rather than planning are what always guide action on the battlefield, or that only fortune and luck—not experience or knowledge—determine the outcome of wars. For do we not often see those ignorant or inexperienced in war prevailing, while those claiming to possess such knowledge fail? "By my life," replies the author (with the first of only two oaths in the treatise), "all this may be true and more." But does the commander have any alternative other than to rely on reason and hope for the best, given that God's inscrutable will determines victory or defeat?

The absence of such an alternative constitutes the author's answer to a third category of objectors: those who question the need for war altogether, or who accept it only under certain conditions. Of them he merely says: "Each doctrine has its adherents, so let us leave off describing them as there is no use in going on any longer." This dismissal of the notion that there is any alternative to war is very much in opposition to the yearning for peace—and its attendant preoccupation with safety—so evident in Byzantine and Sasanian military literature. Indeed, in contrast to Maurice's *Strategikon* and other Byzantine texts cited above, the word "peace" does not appear even once in the *Mukhtasar Siyasat al-Hurub*. Other indications that the *Mukhtasar* reflects a more warlike tradition include its focus on making the enemy submit to one's will rather than just repelling him (chapter 5), its assignment of priority to attacking rather than defending (as in the discussion of sieges in chapters 34 and 35), its emphasis on the various types of courage (chapters 31 and 36), and most notably the absence of injunctions to caution in any of the chapters where the author seems to speak most explicitly in his own voice (preface, 1, 5, 38, 39, 40). Just as victory cannot be assured by recourse to some perfectly illuminating science, in short, safety cannot be secured through the pursuit of an equally spurious perpetual peace. After another apology for a conclusion that does not conclude, the treatise ends with appropriate prayers and benedictions.

The preceding outline reveals the *Mukhtasar* to be a particularly sharp expression, in the tersest and most pointed terms, of a spirit crystallizing among certain elite elements for some decades now. This was a time when the exuberant triumphalism of early imperial expansion had given way to a more mature appreciation of political realities; a time when even authoritative ʿulamāʾ such as the Hanafi jurist al-Shaybani (d. 805) could write that Muslims may conclude treaties with non-Muslims who refuse to pay tribute if "the inhabitants of the territory of war are too strong for the Muslims to prevail against them and it would be better for the Muslims to make peace with them." Indeed, Muslims are even allowed to sign treaties that oblige *them* to pay tribute to non-Muslims if "it were better for the Muslims to do so."[137] Whereas the Umayyads "rarely concluded even temporary truces with non-Muslim polities," accordingly, "under the ʿAbbasids, such truces would become frequent, leading in time to exchanges of embassies, and finally a diplomatic mosque in Constantinople."[138] At such a time, the realization emerges that the most one can realistically hope for is reason without certainty, and empire without utopia.

Despite the *Mukhtasar*'s long-term influence, this was not an insight shared by all, or even by most. The eminent fourteenth-century Mamluk scholar Muhammad ibn Manjli, for example, quoted the *Mukhtasar* virtually verbatim (but without attribution) repeatedly in one of his major treatises on tactics and stratagems, yet insisted on depicting the art of war as a "science" and on devoting page after page to the military applications of incantations, numerology, the occult qualities of colors, and the like—all in hopes of securing certain victory.[139] Within the Islamic tradition, then, the *Mukhtasar Siyasat al-Hurub* reflects the perspective neither of the revolutionary irregular nor of the theoretical dogmatist, but of the seasoned imperial statesman for whom war is an unavoidable but regrettable and uncertain enterprise.

A similar attention to the necessary ordering of worldly affairs, and to the obstacles standing in the way, only now focused on the domestic rather than international arena, is offered by Abu ʿAli al-Hasan, known by his official honorific Nizam al-Mulk (ca. 1018–1092): chief minister to the Seljuq sultans Alp Arslan and Malikshah so powerful that he acted as the empire's "real ruler" for some twenty years, skilled practitioner of the most bare-knuckled court politics as well as more conventional military campaigns, and author of a book on government entitled *Siyar al-Muluk*.[140] In it, he affirms the worldly ends of statecraft: bringing "to pass that which concerns the advance of civilization, such as constructing underground channels, digging main canals, building bridges across great waters, rehabilitating villages and farms, raising fortifications, building new towns, and erecting lofty buildings and magnificent dwellings; [as well as building] inns . . . on the highways and schools for those who seek knowledge."[141] Precisely because "kingship and religion are like two brothers," moreover, Nizam al-Mulk established pious foundations and "madrasas for the propagation of state-approved Islamic thought"; coopted non-subversive Sufi orders and leagues;[142] and advocated ruthless suppression of religious extremists who threaten the civilizing mission of the rulers—especially the Ismaʿili Assassins who, according to most accounts, would ultimately claim his own life. The *Siyar al-Muluk* is filled with examples of the depredations of such extremists, most extensively in chapter 44 where Nizam al-Mulk describes how the high priest Mazdak had tried to establish a cult of his own which advocated communism of property and wives, and made "the common people masters of all" so as to erase "the difference between beasts and men" and cause "differences of rank . . . [to] disappear from the world."[143] Nizam al-Mulk drives home the lesson by describing how the wise and virtuous Sasanian prince Anushirwan intervened to foil Mazdak's plan, having him killed and all 12,000 of his followers buried alive in the ground head-first so that they formed a forest of "legs sticking up in the air."[144]

At the same time, Nizam al-Mulk recognizes that however much wisdom and skill may guide good government, ultimately everything hinges on "the turn of Fortune's wheel." There are no guarantees of continued success: "At any time the state may be overtaken by some celestial accident, or influenced by the evil eye. . . . In such days of discord and disaffection, men of noble birth will be crushed; baseborn men will gain control and whoever has strength will do what he likes."[145] Nizam al-Mulk fell victim to the vagaries of fortune in the end, but in large part because of his many years of artful statecraft, the Seljuq empire transcended its nomadic origins and became a crucible for culture that combined religious orthodoxy with creative advances in science and the arts.

～

This chapter has sought to identify a discrete and coherent outlook that arose in response to the transition of the Islamic polity into an empire—an outlook that in several respects displays features common to realism everywhere. Whereas, for example, the apolitical ascetic idealists viewed worldly concerns as corrupting distractions from more transcendent pursuits and accordingly inclined toward private lives of spiritual contemplation, this outlook's adherents looked to the far less pristine, always conflictual, arena of politics as a critical context for the fullest realization of human ends. And whereas the Kharijis, on the other hand, believed that transcendent or absolute truths are not only within reach, but can—indeed must—be applied to everybody, and therefore adopted the most extreme form of political engagement as revolutionaries seeking to establish an earthly utopia, the adherents of this outlook recognized that gray areas, necessary evils, ongoing conflict, and changing circumstances are inescapable features of political life which rule out perfect or permanent solutions.

At the same time, in contrast to their Western counterparts who operated within a Christian framework, these Muslim realists could avail themselves of a religion much more attuned to their concern with political and military imperatives, and much more accommodating to their focus on the natural diversity of human types. They were consequently able to articulate a credibly orthodox imperial vision that not only benefited from a more warlike and expansionist élan than that of either Byzantine Christianity or Sasanian Zoroastrianism, but that could also call for the concentration of political and especially legal authority at the apex of the state, in pursuit of a type of rule informed by artful statecraft rather than the only apparently more certain strictures of ideological dogma or techniques of political "science;" and that could better negotiate the tension between the principles of equality and difference which constitutes a central vulnerability of all imperial structures, in pursuit of a moral and intellectual hierarchy that seeks the general well-being without having to resort to the leveling lowest common denominator of incentives.

How the various features of this emerging realist tradition were incorporated into political philosophy in an Islamic framework will be taken up in the next chapter.

CHAPTER 3

The Political Turn in Islamic Philosophy

Philosophy is another arena in which the evolution of the Islamic polity demanded radical rethinking. Here too, the central issue was not so much incompatibility between foreign wisdom and indigenous convention, as the tension created by the necessity of adapting existing intellectual principles to the new conditions of an increasingly sophisticated imperial culture. Far from pitting philosophy and religion against each other, most of the philosophers in Islam (the *falāsifa*) who grappled with this tension—including the central figure in this chapter, Ibn Rushd (known in the West as Averroes)—sought to affirm the objective reality of the transcendent Good and the hierarchy of virtues which they maintained religion propounds in its own language.

For Ibn Rushd, such a project entailed delineating clear lines of demarcation between the proper spheres of reason and revelation; accepting the philosopher's obligation to attend to the well-being of his or her political community by actively seeking the establishment of the best regime possible; and recognizing that the vicissitudes of human affairs preclude either philosophical certainty or legal dogmatism, requiring instead artful statecraft in the domestic and foreign policies of a sprawling and diverse empire far beyond the bounds of the self-contained city-states envisioned by his ancient Greek predecessors. In pursuing this agenda, Ibn Rushd could build not only on the political and military literature discussed in the previous chapter, but also on an indigenous philosophical tradition that began over three hundred years before him. This chapter will accordingly begin by reviewing briefly the origins of that philosophical tradition, and particularly the evolution in how Socrates—the paradigmatic philosopher—is presented in the writings of al-Kindi and al-Farabi. It will then turn to Ibn Sina (known in the West as Avicenna), considered by many to be the philosopher who had the most enduring impact in the Muslim world, in order, finally, to assess how Ibn Rushd's highly critical reading of Ibn Sina allows him in turn to highlight the realism of his own political philosophy.

Al-Kindi

Many of the central issues that would define the Muslim philosophers' stance toward the state on one side and the religious establishment on the other are already apparent in the thought of the polymath Abu Yusuf al-Kindi (ca. 801–866), scion of a noble Arab family and companion to the ʿAbbasid caliphs al-Maʾmun and his successor al-Muʿtasim (r. 833–842). More than anyone else, he can be credited with taking the translations of the House of Wisdom scholars and using them to introduce a new philosophical vocabulary in Arabic, and as such may be considered a prototype of the philosopher within Islamic civilization—an early model that would need further refining before a more promising accommodation with the new revealed monotheism could be reached.

Al-Kindi discerned in the anti-Byzantine ideological campaign of the ʿAbbasids, mentioned in the previous chapter, an opportunity to legitimize ancient philosophy and affirm its compatibility with the norms of his own environment. By asserting that Yunan and Qahtan, the mythical ancestors of the Greeks and Arabs, respectively, were in fact brothers, he sought to present the appropriation of ancient Greek wisdom as the reclamation of a shared heritage that had been suppressed by the Christian Byzantines, and thereby at the same time to bolster the ʿAbbasid claim to the mantle of political and cultural hegemony in their place.[1] It was a maneuver that may have won him favor at the Caliph's court, but would ultimately be found too facile an elision of the two traditions by theologians and philosophers alike. While the former remained suspicious of all pagan learning, the latter would complain that al-Kindi's eagerness to effect a resolution led him to neglect logic—relying for example on inadequately supported premises or enthymemes rather than rigorous demonstrative syllogisms—and to embrace a metaphysics that seems to have drawn from a strand of Neoplatonism "associated with . . . the astral theology, heavily influenced by Hermetism, of the Ṣābiʾans of Ḥarrān."[2]

At the same time, it seems clear that having readily accepted the orthodox view of a Creator who brought the universe into being out of nothing, and of a "Seal of the Prophets," Muhammad, after whom the path of revelation to further knowledge is forever foreclosed, al-Kindi felt free to turn to his primary passion: natural science. And indeed, judging by Ibn al-Nadim's bibliographical compendium *al-Fihrist*, the great bulk of his almost 250 treatises dealt with subjects such as mathematics, optics, medicine, astronomy, zoology, and meteorology, as well as techniques of manufacturing goods such as glass, dyes, perfumes, armor, and swords.[3] In conjunction with this natural scientific focus, al-Kindi adopted an epistemological approach which has often been described as abstractly mathematical, and which Dimitri Gutas attributes to an "ideal of unassailable proof" that was "widespread in the ninth century"[4] (with the *Mukhtasar Siyasat al-Hurub* therefore standing as a notable exception).

When applied to philosophy, such an approach yields al-Kindi's famous depiction of Socrates as an exemplar of the ideal philosopher: an apolitical ascetic so preoccupied with his private pursuit of perfect theoretical understanding as to be utterly inattentive to the transient affairs of the world.[5] It is a depiction that has long invited parody, and al-Kindi was certainly subjected to ridicule from several quarters. In the famous debate between the dialectical theologian and grammarian Abu Sa'id al-Sirafi and the Aristotelian philosopher Abu Bishr Matta in 932, for example, al-Sirafi attacked philosophers for assuming too simplistically that wisdom can be conveyed in abstract, quasi-mathematical terms—"Not everything in the world admits of being weighed"—and consequently failing to translate the insights of the Greeks in a way comprehensible to Arabs, Turks, Persians, or Indians, so that in practical terms their logic turns out to be useless for resolving consequential disputes, religious or otherwise.[6] He also pursued this line of critique by mocking their shortcomings, despite professions of expertise, in poetry and rhetoric, and noted pointedly that if Aristotle's "Book of Demonstration" (*Posterior Analytics*) was so indispensable, why did he bother to write treatises on those other subjects as well?[7] Finally, al-Sirafi singled out "your leading light" al-Kindi for particular ridicule on these grounds, depicting him as both a gullible consumer, and in his turn purveyor of incomprehensible philosophical gibberish, adding: "Our Sabean friends have also told me things about him that would make a bereaved mother laugh, an enemy gloat, and a friend grieve."[8]

The central critique leveled here—that al-Kindi did not appreciate the importance of communicating effectively with, or persuading, the various elements of his community—seems also to underlie the "Tale of al-Kindi" in the belletrist and comic writer al-Jahiz's *Book of Misers*. The widespread belief that this is the same al-Kindi is strengthened by the fact that beyond the asceticism he advocated, the philosopher did indeed have a reputation for miserliness.[9] Most of the piece consists of al-Kindi's defense, parodying the philosopher's logical reasoning, of his treatment of tenants in his capacity as landlord. He argues that as the owner, he has a right to guard his "riches," and that it is for this reason that "walls are built, doors hung, chests contrived, padlocks made, seals and seal-rings engraved, accounting and book-keeping taught." By depicting the absurd extremes to which the landlord goes in pursuit of this objective, however, al-Jahiz seems to suggest that al-Kindi's rebuke of tenants displaying neglect or contempt (*tahāwun*) for others can be turned on himself as well.[10]

It is difficult to reach definitive conclusions regarding al-Kindi's thoughts about politics, particularly as he apparently wrote some pieces on governance that are now lost, but the Socrates he himself presents as philosophical exemplar is certainly one who also shows no interest in caring for the well-being of his city or its inhabitants, preferring instead to hoard his philosophical riches. His compendium of anecdotes about Socrates accordingly paints so apolitical a picture that it ascribes to Socrates the story of Diogenes the Cynic telling a king to step aside as he is blocking the sun.[11] The obliviousness of such a stance comes into sharp relief when considered in light of al-Kindi's own fate. Already in his major metaphysical treatise, *On First Philosophy*, he had felt compelled to respond to dogmatic attacks by denouncing those who "traffic" in religion, adding: "it is right that one who resists the acquisition of knowledge of the real nature of things and calls it unbelief be divested of (the offices of) religion."[12] His fortunes declined precipitously after the failure of the inquisition (*mihna*) initiated by Caliph al-Maʾmun, apparently due to a combination of changed political circumstances and personal enmities, and reportedly to the point of being beaten at the orders of the new caliph and having his books taken away for a time. Like al-Jahiz, who reacted to the new conditions by turning to "purely literary activity," al-Kindi seems to have increasingly focused on empirical science and mathematics in the latter part of his life.[13] He expressed his disillusionment in a verse subsequently relayed by one of his disciples:

Real leaders have been replaced by the mob. Therefore
   shut your eyes, and let your head hang low!
Make yourself inconspicuous, and clench your hands
   together! Look for a seat in the innermost part of your
   house![14]

Al-Kindi was famously ignored by his philosophical successors in the Muslim world, evidently dissatisfied with his treatments of philosophy and religion. His ascetic and apolitical Socrates, preoccupied with private happiness to the exclusion of any public concerns, gave way to the Socrates of Abu Nasr al-Farabi (ca. 870–950), recast now as much more attuned to the relationship between the individual philosopher and his community, and consequently much more receptive to what al-Farabi called the "way of Thrasymachus"—the way of connecting with and persuading the multitude.[15] The extent to which such a reorientation adds up to a "political philosophy" in al-Farabi's writings has been much contested, with opinions ranging from Muhsin Mahdi's argument that it was with him that "political philosophy proper emerged in the Islamic community," to Dimitri Gutas's argument that al-Farabi's discussions of political matters were "not central" but instead "derivative" of his primary focus on metaphysics and noetics, and that "the real initiator of political philosophy in Arabic" was Ibn Khaldun almost five centuries later.[16] Corollary to this central dispute are perceived ambiguities in al-Farabi's thought on several other crucial issues, such as the sincerity of his belief in the Neoplatonically inspired emanationist metaphysics conveyed in some of his works; the possibility of demonstrative arguments in ethics or politics, and relatedly of the objective, rationally accessible reality of distinctions between good and evil, or noble and base; the necessity of practical activism in the pursuit of theoretical insight; and the feasibility or even desirability of attempting the realization of more virtuous political regimes. One can find cross-cutting perspectives on these questions even within the same general schools of thought.

An adequate treatment of al-Farabi's thinking on such issues lies beyond the scope of the present study. But the implications for the tension between realism and idealism in Islamic political thought suggested by his new presentation of Socrates can be pursued by considering the differences between two other leading philosophers. One is Abu ʿAli ibn Sina (980–1037) of Khurasan, who, despite the fact that he adhered to the leading *falāsifa*'s line of remaining silent on al-Kindi, nevertheless seems to have studied him carefully and incorporated several of his key insights.[17] The other, a prime example of the approach that rejects hiding in the innermost part of one's house or tending only to one's own garden, is Abu al-Walid ibn Rushd (1126–1198) of Andalusia.

Ibn Sina's Metaphysics

Like other philosophers, Ibn Sina wrestled with the divide between external objective reality and the internal, subjective perceptions of the human intellect. In particular, as someone obliged to justify the practice of philosophy before the bar of revealed Law, he found Aristotle's metaphysics—which describes all existents as (physical) matter or (intellected) form or a combination of the two—wanting, because it fails to provide an adequate grounding for immaterial principles such as God or the concept of the Good. Stephen Menn nicely summarizes Ibn Sina's problem: "If we explain the difference between F and the knowledge of F, as Aristotle and Alexander [of Aphrodisias] do, by applying the concepts of matter and form, we are led to the conclusion that when F has no matter it is identical to the knowledge of F, and indeed to *our* knowledge of F, a conclusion that Avicenna finds clearly unacceptable."[18] It is in pursuit of such an independent grounding that Ibn Sina developed his own metaphysics.

Moreover, Ibn Sina denied that Aristotle's insistence on taking physics as a starting point could yield an autonomous "First Principle" convincingly shown to be a cause not just of motion, but of all being. The proof of the Creator's existence must therefore lie elsewhere—in Ibn Sina's own metaphysical account, which rests on the proposition that every being other than God has a dual aspect. One aspect is that as a being that has been caused to come into existence (since every effect has a cause), in its essential, preexisting or potential state it had been capable of either existing or not; in other words, its existence considered in itself is contingent, and so not part of its essence. The second aspect is that subsequently having been caused in fact, its existence is now necessary, albeit through another (its cause). Ibn Rushd identifies Ibn Sina as "the first to devise this formulation . . . contingent in itself and necessary through another."[19] As one traces back the chain of causation from each effect to its cause, however, the only way to avoid a logically inadmissible infinite regress is to posit an initial cause that is itself uncaused; that is, a being that is necessary in itself. Since the essence of a necessary existent is to exist, in this one case essence equals existence, and the first cause is a unitary and therefore immaterial being: the Necessary Existent (*wājib al-wujūd*), or God.

But how can such a divine entity maintain its absolute, unchanging, and eternal self-sufficiency and still exert providential intervention on the entirety of creation in all its mutable particulars? Since such intervention cannot be direct; since, as he liked to put it, from one thing only one thing can proceed, Ibn Sina adopted the Neoplatonic conception of an intervening hierarchy of celestial entities. In an act endowed with its divine knowledge (*maʿrifa*) and consent (*riḍa*),[20] the unitary Necessary Existent emanates one thing: the First Intellect, which nevertheless has the aforementioned two aspects of being contingent in itself, and necessary through another. Whereas the Necessary Existent thinks only Himself, therefore, the First Intellect can be said to have three objects of contemplation. When it contemplates itself as contingent in itself, it emanates a celestial body; when it contemplates itself as necessary through another, it emanates an angelic soul (or form) which animates that celestial body; and when it contemplates its creator (the Necessary Existent) as necessary in itself—and accordingly as a model to be loved and emulated—it somehow emanates another, still less perfect, celestial intellect. This emanative process continues downward until it reaches the tenth and last of the celestial intellects, the Active Intellect or Giver of Forms (*wāhib al-ṣuwar*), whose level of perfection is such that it can only emanate the multiplicity of the sublunar world, including human thought itself.[21] In this manner Ibn Sina sought to resolve another critical problem confronting philosophy in the age of revealed religion: how to preserve the Aristotelian principles of both efficient and final causation without violating the monotheistic imperative of maintaining a unitary God. As initiator of emanation, God acts as the efficient cause of all that ensues; as a model of perfection which everything below strives to emulate, He acts as final cause.[22]

Transitioning from cosmology to psychology, Ibn Sina emphasized the external, separate existence of the Active Intellect as the repository of the intelligible forms which make human thought possible, and which can only be accessed by the human intellect through "conjunction" (*ittiṣāl*) with it. Since the capacity for acquiring knowledge varies from individual to individual, however, human beings achieve varying levels of such conjunction. In some very rare cases, an individual is able to access the diverse kinds of celestial knowledge in an immediate and perfect manner—intuitively as it were, "dispensing with learning and thought" or routine scientific procedures—and can even prognosticate particular future events.[23] These are the prophets, who convey what needs to be conveyed for the benefit of the rest of humanity. Ibn Sina's account here rests on the composite character of the Active Intellect as a celestial being with an embodied soul, because as such it possesses knowledge of particular things which can be relayed to a prophet.[24] Even after the passing of their perishable bodies, finally, the most intellectually accomplished human beings can attain permanent conjunction with the Active Intellect. In this way, then, Ibn Sina sought to formulate a metaphysics that preserves causality even as it provides an account of how a monad can emanate a pluralistic universe, that maintains independent foundations or standards of right and wrong, and that at the same time goes far beyond Aristotle in trying to accommodate the various features of Islam: from a creative and providential God, to prophetic revelation, to the immortality of individual souls.

Ibn Rushd's Critique of Ibn Sina's Metaphysics

According to Fazlur Rahman, this schema of Ibn Sina's came in response to an "acute crisis" of faith in Islamic doctrine that arose in his time, and that as such—much like the "tripartite theology" with which the Stoics had tried to defend their "popular religion against the onslaught of the Hellenic enlightenment" over a millennium earlier—it can "justifiably" be considered a defense of the faith.[25] If so, Ibn Rushd nevertheless finds much to criticize in it. His central objection to Ibn Sina parallels his central objection to dialectical theologians (*mutakallimūn*) such as the Muʿtazilis and Ashʿaris: their inappropriate admixture of the terminology and procedures of philosophy and religion ends up undermining both. Thus, Ibn Sina's attempt to reconcile Islam to philosophy through his theologized metaphysics succeeded only in enabling Abu Hamid al-Ghazali (d. 1111) to attack him—and through him, philosophers in general—on religious grounds, for example in his influential book *The Incoherence of the Philosophers*. In his response, *The Incoherence of the Incoherence*

(*Tahafut al-Tahafut*), Ibn Rushd is therefore obliged to refute point by point the charge of heresy al-Ghazali levels against the philosophers on three counts: bodily resurrection, God's knowledge of particulars, and the temporal createdness of the universe. Although Ibn Rushd denies that true philosophers contradict Islam on any of these points—even occasionally singling out Ibn Sina for defense[26]—his overall strategy is to ascribe the alleged confusion primarily to Ibn Sina's (and to a lesser extent, al-Farabi's) poorly formulated and eccentric arguments.

Accordingly, Ibn Sina is said to go wrong right from the outset by expanding the domain of metaphysics from the study of immaterial or divine beings to the study of being itself—a departure that led him to conclusions contradicting those of the Aristotelian tradition which Ibn Rushd identifies with true philosophy. The proposition that something can be contingent in itself yet necessary through another, for example, is a "mistaken theory" based on a false essence-existence distinction which Ibn Sina "took from the theologians," and which rested on their unwarranted "assumption that the world in its totality is contingent."[27] In fact, Ibn Rushd adds, "in the necessary, in whatever way you suppose it, there is no contingency whatsoever and there exists nothing of a single nature of which it can be said that it is in one way contingent and in another way necessary in its existence"— unless "contingent" is taken equivocally, to refer to the celestial body's motion as opposed to its existence.[28] Similarly, the celestial bodies, not being subject to generation and corruption, are not composite in the manner of transient sublunary bodies: "the assertion that the celestial body is composed of form and matter like other bodies is something falsely ascribed by Ibn Sina to the Peripatetics."[29] And: "That each body is composed of matter and form is not the doctrine of the philosophers about the celestial body—unless 'matter' is used here equivocally—but of Ibn Sina alone."[30] The collapse of Ibn Sina's dualistic framework, in turn, renders untenable his theory that the mere contemplation by a celestial intellect of its principle or of itself in its various aspects suffices to generate the multiplicity of the cosmos, for, again, the intellect can never be composite: "This, however, is a mistake according to philosophical teaching, for thinker and thought are one identical thing in human intellect and this is still more true in the case of the separate intellects."[31]

Ibn Sina's failure to provide a philosophically convincing account of the universe, according to Ibn Rushd, is equally evident in his depiction of the final stage in the process of emanation, the point of contact between the Active Intellect and the sublunar world. To simplify greatly, Ibn Rushd's criticisms on this score revolve around two key points. The first is the extent to which responsibility for the diversity and dynamism of the sublunar world can be ascribed to an external celestial entity such as the Active Intellect. For Ibn Sina, the Active Intellect does indeed emanate our entire world, because in its aspect as an embodied soul, it is "corporeal, transformable, and changeable," with estimative and imaginative cognitive functions resembling those of human beings, and therefore enabling the Active Intellect to apprehend—as well as emanate—not only abstract universal intelligibles, but also the world's manifold sensory particulars.[32] As even Ibn Sina's follower Nasir al-Din al-Tusi (d. 1274) later acknowledged, this is a clearly un-Aristotelian proposition: "The opinion of the Peripatetics is that the intelligible universals are imprinted in one thing, and the sensory particulars in another."[33]

Ibn Rushd for his part denies not only that the Active Intellect is a composite of form and matter, that it has estimative or imaginative faculties, and that it can thereby apprehend particulars, but more broadly that such an incorporeal entity can "have a general effect on all that comes to be without an intermediary, as maintained by Ibn Sina."[34] To argue that terrestrial beings can be spontaneously generated by such an agent is to undermine natural causality, and thus natural philosophy or science as a whole. Whereas Ibn Sina went beyond even al-Farabi in rejecting naturalistic explanations for the production of sublunar matter,[35] accordingly, Ibn Rushd argues that "Aristotle introduces the separate intellectual principle in the natural sciences only for the human intellect and for the motions of the celestial bodies," leaving other sublunar effects to be explained by natural causes such as heat and motion.[36]

The second key point in Ibn Rushd's philosophical critique on this score is his resistance to Ibn Sina's depiction of human thought as a passive reception of emanations from a wholly external repository of intelligibles, the Active Intellect, and his struggle to locate instead the decisive origins of thought within, as arising from willful human effort.[37] This difference extends also to the two thinkers' treatments of prophecy, with Ibn Sina emphasizing an instantaneous and perfect apprehension of intelligibles emanating from the Active Intellect, and Ibn Rushd recoiling from the suggestion that knowledge can be acquired through any but normal scientific means: "It is therefore impossible that a theoretical art be fully acquired by a person, by

God, unless a person assumes that we have here a species of man that can comprehend the theoretical sciences without training. Now this species, if indeed it existed, would be called 'man' only equivocally, but actually it would be closer to the angels than to man."³⁸ On both scores, then, the overall thrust of Ibn Rushd's account of his philosophical differences with Ibn Sina is to highlight his own preference for moving natural and intellectual agency away from the Active Intellect and back to our sublunar world.

At the same time, Ibn Rushd asserts, his faulty theologized philosophy led Ibn Sina to questionable *religious* conclusions that drew the ire of theologians as well. When Ibn Sina divided existence into that which is necessary and that which is contingent, for example, he could "no longer prove the impossibility of the existence of an infinite causal series," he thereby undermined the foundations of belief in an ultimate Creator, and he was unable to avert the "objections" al-Ghazali consequently "directed against him"—and by extension, against philosophy as a whole.³⁹ Most generally, Ibn Rushd concludes, Ibn Sina's emanationist model, far from constituting a successful defense of the faith, ends up satisfying the sober strictures of religion no better than it does the logical standards of philosophy:

> All these are senseless statements and assertions, weaker than those of the theologians, extraneous to philosophy, and not congruous with its principles, and none of these affirmations reaches the level of rhetorical persuasion, to say nothing of dialectical persuasion. And therefore what Ghazali says in different passages of his books is true, that the metaphysics of Farabi and Ibn Sina are conjectural.⁴⁰

Ibn Rushd's Alternative Account

The outlines of Ibn Rushd's alternative account are already evident in his critique of Ibn Sina's metaphysics. Both begin from the same starting point: the affirmation that there are real, unchanging things—God, the Good—beyond the material world. Both claim to confront adversaries on two fronts: on one front, the atheistic materialists (*dahriyya*) who deny any such transcendent entities; on the other, dialectical theologians (such as the Ashʿaris) who reject natural causation and human agency altogether, and who instead ascribe to God an absolute control over all effects that cannot be constrained even by independent standards of good or evil. Both Ibn Rushd and Ibn Sina, finally, continue to adhere to the paradigm of a hierarchy of celestial beings; a paradigm that for centuries proved so appealing because it seemed to provide a grounding that could accommodate the imperatives of philosophy and religion simultaneously. Within this paradigm, however, Ibn Rushd seeks to correct what he identifies as Ibn Sina's fatal deviations.

Thus, dismissing Ibn Sina's theory of emanation as a "false fabrication" and "something the community [of Aristotelian philosophers] does not recognize," Ibn Rushd shifts the emphasis back from efficient to final causality, whereby the higher entities come to serve more as models to be contemplated, desired, and emulated.[41] The Active Intellect in particular is stripped of responsibility for the generation of natural forms, and downgraded into a catalyst for the abstraction and understanding of intelligibles *within* the human mind—two activities Ibn Rushd stresses are products of "our will" (*mashīʾatuna*).[42] Increasingly prominent, by contrast, is the Material (or Potential) Intellect (*al-ʿaql al-hayūlānī*), which assumes the role of primary arena where Ibn Rushd struggles with the old problem of how to posit any conjoining between the perishable individual human mind and the enduring universals that must exist. Not surprisingly, therefore, as Alfred Ivry points out, the Material Intellect's "nature and location . . . troubled him through much of his career."[43] In his Short Commentary on Aristotle's *De Anima*, Ibn Rushd describes it primarily as a receptive disposition located in the individual soul (and hence a human faculty); in his Middle Commentary on the same work, he focuses on the argument that it is at the same time somehow a separate substance, immaterial and unchangeable (and hence capable of apprehending universal intelligibles); and in his Long Commentary he presents the Material Intellect as "a being which is other than form and matter and the composite of these," an altogether "fourth kind of being" which is no longer grounded in each individual human soul, but rather a single transcendent and eternal intellect shared by all mortal humans.[44]

Coupled with an expanded emphasis on the cogitative faculty of individual human minds, this novel conception of the Material Intellect was the best Ibn Rushd could do to affirm human agency in the process of intellection. It is a solution that has satisfied few readers. Herbert Davidson, for example, assuming a progression in Ibn

Rushd's thought from his Short to Middle to Long Commentary on the *De Anima*, wishes that he had "returned to his original naturalistic construction of the material intellect, and incorporated the original construction into his new, hard-won naturalistic account of biological processes."[45] To have done so, however, would have brought him too close to "those who deny agent [efficient] causes and those who allow only material causes," and that is something Ibn Rushd will not countenance.[46] Still, he himself clearly recognizes the inadequacy of his solution, and underscores its tentative character:

> Since there are all those things [which can be raised regarding the material intellect], for this reason it seemed [best] to me to write what seemed to me to be the case on this topic. If what appears to me is not complete, it will be a start for a complete account. So I ask my brothers seeing this exposition to write down their doubts and perhaps in that way what is true regarding this will be found out, if I have not yet found [it].[47]

Similarly, Barry Kogan notes that Ibn Rushd prefaces his account of divine and celestial causation in the *Tahafut al-Tahafut*—much of which Kogan finds "inadequate on philosophical grounds"—with an acknowledgment that many of his arguments will not be demonstrative.[48] Here, then, is the second of three key general differences between Ibn Sina and Ibn Rushd, after the latter's greater emphasis on natural causation and human agency. It has been observed that the "Socratic way of doing philosophy . . . is totally alien" to Ibn Sina; that his "reworking" of Aristotle's *Metaphysics*, for example, sought to replace its "non-demonstrative procedures" with more "assertive" ones.[49] In sharp contrast to this "systematic, apparently 'complete' character" of Ibn Sina's theologized philosophy,[50] Ibn Rushd—particularly when dealing with divine or celestial matters—prefers to display much less certitude.

One way Ibn Rushd does so is by highlighting the incommensurability of certain key terms when discussing celestial as opposed to sublunar phenomena. His criticism of Ibn Sina for comparing the form and matter, as well as cognitive functions, of celestial bodies to those of earthly ones has already been noted. Evoking the Qur'anic verse (42.11) about God that "Nothing is like unto Him; He is the All-Seeing and the All-Hearing," he likewise insists on the equivocality of concepts such as God's "knowledge," "will," and "justice" regarding sublunary particulars: they mean different things than when applied to mortal creatures.[51] Ibn Rushd reiterates the need to maintain a sharp distinction between the terminology and procedures of philosophy on the one hand, and those of theology on the other, when criticizing what he describes as Ibn Sina's characteristically and eccentrically definite views on prophetic miracles:

> As for the discussion of miracles, this is something about which the ancients had nothing to say, because according to them they are among the things which must not be examined and questioned; for they are principles of religions, and the one who inquires into them and doubts them, according to them, merits punishment, like the one who examines the other general religious principles, such as whether God exists, or happiness (sa'āda) exists, or the virtues (faḍā'il) exist. For their existence cannot be doubted, and the mode of their existence is a divine matter beyond the apprehension of human minds.[52]

The full extent of Ibn Rushd's concerns about Ibn Sina's assertions of certainty in matters beyond the limits of theoretical philosophy, and about the consequences of such transgressions for the affirmation of transcendent principles such as God or the Good, can be further clarified by a consideration of his comments on Ibn Sina's famous "Eastern philosophy."

Ibn Rushd's Critique of Ibn Sina's Politics

The extent to which Ibn Sina's metaphysics injected an irrational or mystical element into the philosophical tradition in the Islamic world is a question that has long been highly contested (see chapter 5 for the views of some contemporary Arab scholars). One of the earliest interventions in this debate came from Ibn Tufayl (d. 1185), the Andalusian philosopher and contemporary of Ibn Rushd, in the introduction to his version of the fable *Hayy ibn Yaqzan*. There, Ibn Tufayl wrote that whereas Ibn Sina set out to convey Aristotle's teachings and methods in his *Shifa'*, he "stated explicitly that in his opinion the truth is something else, that he wrote the *Shifa'* according to the doctrine of the Peripatetics only, and that 'whoever wants the truth without indirection should seek' his book on Eastern philosophy" instead.[53]

Dimitri Gutas has argued that Ibn Tufayl distorted Ibn Sina's words in order to imply that the latter's true ("Eastern") teaching was much more mystical than rationalistic—and hence less objectionable to theologians such as al-Ghazali—the better to invoke Ibn Sina's authority on behalf of his own philosophical fable; that the difference Ibn Sina pointed to between his works was in reality one of style more than doctrine; and that the widespread subsequent reading of Ibn Sina as a mystic and wellspring of the "Illuminationist" theosophy of Shahab al-Din Suhrawardi (d. 1191) and his followers is accordingly altogether unfounded.[54] Gutas acknowledges Ibn Sina's "occasional use of sufi vocabulary . . . in an effort to incorporate its referents . . . into his philosophical system,"[55] and he acknowledges also that Ibn Sina's attempt to articulate his differences with the Aristotelians explicitly through his "Eastern philosophy" ultimately proved "too much neoterizing for his milieu to take," so that "in his final years" he "tacitly disowned the idea of the Easterners."[56] Nevertheless, Gutas insists: "In all of this, Avicenna makes no concessions to any kind of knowledge that could not be explained within his rationalist and empiricist analysis of the faculties and abilities of the human soul."[57]

Since the writings that contain what Ibn Sina called his Eastern philosophy are largely lost, it is difficult to reconstruct their intent precisely. It is possible, however, to propose a third alternative between characterizing them as merely stylistic variations on Ibn Sina's for the most part straightforwardly rationalistic body of work, and depicting them as his genuinely mystical secret teachings. Scattered here and there among Ibn Rushd's writings is a set of comments regarding Ibn Sina from an altogether different perspective. One of the most extensive is from a relatively obscure treatise, hitherto extant only in Latin, devoted to arguing "against some Avicennians" on the proof of God's existence, and which the translators suggest he wrote "near the end of his life," in which Ibn Rushd says the following:

> When there was a revolution in the country of the Berbers, I met someone who had studied the books of that man [Ibn Sina]. This person was a renowned specialist of those books, and he propagated them and praised Avicenna <for his theory> of the necessary being. But I noticed that an abominable opinion had developed in the science he had

recently discovered. For <in his view,> Avicenna had never meant by the 'necessary being' something abstracted from the universe or separated from it, but rather he meant the whole universe. . . . When I talked with those <philosophers> they said in plain language that Avicenna had concealed something in his doctrine so as to agree with his contemporaries. That man thought that it was impossible to prove the existence of a being separate from matter, a being which is not a body and does not exist in a body; and he thought that this was the viewpoint that Avicenna had secretly demonstrated in his Oriental Philosophy. He believed that Avicenna had explained the truth only in that Philosophy, whereas he had established in his writings many other theses to agree with his contemporaries. <Armed> with this opinion he attempted to abolish science and, what is even worse, to destroy the nature of being as a whole.[58]

Elsewhere, in another piece on physics, Ibn Rushd repeats his allegation that "many of the recent philosophers . . . who follow the doctrine of Avicenna" believe their master held that "there is no being here, which is incorporeal, subsisting in itself, separate from the [celestial] bodies."[59] And in his *Tahafut al-Tahafut*, Ibn Rushd writes that "we see nowadays that many of Ibn Sina's followers . . . say that he does not believe that there exists a separate existence," and that he called his book Eastern Philosophy because "according to the doctrine of the people of the East, the Gods (*al-āliha*) are the celestial bodies, as he [Ibn Sina] had come to believe (*'ala mā kāna yadhhab ilayhi*)."[60] According to Ibn Rushd, then, the real secret in Ibn Sina's writings—at least according to his unnamed followers—was not adherence to some theosophical mysticism, but to an atheistic materialism that rejected transcendent realities altogether.

In the course of discussing Judah Halevi's *Kuzari* (*Kitab al-Khazari*), Leo Strauss advances three points apparently inspired by Ibn Rushd's allegations. First, citing Maimonides's conjecture that the author of a tenth-century book on Sabean magic deliberately "presented his ridiculous nonsense in order to cast doubt on the Biblical miracles," Strauss suggests: "It is perhaps not absurd to wonder whether books such as the *Nabatean Agriculture* were written, not by simple-minded adherents of superstitious creeds and practices, but by adherents of the philosophers." He then immediately notes that "the basic tenet of the Sabeans is identical with what adherents of Avicenna declared to be the basic tenet of Avicenna's esoteric teaching, viz., the identification of God with the heavenly bodies."[61] Second, Strauss adds: "The same would be true *mutatis mutandis* of the rational *nomoi* composed by the philosophers in so far as they served the purpose of undermining the belief in Divine legislation proper."[62] He thus indicates that not just Ibn Sina's "Eastern" musings but the entirety of his theologized metaphysics served a double purpose: to accommodate the religious sensibilities of the majority of his readers while at the same time undermining the same sensibilities of the select few qualified to engage in true philosophy. Third, however, Strauss concludes by recoiling from the "enormously dangerous" implications of this approach—specifically, its atheistic denial of transcendent or natural morality—and validating instead Halevi's defense of the rationality of religion against such philosophizing; a defense Strauss stresses is "identical with the aim of the [Islamic] kalâm."[63]

If this was indeed Ibn Sina's intention; if his cosmological fables really were designed to secure himself and his philosophical followers against the gullible masses and their religious leaders, then for Ibn Rushd it was a strategy that backfired disastrously. Far from establishing a successful accommodation between philosophers and their community, Ibn Sina succeeded only in bringing about a situation where religion was left largely to the likes of either the dogmatic theologians or the various kinds of mystics, and where philosophy itself devolved into a self-indulgent, amoral, and socially irresponsible preoccupation with sterile theorizing: "Perhaps this is one of the reasons why we see that the customs and habits of most of those devoting themselves to philosophy in this time are corrupt."[64] Ibn Rushd's implicit critique of Ibn Sina here—the third general difference between them—is that the latter failed to grapple adequately with the moral and political consequences of his Eastern philosophizing.

In contrast to Ibn Sina's widely noted neglect of politics and public morality, for which he spared just a handful of pages in his mammoth compendium *al-Shifa'*, Ibn Rushd makes clear the centrality of such concerns for him even in apparently unlikely places; beginning his Long Commentary on Aristotle's *De Anima*, for example, by stressing the political significance of its subject matter: "it supplies more principles for more sciences, for example, for moral science—that is, [the science] of governing states—and for divine science."[65] In this, Ibn Rushd follows the approach of al-Farabi before him, who denounced the pursuit of theoretical sciences without "the faculty for exploiting them for the benefit of others" as "defective," and who described one particular type of such defective philosophy thus: "The vain philosopher is he who learns the theoretical sciences, but without going any further and without being habituated to doing the acts considered virtuous by a certain religion or the generally accepted noble acts. Instead he follows his own inclination and appetites in everything, whatever they may happen to be."[66] For one representative of a certain strand within the "Straussian" school, such valorization of practical philosophy reveals al-Farabi's "idealism," while Ibn Sina's relative indifference to politics and ethics indicates his clearer appreciation of the ultimate futility of political action, his retreat into private contemplation, and thus of his "realism."[67] For a fuller consideration of this distinction, it is necessary to turn now to Ibn Rushd's more explicitly political writings.

Ibn Rushd's Political Philosophy

Ibn Rushd's political realism flows from the three primary differences he draws between himself and the Ibn Sina he depicts. His rejection of theologized metaphysics leads him to seek a new, mutually respectful accommodation between religion and philosophy which acknowledges the distinctions between the terminology, procedures, and objectives proper to each. His rejection of "vain philosophy" leads him to valorize the practical sciences that make decent communal life possible in this world, and to the conviction that the optimal conditions for such a life—the best political regime—can and should be implemented in deed. And his rejection of unwarranted claims to certainty leads him to value pragmatic statecraft over a dogmatic legalism incapable of taking into account the vicissitudes of human affairs.

Ibn Rushd begins, accordingly, by insisting in the strongest possible terms that philosophers not dispute the principles and doctrines of their religion: "The denial and discussion of these principles negates human existence, and therefore heretics must be killed. Of religious principles it must be said that they are divine things which surpass human understanding, but must be acknowledged although their causes are unknown."[68] This is because true philosophers understand that "religious laws are necessary political arts"—that is, they are necessary for the moral development and social well-being of the learned and ignorant alike.[69] At the same time, as Ibn Rushd elaborates in his

Decisive Treatise Determining the Connection Between the Law and Wisdom, religion not only sanctions but mandates the use of God-given reason to reflect on His creation—particularly by means of the most perfect kind of syllogistic reasoning, which is demonstration—and to benefit in the process from the insights of those "who reflected upon these things before the religion of Islam."[70] It is therefore "evident that reflection upon the books of the Ancients is obligatory according to the Law, for their aim and intention in their books is the very intention to which the Law urges us."[71]

The basis for this new accommodation is that philosophy and religion articulate the same ultimate truths in different ways, which in turn is due to the fact that capabilities for comprehension vary between individuals—a few are by nature responsive to demonstration, others require dialectical instruction, and still others (the great majority) can be moved only by rhetoric.[72] Since religion addresses all humanity, it employs all three methods; and since rhetoric employs non-demonstrative arguments and analogies, its explicit rhetorical statements occasionally seem to contradict what demonstration would indicate. In such cases, Ibn Rushd affirms, "whenever demonstration leads to something differing from the apparent sense of the Law, that apparent sense admits of interpretation (*ta'wīl*)."[73] He emphasizes, however, that it is *only* in such cases that interpretation is sanctioned, and then "only in books using demonstrations" addressed to the first category of people.[74] Since "consensus is not to be determined with certainty about theoretical matters" at least, presenting such necessarily tentative interpretations to the public at large, and in books that mix up the different categories of argument, can only incite dogmatic factionalism, provoke a backlash against philosophical inquiry, or undermine faith altogether—in short, it is to commit "error against the Law and against wisdom."[75] And indeed, Ibn Rushd concludes, when theologians belonging to the intermediate dialectical class such as the Muʿtazilis and Ashʿaris did engage in such reckless interpretation, "they threw people into loathing, mutual hatred, and wars; they tore the Law to shreds; and they split the people up into every sort of faction."[76]

Ibn Rushd expands his attack on such theologians in his treatise *Uncovering the Methods of Proofs with Respect to the Beliefs of the Religious Community*, where he again begins by distinguishing between different categories of people, this time citing a Prophetic Tradition: "We, the prophets, have been ordered to put people in their places, and to address them according to their rational capacities."[77] Unlike either the general public or the learned few, each of which accepts the truths intended by religion in its own characteristic way (the former literally; the latter also through tentative interpretation where appropriate), the "adepts of dialectic (*Jadal*) and of theology (*Kalam*)" in their folly offer the public half-baked and often conflicting interpretations that are even less "convincing" or "believable" than the explicit religious texts themselves,[78] and demand acceptance of these interpretations with dogmatic insistence, provoking division and strife within the "great medication" of religion:

> The first group to change this great medication were the Kharijites, followed by the Muʿtazilites, the Ashʿarites and then the Sufis. Then Abu Hamid [al-Ghazali] came and opened the flood-gates of the valley so that all the towns were swept away. For, he divulged all [the secrets of] philosophy to the general public, as well as the opinions of the philosophers, to the extent that he was able to understand them.[79]

The net "result of this confusion and muddling" is to drive "many people away from both philosophy and religion."[80] It would have been much more politically responsible to have respected the proper order of natures and discourses. Now that the flood-gates have been opened, however, there is no going back, so Ibn Rushd is "compelled" to do what he would rather not do: to subject a series of controversial religious principles to direct analysis in order to show that in reality the truths of philosophy do not contradict the truths of Islam.[81] His discussion of contingency and causality, for example, takes aim at the occasionalist Ashʿari premise that since there can be no active agent other than God—so that every effect must be the product of a divine will that cannot be circumscribed in any way—"it is possible for the world, with everything in it, to be the opposite of what it actually is."[82] Such rejection of necessary causality, Ibn Rushd argues, "abolishes wisdom, because wisdom is nothing more than the knowledge of the causes of existing things." Not only are the natural and philosophical sciences thereby abolished, religion too is undermined because believers are left with no means to rebut the atheistic advocates of pure chance.[83] Ibn Rushd cannot resist observing at this point that "Ibn Sina accepts this premise in a certain respect, since he believes that every existing entity, other than the Agent, if considered in itself, is possible and contingent," but then reminds himself: "This, however, is not the place to argue with this man."[84] Most fundamentally, at any rate, since "all people consider that only base products could have been made differently," the notion that everything is contingent undermines belief in eternal or necessary noble truths and virtues. Once again, both philosophy and religion undergo serious harm.[85]

Ibn Rushd returns to this point in his discussion of justice, where he brings up the "very odd" Ash'ari view that "there is nothing here on earth that is just in itself or unjust in itself."[86] Again, this is because such theologians deny that God can be constrained by any absolute standards of good or evil. As Ibn Rushd notes elsewhere: "According to this, there is nothing beautiful or base other than by fiat."[87] In their effort to establish God's complete autonomy, the dialectical theologians undermine the objective or natural grounding of a distinction that is crucial for the learned and the multitude alike; for any kind of decent polity at all. Instead, argues Ibn Rushd, one must affirm the reality of the noble and the base, of justice and injustice, and conclude that God allows the latter to exist for the sake of some greater good: "It is self-evident that the coexistence of the greater good with the lesser evil is better than nullifying the greater good altogether lest the lesser evil should exist."[88] In this way God's autonomy and His justice can both be maintained as long as it is kept in mind that He "is not described as just in the same sense in which the human being is so described."[89] Ibn Rushd appeals to similar equivocation, finally, when he turns to the contentious debate about God's attributes in general. Rather than recognizing that attributes such as corporeality or directionality are spoken of God "in a different manner" than of terrestrial beings,[90] the practitioners of *kalām* simply deny them altogether and publicly, and in doing so undermine the representations that make God above imaginable to common people.

His appreciation of the damage caused by an inadequate understanding of the objectives and methods specific to theology and philosophy, respectively, then, leads Ibn Rushd to a political conclusion: the interpretation of ambiguous theoretical statements in religion cannot be left in the hands of the poorly educated and reckless dogmatists of *kalām*, but should be entrusted instead to those with the requisite philosophical training to recognize where "consensus is never to be had," and to judge how to address different audiences so that philosophy and religion do not come into conflict with each other.

This in turn obviously entails a much greater legal and political role for philosophers, the shirking of which would constitute irresponsible self-indulgence. The importance of the practical sciences for Ibn Rushd is accordingly elevated to a higher degree than with Ibn Sina. Political science in particular emerges as the highest of these practical sciences, and Ibn Rushd goes so far as to argue—contrary even to Aristotle—that it has itself a theoretical part where demonstration, not just convincing rhetorical or dialectical arguments, becomes possible.[91] This emphasis on political philosophy is especially apparent in Ibn Rushd's commentaries on Aristotle's *Rhetoric* and Plato's *Republic*. In the former, he sets out by recapitulating the classical types of political regime as monarchy, which has honor as its end; oligarchy, with wealth as its end; democracy, with freedom as its end; and aristocracy—called by Ibn Rushd "the regime of good dominion" (*siyāsat jūdat al-tasalluṭ*)—with "virtue [*faḍīla*] and holding fast to law" as its end.[92] He describes this last regime as "the dominion by which the well-being of the citizens and human happiness is attained." Its rulers "possess virtue and are capable of the actions that improve the city; and they possess discernment and are wary of whatever might corrupt the city from without or from within." A virtuous regime, in short, is one that manifests justice by attending to the well-being of the whole city and not just of its rulers.[93]

Then, in another departure from Aristotle, Ibn Rushd makes a further distinction within this fourth, virtuous, type of regime: (a) "rulership of the king [*riyāsat al-malik*], which is the city whose opinions and actions are in accordance with what the theoretical sciences prescribe" and which in fact evidently corresponds to the ideal city ruled by Plato's philosopher-king; and (b) "rulership of the best [*riyāsat al-akhyār*], which is the one whose actions alone are virtuous and is known as the imamate. According to what Abu Nasr [al-Farabi] said, it existed among the ancient Persians."[94] This identification by Ibn Rushd as one of the two kinds of best regime, one where the actions but not opinions of the city are in accordance with what philosophy prescribes, has puzzled modern readers such as Charles Butterworth: "Part of the enigma behind his identification of the 'rulership of the best,' that is, the Imamate or priestly regime, as the second kind of best regime . . . is that he never explicitly criticizes it and certainly never rejects it. It remains not merely as one of the kinds of virtuous regime, not merely as the best possible regime, but as the one regime whose merits have actually been tested."[95] Since this is a decisive question that goes to the very heart of how al-Farabi and Ibn Rushd understand the relationship between philosophy and governance, it is worth looking at in some detail.

Patricia Crone approached the problem by going back to al-Farabi himself.[96] Al-Farabi's reference to the ancient Persian regime, however, cited also by Ibn Rushd's older contemporary Ibn Bajja, is apparently not found in his extant writings, though it has been speculated that it appeared in one or the other of his lost works.[97] Crone therefore turned to al-Farabi's *Selected Aphorisms* instead, where he identifies two pairs of virtuous cities. The first pair are ruled either by a founder (*al-raʾīs al-awwal*) who unites all the necessary leadership qualities—including wisdom (*ḥikma*), prudence (*taʿaqqul*), the power to persuade, and the ability to wage jihad—in himself, or by a group of founders in whom the necessary qualities are dispersed. The second pair are ruled either by a successor or a group of successors who have the "excellence of discernment" to understand the intentions of the founders (*maqṣūd al-awwalīn*) and adapt their laws to changing circumstances and new exigencies.[98] Even though al-Farabi begins by stating that all four kinds of virtuous *city* contain "wise" and "prudent" individuals who "have opinions on great matters," the fact that he does not explicitly say here about the second pair of *rulers* what he says about the first—namely, that they possess wisdom—led Crone to conclude that this second pair of rulers are "less outstanding," in that they are merely faithful implementers rather than formulators of the law, and their regimes consequently philosophically "inferior."[99] Although al-Farabi must therefore have intended the point about actions but not opinions being virtuous to refer to these second, inferior pair of regimes, a copyist (here Crone admits to "venturing into deep conjecture") might have mistakenly attributed it to the "highest form of government" instead. The resulting corruption of al-Farabi's text would then be the reason for Ibn Rushd's "odd" and "problematic" identification of this non-philosophic rule as a version of the highest kind of regime.[100]

This explanation cannot be correct because al-Farabi's wording is consistent with what he writes elsewhere. In another of his books, *The Principles of the Opinions of the Inhabitants of the Virtuous City*, he again outlines the four types of virtuous city. Here, however, he explicitly describes the second pair as one ruled by a successor (*al-raʾīs al-thānī*) who is "a philosopher [*ḥakīm*] . . . powerful in his deductions to meet new situations for which the first sovereigns could not have laid down any law," and the other ruled by a group of successors in whom the necessary qualities are dispersed.[101] The key point is that all four virtuous cities must incorporate philosophy (*ḥikma*): "But when it happens . . . that philosophy has no share in government . . . then, after a certain interval, this city will undoubtedly perish."[102]

Although Charles Butterworth's treatment of this "enigma" is cognizant of al-Farabi's *Principles*, he likewise concludes that the "imamate" which "concentrates on actions alone" must be a regime ruled "by one competent only in administering the laws set down by the founder—one adept, that is, in the art of jurisprudence—who is also a capable warrior," and as such is a regime in which "philosophy . . . is not available to the ruler or rulers."[103] His more circumspect explanation seems to be that Ibn Rushd's presentation of this regime, which "does not even explain how these best rulers come to have virtuous actions," is a "model" meant primarily to suggest "the need to reconsider" the philosopher's imperative of going beyond merely understanding what wise rule would look like, to actually undertaking the task of training such rulers.[104]

The apparent contradiction in Ibn Rushd's depiction of a city in which actions but not opinions are virtuous, but in which philosophy nonetheless has "a share in government," disappears, however, when one keeps in mind the difference—highlighted in the previous chapter as a prominent element in medieval Islamic political thought—between the common citizenry (*ʿāmma*) who constitute the "city," and the political or philosophical elites (*khāṣṣa*) whose "opinions on great matters" shape the governance of that city. Ibn Rushd's distinction, in his *Middle Commentary on the Rhetoric*, between virtuous cities in which both opinions and actions are in accordance with what philosophy prescribes, and virtuous cities in which only actions are in such accordance, is then a distinction drawn only at the level of the citizenry. Ordinary citizens do not need to be philosophers. In fact, as the failure to provide any actual examples of the first kind of virtuous regime by both al-Farabi and Ibn Rushd indicates, that can never be the case. But their actions can be rendered virtuous through other means: a true religion, for example, or the kind of belief system that prevailed among the ancient Persians. At the level of rulers, by contrast—founders as well as successors—philosophy must in all cases have a "share in government" for the city to manifest virtue and thus longevity. Without philosophical guidance in the implementation of law, or virtuous statecraft, even the best legislation will atrophy as circumstances change, and the polity will perish. Only in this way,

Ibn Rushd indicates, is it indeed possible to have a virtuous or best kind of regime.

Elsewhere, in his commentary on Plato's *Republic*, Ibn Rushd repeats the distinctions between virtuous regimes ruled by single versus multiple rulers, and between cities that are virtuous in both opinions and actions versus those (the ancient Persian example is given again) that are virtuous in actions alone.[105] Then, after explicitly stating that he is now turning to Plato's discussion of "nonvirtuous governances," Ibn Rushd describes successors who are of lower "rank" than the virtuous ruler or rulers. Whereas the latter possess (singly or collectively) five necessary qualities—"namely, wisdom, perfect understanding, good persuasion, good imagination, and capability for war"—the lower-ranking successors have expertise only in jurisprudence (*fiqh*) and in warfare. Ibn Rushd adds that when these two qualities "are not found in a single individual, the warrior being other than the judge [. . .] the two of them must [then] necessarily share in leadership, as was the case with many of the Muslim kings."[106] In short, Ibn Rushd ranks "many of the Muslim kings"—who defer to the jurisprudential authority of the religious scholars—below their ancient Persian counterparts. The ancient Persians were virtuous rulers who had access to the philosophical insight required to understand the spirit of their foundational laws and adapt them to new circumstances. Many of the Muslim kings, by contrast, not having such access, apply their own law in a less creative, more dogmatic manner—ultimately to the fatal detriment of their polities.

At the same time, moreover, even nonvirtuous governances can be improved significantly. Ibn Rushd highlights the critical role philosophy can play in this regard when he discusses the democratic city, singled out by al-Farabi as "the marvelous and happy" one among the imperfect cities.[107] Ibn Rushd likewise admires the variety of character types produced by democracy and its core principles of freedom and equality—he echoes Plato's likening it to "a many-colored garment"—and affirms that it may even produce virtue: "Hence there will emerge in this city the totality of things that exist separately in those [other] cities. . . . Nor is it farfetched that there be among them one who has the virtues and is moved by them. Hence all the arts and dispositions emerge in this city, and it is so disposed that from it may emerge the virtuous city and every one of the other cities."[108] Nevertheless, its primary focus on the autonomy of the self and the private sphere, "contrary to what is the case in the virtuous city," generates a selfishness and lack of civic-mindedness that can lead to "ruin" at the hands of foreign invaders or domestic tyrants.[109] "Unless strengthened by virtue or honor," Ibn Rushd warns, the democratic city "perishes rapidly." That is why "the wise ought to attend to such cities"—not necessarily by ruling themselves, but by formulating, in al-Farabi's words, "opinions on great matters" which they make available to the rulers, and thereby having a "share in government."[110]

Two important conclusions emerge. First, Ibn Rushd's repeated insistence on citing the ancient Persians as actual exemplars, and his advocacy of philosophical reformism even in cities of lower rank, indicate that he views the virtuous regime as far from a utopian or merely heuristic idea. The nature of things does in fact permit the realization of political rule guided by "the wise," and consequently mandates the pursuit of happiness in this world—not just the private happiness of a select few, moreover, but the well-being of the citizenry in general. It is here that Ibn Rushd distances himself most sharply from the "vain philosophy" of those who seek merely to placate the multitude the better to wash their hands of political affairs and tend exclusively to their personal contemplative pleasures. Second, it is above all the imperative of applying law correctly or prudently that provides the rationale for an alliance between rulers and philosophers in a virtuous regime.

The core issue here is the inherently problematic character of all law. On matters other than basic eternal truths which no one may deny, changing circumstances periodically necessitate rectification of the law in accordance with its original intent:

> No one can establish laws that are comprehensive and general with respect to all people at all times, because that is infinite—I mean the alternation of the beneficial and the harmful. . . . And if matters are such, then by necessity the laws ordained will not be true for ever and always—I mean for every individual and at every time—and therefore may require addition or subtraction to be made in them. This is evident to you from the written religions in these our times.[111]

Given that variations in circumstances are infinite, and the literal application of even sound prior interpretations will not suffice, every age needs its own *mujtahids*—scholars possessing the requisite skill to interpret independently the true, underlying or non-figurative, intent of the law in light of prevailing conditions. Ibn Rushd's dissatisfaction with the dialectical theologians (*mutakallimūn*) in this regard has already been reviewed. In an early treatise on the principles of jurisprudence, he focuses his attacks on the more conventional jurists (*fuqahā'*) of "our time" whose blind literalism renders them incapable of even recognizing the exigencies of changing circumstances, let alone of the faulty interpretation attempted by the likes of the Mu'tazilis and Ash'aris. All they can do is engage in mere "imitation" (*taqlīd*) of prior authorities, and in doing so too often "transgress" against the interests of the political community as a whole by drawing inappropriate analogies for new situations.[112] Hence Ibn Rushd's advocacy of an alliance between government and philosophy, for only the political ruler has the wherewithal to implement what reason decrees. As he puts it in his *Decisive Treatise*, addressing a particularly well-inclined ruler of his time: "God has removed many of these evils, ignorant occurrences, and misguided paths by means of this triumphant rule . . . [which] calls the multitude to a middle method for being cognizant of God (glorious is He), raised above the low level of the traditionalists yet below the turbulence of the dialectical theologians, and alerts the select to the obligation for complete reflection on the root of the Law."[113]

Such a rationale, then, explains Muhsin Mahdi's surmise that Ibn Rushd's addressee in the *Decisive Treatise*, the Almohad caliph Abu Ya'qub Yusuf (r. 1163–1184), had in fact already launched an initiative to curtail the political influence of the dogmatic theologians, so that this text is meant not just to advocate for, but to "justify and defend . . . an established policy,"[114] as well as Maribel Fierro's hypothesis that Ibn Rushd's major work on jurisprudence, the *Bidayat al-Mujtahid*, was designed "to achieve something similar to what Ibn al-Muqaffa' had suggested, that is, a first step (collection of different legal opinions) towards a further stage (election on the part of the caliph of certain solutions which would eventually be codified)."[115] And indeed, in his introduction to the *Bidaya*, Ibn Rushd once again emphasizes the elusiveness of certainty regarding the law—"since the situations that may arise between people are infinite in number, whereas the texts, actions and tacit approvals of the Prophet are finite in number," so that "differences of opinion" among even qualified interpreters is "inevitable"[116]—and thereby suggests the need ultimately for a political act of will, an assertion of executive authority to suppress false opinion and select from the range of legitimate interpretations what is best suited for a particular circumstance.

Thus in Book Ten of the *Bidaya*, which is devoted to the laws of jihad, Ibn Rushd goes through the points of contention among jurists on virtually every aspect of the subject—from the legitimate justifications for waging war, to the various forms of proper conduct before, during and after hostilities.[117] On issue after issue, he shows how disagreements stem from apparent contradictions between different Qur'anic verses, or between a Qur'anic text and the practice of the Prophet, or between the words and actions of the Prophet, or between different actions of the Prophet, or between the general implications of a rule and a specific injunction. On yet other issues, disagreements stem from the absence of any specific determination at all in the Law. As a result, the jurists do not agree on even the most fundamental questions relating to war, including the underlying rationale for slaying the enemy: "those who maintained that the effective underlying cause for this is disbelief (*kufr*), did not exempt anyone of the polytheists, while those who maintained that the underlying cause in it is the ability to fight, there being a prohibition about the killing of women though they be non-believers, exempted those who do not have the ability to wage war, or those who have not affiliated themselves with it, like the peasants and the serfs."[118] Similarly, on the crucial question of whether it is permissible to suspend hostilities even in the absence of compelling circumstances such as the clear military superiority of the enemy: "A group of jurists permitted this . . . if the *imām* considered it to be in the interest of the Muslims. Another group of jurists did not permit it, except on the basis of a compelling necessity."[119]

Given such contention Ibn Rushd does not hesitate on occasion to criticize the reasoning of even the most authoritative jurists of the past, such as Abu Hanifa and Malik.[120] With only a few exceptions, however—for example concluding that the evidence favors understanding jihad as generally constituting a collective obligation (*farḍ kifāya*) rather than an individual one (*farḍ ʿayn*), or agreeing with the interpretation that gives rulers discretion in determining the amount of the poll tax (*jizya*)[121]—Ibn Rushd for the most part refrains here from offering his own opinions. Instead, his focus remains on highlighting the inevitable uncertainties, and consequent range of opinions, surrounding specific applications of the law. He makes his own preferences more explicit elsewhere. In his commentary on Aristotle's *Nicomachean Ethics*, for example, he illustrates the need to interpret the true intent of a general law in light of changing circumstances by discussing the Islamic imperative to wage jihad:

And you can understand this from the laws laid down with respect to war in the Law of the Muslims because the command in it pertaining to war is very general to such a point that they destroy, root and branch, whoever differs with them. Now there are times in which peace is more to be preferred than war. However, since the Muslim multitude make this edict of war generally valid despite the impossibility of destroying their enemies completely, great damage has attained them on account of their ignorance of the intention of the Lawgiver, the blessings of God be upon him. It is therefore proper to say that peace is preferable at times to war.[122]

Ibn Rushd is far from advocating pacifism here. His intention is to replace dogmatic inflexibility with reasoned discretion when considering war and peace. Indeed, in his capacity as jurist he often delivered sermons in the grand mosque at Cordoba exhorting jihad.[123] And he begins Book Ten of the *Bidaya* by noting that the jurists "agreed unanimously" on the obligation to wage collective jihad, reinforcing the point with a quote from the Qurʾan (2.216): "Fighting is prescribed for you, though it is hateful to you. But it may be that you hate a thing which is good for you, and it may be that you love a thing which is bad for you. God knows, and you know not."[124] In his capacity as philosopher he adopts a parallel stand. It has already been noted that one aspect of Ibn Rushd's realism consists of his denial that a virtuous regime (one in which philosophy has a share in government) attends only to the well-being of a select few, and not of the common citizens—a view for which he "takes Plato to task" in his commentary on the *Nicomachean Ethics*.[125] In his commentary on the *Republic* he criticizes Plato again, this time for seeming to suggest that only Greeks qualify for inclusion in the "class of humans disposed to the human perfections and especially to the theoretical ones."[126] If this suggestion is true, there would be no point in trying to reform the non-Greek nations. If it is false, on the other hand, then the rationale for a much more interventionist foreign policy emerges: since there is often no way of bringing political rule guided by the wise to non-virtuous nations other than "to coerce them through war," war can be justified on philosophical grounds as well.[127]

Plato's lack of interest in expansionism is also reflected in the *Republic*'s injunction to maintain the virtuous polity as a compact city-state that is not allowed to grow beyond a very limited size. Here again, Ibn Rushd takes sharp issue. If virtue and happiness are accessible to many more people than Plato apparently envisaged, then the virtuous polity can be—indeed should be—of much greater, potentially even universal, size: "This is alluded to in the saying of the Lawgiver [the prophet Muhammad]: 'I have been sent to the Red and the Black' [i.e., to all mankind]."[128] Hence the need for the inculcation of courage. For the guardians, "practical music" is particularly useful as an "art" that "conduces the soul to courage and perseverance in wars" as well as to "whichever of the virtues he [the wise legislator] intends for it to accept with ease, calmness, and quietness."[129] Without such inculcation the citizens of an increasingly thriving and prosperous polity can grow "contumacious" and unwarlike, and finally fall prey to rougher and tougher adversaries. Ibn Rushd notes that this is what happened after all to the Persian Empire at the hands of the conquering Arabs.[130] For wise legislators, the inculcation of courage is necessary both in their capacities as military commanders and in their capacities as the ultimate authorities in jurisprudence: "For one who has no courage will be unable to despise the nondemonstrative arguments on which he has grown up, and"—adds Ibn Rushd, digressing yet again from his commentary to refer explicitly to the circumstances of his own time and place—"especially if he has grown up in these cities."[131]

Ibn Rushd has been charged with misrepresenting a number of points in Ibn Sina's metaphysics, including his treatments of necessity and contingency, efficient versus final causality, and the Active Intellect. However that may be, the Ibn Sina Ibn Rushd chooses to present to his readers is one designed to serve as an instructive example of philosophical hubris. Ibn Rushd's Ibn Sina presumed to supplant the dialectical theologians with an altogether new metaphysical dogma of his own devising that would keep the multitude pacified while simultaneously attracting the brightest young minds to a life of private contemplation untroubled by social or political concerns. Instead, this presumption proved too clever by half, damaging the reputation of philosophy in Islam almost beyond repair. Ibn Sina's more gullible acolytes, meanwhile, drifted off into mysticism, while the more cynical ones sank into a nihilistic hedonism that ultimately called into question both the distinction between noble and base and the very possibility of scientific reasoning.

Much of Ibn Rushd's own metaphysics, presented with considerably less certitude, can be seen as an attempt to forestall such tendencies and to safeguard a conception of the Good that is both moral and rational. The same can be said of his politics, which is at the same time more prudently realistic and more engaged than that of the Ibn Sina he depicts. Muhammad being the seal of the prophets, statecraft replaces prophecy at the center of Ibn Rushd's new approach, as the art—informed by philosophy—of attending to the well-being of the political community as a whole, in accordance with the needs and capabilities of each citizen, in accordance with the changing requirements of the times, and in accordance with the persuasive or coercive methods appropriate to each case.

And yet there seems to be widespread consensus that it is Ibn Sina and not Ibn Rushd whose ideas found more lasting resonance in the Islamic world. Precisely because of his "theologized presentation of the theoretical sciences," according to James Morris, Ibn Sina achieved "overwhelming"—if, from a philosophical perspective, ultimately "Pyrrhic"—"historical success" over his rivals. Less reservedly, Dimitri Gutas has argued that because Ibn Sina was able to "enlarge philosophy to accommodate religious phenomena to a larger extent than his predecessors did and to prosecute this goal with unswerving philosophical vigor and consistency," he "represents the culmination of the tendencies that preceded him and constitutes the fountainhead of everything that came after him." Ibn Rushd, by contrast, "for all his brilliance as an Aristotelian commentator whom we can appreciate even today, failed to impress Arabic philosophy after his death."[132]

Before reconsidering this conclusion in light of current circumstances, it is necessary first to turn to Ibn Khaldun, a thinker upon whom at least Ibn Rushd did have some notable influence, and who brought together all the central elements of the realist tradition outlined in this and the previous chapter.

CHAPTER 4

Ibn Khaldun's Synthesis

The previous chapters identified an emphasis on imperial war and expansion as a distinguishing feature in at least some currents of Islamic political thought. On these issues as well, however, much of the scholarship continues to draw a sharp distinction between religious and rationalist approaches. Joel Kraemer, for example, argues that: "Despite the patina of Islamic vocables on the linguistic level, the Falāsifa diverge radically from true Islamic doctrine on the substantive questions concerning the nature of the best polity and the purpose of justified warfare."[1] He accordingly contrasts the *falāsifa*'s conception of just war "aimed at spreading philosophical enlightenment throughout the world" with the Islamic conception of jihad aimed at spreading Islam throughout the world.[2] This chapter will focus on the most systematic treatment of war and empire in Islamic political literature—that of Ibn Khaldun (1332–1406)—in order to assess where he stands relative to such a contrast.

For all the ink that has been spilt about him, Ibn Khaldun remains an elusive and enigmatic figure. Some have associated him with the amoral "kernel of derangement" Hamilton Gibb described as being so "foreign" to the "inner spirit" of the "Islamic ethic."[3] Thus, Majid Khadduri asserts that the "question of making a distinction between just and unjust wars is . . . irrelevant" for Ibn Khaldun, and that his characterizations of jihad as just war in his masterpiece the *Muqaddima* are mere rhetorical "concessions to [Islamic] Law."[4] Others by contrast have identified him as a pious Muslim for whom the concept of just war is entirely comprehended by jihad for the propagation of Islam.[5] The objective of what follows is to demonstrate that Ibn

Khaldun takes the insights of the preexisting intellectual tradition extending from Ibn al-Muqaffaʿ through al-Jahiz and the author of the *Mukhtasar Siyasat al-Hurub* to Ibn Rushd, and synthesizes them into a comprehensive political theory that remains true both to the "inner spirit" of Islam and to the standards of rational realism. In the process, it will be shown that a central component of successful statecraft for Ibn Khaldun is nurturing a sense of political solidarity (*ʿaṣabiyya*) that is powerful but also capable of accommodating new elements into an expanding polity, and that his animating concern is to counter those tendencies—ranging from asceticism to hedonism—which enervate such solidarity.

The Drive to Civilization: *ʿAṣabiyya* Evolution

The fundamental purpose of all political action for Ibn Khaldun is to advance culture (*ʿumrān*), "the object of the science under discussion."[6] This is because advanced culture or civilization (*ḥaḍāra*) provides the context in which human beings can realize their distinctive potential: the cultivation of "sciences and arts resulting from that ability to reflect by which the human being is distinguished from animals and exalted over all creatures."[7] Such a civilization is necessarily urban in character, as indicated by Ibn Khaldun's famous central dichotomy between civilized culture (*ʿumrān ḥaḍarī*) on the one hand, and primitive culture (*ʿumrān badawī*)—denoting not just nomadism but small-scale settlements as well—on the other. It is also characterized by its substantial size and complexity, since it takes a large population living in large cities and engaged in a multitude of specialized tasks to generate the economic production and well-being necessary for the arts, sciences, and crafts to flourish: "Know that the improvement of conditions and the increase of prosperity in [civilized] culture are consequent to its magnitude."[8] In order to ensure maximum access both to the material prerequisites of civilization and to its intellectual products, moreover, such cities must be open to foreign commodities and ideas. Care should therefore be taken to situate them "close to the sea," in order to facilitate the importation of necessities from faraway lands.[9] Ibn Khaldun emphasizes the importance of such cosmopolitanism by including "merchants and foreigners" with men of religion, descendants of the Prophet, and other "well-born persons" in the category of those who should be afforded particular respect.[10]

Next, the entire agglomeration of commercial urban centers needs to be bound together by an overarching political structure. The centrality of this institutional framework for Ibn Khaldun is indicated in his statement that "state [*dawla*] and regime [*mulk*] constitute the form of the world and of culture, and all of it with its subjects, cities, and all other things, constitute their matter."[11] *Dawla* in pre-modern Arabic denotes a "turn" in power, or period of rule by an individual or group, and hence is more usually translated as "dynasty." As Muhsin Mahdi points out, however, the distinction between ruling dynasty and state in Ibn Khaldun's writings "is not very clear. In certain places, Ibn Khaldun seems to think they are one and the same. . . . But Ibn Khaldun also states that within a large nation made up of many peoples (*shuʿūb*), various peoples (and hence dynasties) may follow each other in ruling the same state."[12] In this context, the state understood as an institutionalized structure of governance fits Ibn Khaldun's notion of what constitutes the "form of the world and of culture" better than would an individual ruler or dynasty. Similarly, whereas *mulk* denotes kingship or royal rule, it is rendered as "regime" here in order to emphasize its connotation as form of government. Ibn Khaldun's primary concern for the cultivation of the fruits of reason (the arts and sciences), at any rate, thus necessitates a centrally governed polity comprised of populous cities engaged in busy intercourse across the seas—not a small isolated inland city-state such as the one envisioned by Plato's Athenian Stranger in the *Laws*, but an empire.

Ibn Khaldun delineates the trajectory leading to civilization through his famous investigation, illustrated with historical examples both Islamic and non-Islamic, of the rise and fall of dynastic states. He begins by tracing the origins of political structures back to their natural biological beginnings—to the family and its patriarch. The primordial political unit is thus the family or clan, constituted by blood ties and the shared exigencies of survival under primitive conditions. The primordial mode of government is the rule of the patriarch and subsequently of his offspring in the noble house he founds. The primordial bond of social solidarity holding this unit together Ibn Khaldun calls *ʿaṣabiyya*—a word derived from a root referring to binding, as in a tightly twisted rope or a "convolvulus that winds itself up round a tree or some such thing" or, by extension, a close-knit kinship group.[13] In its initial Islamic usage it had the negative connotation of a clannish or tribal parochialism that fosters division and aggression instead of the broader communal unity Islam sought to create, and it continued to be used primarily in this negative sense for several centuries until Ibn Khaldun rehabilitated the term.[14]

From the very beginning, at any rate, human interactions manifest a dual aspect. Negatively, the predatory but natural human desire for dominance and gain generates destructive conflict: "Each one will stretch his hand out for what he needs and take it from its owner, in accordance with the iniquity and aggressiveness of animal nature. . . . So strife breaks out, leading to combat which leads to disorder and the spilling of blood and loss of life, which leads to the extinction of the species."[15] The same logic applies to relations between clans: "aggressiveness is natural" so war itself is also "something natural among human beings."[16] The default mode of human interaction in this natural primordial state, then, is one Ibn Khaldun characterizes as "evil" (*sharr*): "Human character includes iniquity and mutual aggression, so he who casts his eye upon the property of his brother will lay his hand upon it to take it, unless there is a restraining influence (*wāziʿ*) to hold him back." Ibn Khaldun quotes the great poet al-Mutanabbi to drive home the point:

> Iniquity is a characteristic of souls, so if you find
> a restrained person, there is a reason he does not do wrong.[17]

Positively, however, those same predatory but natural human impulses also contribute to the creation of precisely that "restraining influence" needed to counteract the destructive effects of civil strife. They explain, for example, the emergence of clan chieftains in the first place: "kingship is a noble and enjoyable position that comprises all worldly goods, bodily desires, and psychic pleasures."[18] The ambitious clan chieftain accordingly seeks to consolidate and centralize his power, and in so doing comes to replace the state of "anarchy" with a political authority that keeps his subjects apart and restrains them from waging war against each other.[19] At the same time, moreover, the centralization of power within the clan and the prosecution of campaigns against other clans combine to engender a stronger sense of collective identity and solidarity—a stronger *ʿaṣabiyya* that harmonizes the polity internally while making possible the acquisition of ever-greater domains, thereby setting in motion a process that may ultimately lead to the establishment of a much larger-scale, imperial, order in the external realm as well.

Long before then, however, the biological basis of the primordial political arrangements must erode. Leadership cannot always devolve from father to son—other, more distant, members of the clan sometimes seize power if they happen to be bigger and stronger, or are otherwise able to mobilize greater support. The clans themselves conquer and absorb neighboring clans and tribes in the course of their incessant wars. In a process Ibn Khaldun studied in some detail, those conquered clans and tribes become the wards or clients of their conquerors, and eventually come to claim common descent. Some of their abler members may rise to take the throne. In this way blood lineage, the basis of primitive kingship and solidarity, assumes an increasingly "imaginary" (*wahmī*) or mythological character over time.[20] Natural bonds give way to political ones at both the leadership and communal levels.

Ibn Khaldun underscores this distinction between biological (imaginary) and political (true) *ʿaṣabiyya* through his discussion of the prestige of noble houses. Taking issue with what he asserts to be Ibn Rushd's understanding of prestige (in the latter's commentary on Aristotle's *Rhetoric*) as a function simply of long-established presence in a community—as something that "belongs to people who are ancient settlers in a town"—Ibn Khaldun argues that "true and unqualified" prestige (*ḥasab*) entails the ability to sway the people who count, and this requires more than a distinguished pedigree.[21] It requires also the backing of a band or "group" (*ʿuṣba*) with coercive capability. As always with Ibn Khaldun, normative phenomena such as kinship affection and communal prestige must be undergirded by power relations in order to remain viable. The dual character, positive and negative, of *ʿaṣabiyya* thus operates at both levels: a leader requires coercive power to keep his immediate (kinship) group bound to him, and this in turn enables him to maintain his prestige among the broader (communal) group which he seeks to bind together and to exert authority over. Ibn Khaldun illustrates the centrality of power in true prestige and effective solidarity through a discussion of the Jews of his time, a people bound together by an extraordinary sense of distinction who "originally had one of the greatest 'houses' in the world"—as reflected in the "great number of prophets and messengers among their ancestors"—and who still take pride in the lineage of their tribes. Because they have been "destined to live as exiles on earth" and subjected to the power of others for "thousands of years," however, this pride is a "delusion" and in reality their practical "ʿaṣabiyya has disappeared."²² At the same time, the normative dimension of ʿaṣabiyya cannot be discounted either, for the distinctive hegemonic potency of the phenomenon rests on the feelings of fraternity and solidarity that allow it to serve effectively both as a marker of group identity (on the communal level), and as the basis of a political legitimacy that goes beyond mere coercion and domination (on the leadership level).

This remains the case even as the political unit evolves further and further away from its primordial origins. As a first step, the primitive chieftain and his clan embark on campaigns against neighboring groups motivated by the quest for security as well as a more aggressive "pressing of claims" (muṭālaba) fueled by the old desire for dominance and gain.²³ Mobilized by their powerful ʿaṣabiyya—because "in fighting one cannot do without ʿaṣabiyya"²⁴—these barbarians constitute a formidable force capable of sweeping away more sedentary cultures, along with all their artifacts, before it: they are to settled communities "what predators are to dumb animals. . . . They do not stop at the borders of their horizon, but conquer distant regions and overcome faraway nations."²⁵ Clans consequently give way to tribes, tribes to tribal confederations, tribal confederations to nations, nations to still broader empires. As the polity grows in size and complexity, its dominant ʿaṣabiyya is transmuted into new forms that go far beyond the original kinship group. A new "greater solidarity" (ʿaṣabiyya kubrā), subsuming narrower parochial attachments, must be manufactured—for it can no longer be "natural"—in order to stabilize the expanded polity and unite it against outsiders. Each stage of political development, then, from clan to empire, needs to manifest its own distinguishing and integrating dominant ʿaṣabiyya.²⁶

Ibn Khaldun's emphasis on the natural lineage-based origins of social solidarity has misled some of his readers into viewing ʿaṣabiyya as a primitivist concept arising from his roots in the tribalized society of the Maghrib, a concept said to be irrelevant even to the more advanced Egyptian society of his time, let alone to modern societies.²⁷ But Ibn Khaldun's explicit description of ʿaṣabiyya as emerging from shared lineage "or something corresponding to it,"²⁸ his discussion of the "greater ʿaṣabiyya" of successively broader polities, and (as will be discussed presently) his analysis of the relationship between ʿaṣabiyya and virtuous religion, all make it clear that the concept he has in mind retains its salience at all stages of political development. More specifically, it retains a crucial role in the development that is of central importance for Ibn Khaldun: if all goes well and the evolution of ʿaṣabiyya runs its proper course, the states that crystallize in domains conquered by barbarian hordes may ultimately acquire the features necessary for human culture to attain its fullest flowering. From savage beginnings, civilization can emerge.

A parallel dynamic unfolds on the leadership level. Here too, the evolution and refinement of domestic regimes requires a transmutation of ʿaṣabiyya from its natural or biological origins into increasingly complex political manifestations. Ibn Khaldun expresses this parallelism by saying that "the goal toward which ʿaṣabiyya drives is kingship."[29] At the root of the process, as always, lie human impulses that are less than sublime. As Muhsin Mahdi puts it, noting Ibn Khaldun's distinction between primitive and advanced modes of government: "unlike civilized kingship (mulk ḥaḍarī), primitive kingship (mulk badawī) cannot completely satisfy man's lust for absolute power and even less his desire for riches."[30] As soon as he can, therefore, the chieftain who would be king "pushes away" the kinfolk who helped him rise to power in the first place, and on whom he initially relied to staff the key offices of his administration. They become his "enemies" as a result, and in order to ward them off he turns to "other, unrelated assistants" instead.[31] An additional compelling motive is that the bureaucratic efficiency of an increasingly complex state structure itself mandates the replacement of the ruler's kinsmen with personnel selected on the basis of expertise and merit.[32]

The abandonment of the ruler's primordial base of support, however, means that he is no longer sustained by natural ʿaṣabiyya. If a new and broader principle of solidarity capable of binding the people to its leadership can be found, the development of an increasingly civilized polity can proceed smoothly. If not, the ruler must rely instead on coercion to maintain his position, leavened only by the opportunistic distribution of material rewards to those who are useful to him at any given time. But this is a condition so unstable that Ibn Khaldun describes it as a pathology: it "heralds the destruction of the dynasty and indicates the chronic disease that has befallen it. . . . There can be no hope of recovery."[33] The regime degenerates into a reprehensible tyranny, serving only the selfish and base "intentions and appetites" of the ruler. It cannot maintain itself for long either internally or externally, for its main effect is to enervate its subjects.[34] They "are suffused with fear and abasement, and seek to protect themselves against him through lies, duplicity, and deceit.

This becomes a character trait of theirs, and their discernment and moral habits are corrupted." Externally, the "corruption of sincerity degrades the ability to defend" against foreign enemies.[35] Internally, insubordination takes root and eventually gives rise to "disorder and bloodshed."[36] On both fronts—and this is what Ibn Khaldun cares about most—the drive toward a greater polity capable of sustaining advanced culture and civilization is stymied.

Engines of Decay

The crisis of ʿaṣabiyya encountered by the political leadership during the transition to an increasingly complex polity is one of an array of internal contradictions that emerge at every level to threaten the incipient civilization almost as soon as it begins to take shape. At the level of the army, for example, once military expansion goes beyond localized raiding a transformation in military organization becomes necessary. Tribal warriors motivated by individual glory and booty must become disciplined soldiers fighting for a greater cause. Among other things this involves discouraging individual duels between champions in favor of combat in arrayed units, and suppressing the propensity to break ranks in order to flee or plunder or pursue the enemy prematurely. More generally it requires a transition from the hit-and-run tactics (al-karr wa-l-farr) characteristic of bedouin and other primitive peoples, to the fighting in closed formation (al-zaḥf ṣufūfan) characteristic of the armies of more advanced polities. Ibn Khaldun spells out as explicitly as possible this connection between military and social organization—"in fighting in closed formation, the lines are orderly and evenly arranged, like arrows or rows of worshipers at prayer"—and reinforces the point by citing a Qurʾanic verse (61.4) that likewise evokes the link between new fighting techniques and a polity in the process of evolving into an urban civilization: "God loves those who fight for His cause in a line, as if they were a solid building."[37]

The necessary transformation is reflected in the rules of engagement as well. Martial ferocity can no longer be driven by mere bloodlust, but rather must be harnessed to the logic of the emerging civilization. In the Kitab al-ʿIbar, his broader history for which he intended the Muqaddima to be an introduction, Ibn Khaldun invokes the Prophet Muhammad and other authorities in this regard, citing their prohibitions against killing protected noncombatants such as women and children or engaging in wanton destruction of property.[38] He also depicts exemplary figures who display an aversion to bloodlust even as they go about the hard business of state building; figures such as Abu Hanifa, who convinced Caliph al-Mansur to show mercy to his enemies, or al-Mansur himself, who secured his realm by war but warned against spilling innocent blood in his testament to his son.[39] Finally, Ibn Khaldun underscores the importance of subordinating fighting spirit to political guidance through his recurrent depictions of commanders who threaten to turn their destructive energies inward—for example the brilliant Khalid ibn al-Walid, responsible for many of the most spectacular victories of Islam's early conquests but also a man whose irascibility and self-regarding willfulness led the caliphs to discipline him repeatedly.[40]

Military expansion, then—the necessary first step in the state-building process—entails two distinct imperatives. One is nurturing the well-springs of martial irascibility (*ghaḍab*) and vigor: the Prophet, Ibn Khaldun points out, "did not censure *ghaḍab* with the intention of eradicating it from human beings, for if the power of *ghaḍab* were to disappear, man would lose the ability to help the truth become victorious."[41] The other is inculcating submission to political-legal discipline. The problem is that the latter imperative undermines the former. Submission to laws tends to have an enervating effect, because "one grows up in fear and docility and does not rely on one's own fortitude. For this reason we find that the savage Arab bedouin have greater fortitude than those who are subject to laws, and also that those who submit to and internalize laws from the beginning of their education and instruction in the arts, sciences, and religions exhibit a decrease in their fortitude." If warriors lose their fortitude, their lines crumble and the states and civilizations they are supposed to protect are put in peril, as "they can hardly defend themselves against hostile acts at all."[42] Since both martial spirit and military discipline remain necessary, in short, maintaining the proper balance becomes a crucial element in the management of warfare.

At the level of the city as well, a similar contradiction quickly arises. The development of urban culture in terms of size, complexity, and openness to outside influences accords, as has already been noted, with the requirements of a flourishing civilization. But it also entails a break with earlier conventions. Ibn Khaldun illustrates the ensuing tension by describing an inquiry the second caliph, 'Umar ibn al-Khattab, received informing him that the reeds used to construct dwellings for troops in the new settlement of Kufa in Iraq had caught fire, and requesting permission to use stones instead. Although ʿUmar is traditionally credited with the growth of garrison cities such as Kufa and Basra, Ibn Khaldun highlights the hesitation evident in his reply: "Do, but let no one exceed three houses, and do not compete in building. Adhere to the Sunna, and your rule will endure."[43] Ibn Khaldun's account of the reasons implicit in ʿUmar's hesitation constitutes his famous elaboration on the decadence of polities at the end of their life cycles. Urban prosperity leads to abundance and luxury, which in turn breed "dissipation" among the citizens: "the decline in their courage matches the decline of their savage and primitive condition."[44] Just as their bodies are enervated by rich foods, their souls succumb to a jaded sophistication prone to "foul habits" and "base, reprehensible practices." Depending now on a professional army for protection, feeling safe behind the "walls" and "fortifications" of their cities, the mass of the citizenry lose their martial qualities and are "reduced to the position of women and children who are dependent on the patriarch of their home."[45] Once again, an evolution that fosters civilization also carries the seeds of its mortality: "Time feasts on them," their vigor drained by luxury and decadence: "They reach their limit, the limit set by the nature of human urbanization and political dominance."[46] Soon, they will fall prey to the next wave of warlike barbarians gathering beyond the horizon.

At the level of society, finally, the central problem manifests itself primarily as an erosion in the bonds that underlie political solidarity. It appears first as a literal loss of grounding, when further expansion makes it necessary to take to the sea—an unsettling prospect for Hijazis with no maritime experience such as the first Muslims. Ibn Khaldun relates the well-known story of Caliph ʿUmar reacting to requests for naval expeditions by asking a commander to describe the sea. When the commander wrote back that "the sea is a mighty creature upon which puny creatures ride, like worms on a piece of wood," the caliph instructed that Muslims be barred from seafaring. "Thus it remained until Muʿawiya's reign [661–680], when he permitted the Muslims to ride the sea and wage jihad in ships."[47] In the most basic sense, the fluid innovations necessary for imperial expansion come into conflict with the conventions that are the grounding for primitive ferocity and solidarity. As military expansion takes the conquerors farther and farther away from their roots, the problem assumes deeper and more acute dimensions. New populations are incorporated, each with its own affinities and orthodoxies, giving rise to the danger that preoccupied al-Jahiz so greatly: the empire's greater ʿaṣabiyya devolves into an atomizing shuʿūbiyya, diluting the polity's core solidarity and reducing its ability to fight effectively, so that it can neither expand any further nor even defend what it has.[48] Ethnic diversity turns out to be yet another hallmark of advanced civilization that bears the seeds of its demise.

The same basic dynamic, then, operates at each level—army, city, society—to create the conditions that characterize the kind of polity in which human potential can most fully be realized, and yet that are also ultimately destructive for the *sine qua non* of any such polity: its war-fighting ability. Noting that the life-span of a dynasty is typically limited to about three generations, Ibn Khaldun provides a succinct illustration with his account of the rise and fall of the Tulunid state.[49] It was founded by Ahmad ibn Tulun, a war-loving and pious governor of Egypt who broke away from the ʿAbbasids and inaugurated a reign marked by urban construction, economic growth, and the promotion of arts and crafts. In the end, however, he proved incapable of disciplining the appetites that all along underlay his ambitions: exacerbating an illness by ignoring his doctors' orders not to over-eat, then sinking into an orgy of cruelty by having various officials beaten or killed before finally succumbing to his disease. His son Khumarawayh, less adept and even more self-indulgent, was murdered by his eunuchs when he began investigating reports of adultery in his harem. He was succeeded by Jaysh, a degenerate libertine ousted by generals who then supplanted his brother as well and plunged the state into chaos and finally extinction.[50]

This prototypical trajectory highlights the fragility of civilized culture, dependent as it is on the stability of a vigorous political regime. But the vigor of the regime is in turn subject to the enervating effects of legal discipline, urban life, and dynastic succession. Civilization accordingly enters a phase of senescence, as its host state grows progressively weaker—first less able to incorporate further lands and new populations (with their ever greater "differences in opinions and desires" and consequently solidarities as well), then less able even to defend itself, until finally it is overwhelmed by new conquerors who still possess the martial virtues.[51] Thus, just as bedouin Arabs supplanted the Persian Empire, the states they constructed eventually gave way to nomadic Turks and Berbers, who in turn underwent their own cycles of dominance and decay.[52]

Small wonder then that so many commentators have viewed Ibn Khaldun's work as "an extended commentary on the futility of human aspiration," a "dark and gloomy" account of how the inadequacy of reason and the failure to live up to the dictates of divine guidance combine to condemn mankind to "an empty and unending cycle of rise and fall"—an account that is also said to explain Ibn Khaldun's own alleged retreat into mystical contemplation.[53] However this is not Ibn Khaldun's final word: the imperative of statecraft is no more negated by the mortality of empires than the imperative of virtue is negated by the mortality of human beings. In the first place, the historical record reveals significant deviations from the normal life expectancy of dynastic states. Ibn Khaldun mentions Persian and other states that lasted "thousands of years. . . . They had a great deal of time, and the arts became firmly established among them. Thus, their buildings and monuments were more numerous and left a more lasting imprint."[54] In the early Islamic state as well, submission to religious law, for example, did not engender the usual diminution in fortitude that eventually cuts short imperial expansion and begins the process of internal decay.[55] In the second place, the historical record also shows that even when regimes or states do collapse, the civilizations they nurture may survive and endure. One example Ibn Khaldun provides is the transition from Arab to Berber rule in the Maghrib within the framework of the same Islamic civilization.[56] Most generally, skills and specializations—all the accumulated expressions of human reason and productivity—can be passed on from generation to generation, so that civilizations do not "start completely afresh."[57] The mortal character of individual states, in short, does not obviate the imperative of struggling against the internal contradictions, or engines of decay, that undermine the magnitude, quality, and duration of civilization.

Models of Virtuous Statecraft

A statecraft aiming to counter the engines of decay that threaten civilization, then, entails maintaining appropriate balances between requirements such as ferocity and discipline, fortitude and urbanity, solidarity and diversity, orthodoxy and innovation, royal (or regime) authority and regime change. An apt model for such statesmanship is excellent generalship. In war as well, different circumstances call for different balances—the challenge in the early phase of expansion may be to stress discipline at the expense of ferocity, for example, whereas at a later date, when a degree of refinement and enervation has set in, the contrary may hold.

On the battlefield, the interplay of multiple factors and unforeseen contingencies creates a fog of uncertainty that makes it futile to rely mechanically on formulas and techniques. Ibn Khaldun draws a distinction between "apparent" and "hidden" factors in the outcomes of wars. Apparent factors include "armies and their numbers, perfection and excellence of weapons, abundance of courageous men, orderly arrangement of line formations, efficient battle tactics, and similar things."[58] They refer to the laws of war or the science of war—the logistical and tactical techniques that can be set down in military manuals and taught at military academies, so that they can be handed down from one generation of officers to the next. They are a necessary component of the virtuous commander's expertise, to be sure, but they do not suffice. Ibn Khaldun illustrates the point in his critique of the scholar Abu Bakr al-Turtushi (d. 1126), who he says "circled around the same idea" and organized his masterpiece in a way that came "close to the chapters and problems of our work," but failed to "treat the problems adequately" or to make his "natural demonstrations" (*barāhīn ṭabīʿiyya*) evident and so "did not realize his intention."[59] Later Ibn Khaldun explains that one of al-Turtushi's great failings is that he exaggerated the importance of apparent factors such as numerical superiority.[60] Instead, echoing the author of the *Mukhtasar Siyasat al-Hurub* and anticipating Clausewitz, Ibn Khaldun writes: "It is thus clear that victory in war is as a rule the result of hidden, not apparent, factors."[61] These hidden factors include intangibles such as morale and surprise, and have two primary sources: (1) "human deception and artifice" and (2) "celestial matters which human beings have no power to acquire for themselves."[62]

If "apparent factors" constitute the realm of military matters amenable to technical or scientific application, "human deception and artifice" refers to the art of war—the approach that becomes necessary when the dogmatic application of codified blueprints becomes dysfunctional. Most critically, it includes the Clausewitzian element of quick discernment (*coup d'oeil*) that allows a commander to act on sudden opportunities and challenges in rapidly changing battlefield conditions, for example by seizing on positions from which one can fool or surprise a moving enemy, or by emboldening one's troops while causing dissension and loss of heart among the enemy at precisely the right time.

Ibn Khaldun highlights this artistic component of good generalship in his discussion of war music, the "beating of drums and the blowing of trumpets and horns" (often accompanied by the display of vivid banners and flags) for psychological effect on the battlefield. He cites Aristotle on the objective of causing fear among the enemy, but adds that war music has much broader emotional (*wijdānī*) uses: when the soul hears the right tunes and melodies it is "seized" by "an elation which eases difficulties and enables one to defy death in whatever situation one finds oneself." Ibn Khaldun adds that this elation generates courage in the soul in the same manner as the elation induced by alcohol.[63] War music skillfully employed can whip up the troops or rein them in; it can inspire feelings of transcendence that induce warriors to put their lives on the line under the discipline of closed formations—"the fighting technique more suitable for one willing to risk death"[64]—while amplifying their fighting spirit by evoking powerful solidarities that bind together the diverse elements of an imperial army. War music, in short, allows the military commander to modulate the temper of his troops (and even the temper of enemy troops) in accordance with the ever-shifting requirements of the battlefield. As such, it is not something that can be applied mechanically.

Ibn Khaldun's discussion of war music and his emphasis on "human deception and artifice" more generally indicate the centrality of ingenuity in an unpredictable world. Such is the importance he attaches to this factor that he quotes the Prophet Muhammad's saying "war is deception" not once but twice in the same chapter of the *Muqaddima*, adding in his own voice that "deception is one of the most useful things employed in war, and the most likely to bring victory," and then as usual presenting exemplary commanders in the *Kitab al-'Ibar* to reinforce the point.[65] Perhaps more than anything else, it is this emphasis on human ingenuity that argues against the depiction of Ibn Khaldun as a fatalist resigned to the relentless repetition of history's grand cycles.

At the same time, Ibn Khaldun makes it clear that human agency can always be impinged upon—for good or ill—by the second main category of hidden factors: the "celestial matters, which human beings have no power to acquire for themselves." These may be divine interventions, and Ibn Khaldun provides several illustrations of God striking fear into enemy hearts at crucial junctures, or sending desperately needed sustenance—in several examples, water—to the Muslims just in time to turn the tide of battle.[66] A particularly consequential example is the infusion into Islam of Central Asian and Caucasian converts following the decadence and decay of late ʿAbbasid rule: "it was by the grace of God, glory be to Him, that He" sent "to them (the Muslims) out of this Turkish people and out of its mighty and numerous tribes, guardian amirs and devoted defenders" who "embrace Islam with the determination of true believers, while retaining their nomadic virtues which are undefiled by vile nature, unmixed with the filth of lustful pleasures, unmarred by the habits of civilisation, with their youthful strength unshattered by excess of luxury." As a result, "Islam rejoices in the wealth which it acquires (by means of them) and the boughs of the kingdom are luxuriant with the freshness and verdure of youth."[67] Ibn Khaldun takes care to point out that divine intervention can work in the opposite direction as well, however, and so—along the lines of the *Mukhtasar Siyasat al-Hurub*—recounts several occasions when God, for whatever obscure reasons, put Muslims to the test with defeats at the hands of the enemy.[68]

The celestial matters may also include other, less divine, forms of supernatural factors, such as the use of charms or talismans (though a portion of these may turn out to fall under the category of human "deception and artifice"). Ibn Khaldun mentions a pseudo-Aristotelian treatise on how to conquer cities and fortifications using such devices, including charms to induce rain and bring forth water.[69] These too can act either to further or foil the designs of the virtuous. Finally, Ibn Khaldun introduces a particularly crucial element—fortune (*bakht*): "There is no certainty of victory in war. . . . Victory and superiority in war come from fortune and chance."[70] Once again, as the author of the *Mukhtasar* also notes, virtue, moral or intellectual, does not assure success: "The idea of victory in wars depending on hidden and unnatural causes is related to the situation with fame and renown. . . . Many have gained fame without deserving it, and many have been passed over by fame although they are worthier and more entitled to it."[71] While "deception and artifice"—along with the tactics and techniques that fall under the rubric of apparent factors—describe human agency in historical processes, then, "celestial matters" delineate the limits of human control.

The implications of the facts that ingenuity can be foiled by fortune, and that virtue often fails to guarantee success, are significant. The first conclusion argues for prudence even when one enjoys superiority in numbers and skill. Ibn Khaldun once again invokes the authority of ʿUmar ibn al-Khattab, quoting him to the effect that "it is more appropriate to be heavy-footed than light-footed in war, until the situation becomes clear."[72] The second conclusion—that God will not necessarily allow the Muslims to prevail in war—suggests that a triumphalism based on dogmatic faith in divine favor is no more warranted than a triumphalism based on dogmatic faith in science.

Another apt model for virtuous statecraft is provided by the art of religious guidance. Here as well there are crucial balances that must be maintained. On the one hand, excessive dogmatism must be suppressed, lest it lead to an inability to distinguish between friend and foe or between legitimate and illegitimate targets of violence—Ibn Khaldun cites in this context religious zealots such as the Khariji Azariqa and the Ismaʿili Assassins, who disrupt the order of the imperial state and destroy the underpinnings of its civilization by engaging in terrorism against those who do not conform to their opinions and spilling the blood of innocents.[73] But excessive laxity cannot be tolerated either, so Ibn Khaldun does not hesitate also to denounce Sufis who succumb to a moral subjectivism and self-absorption leading to "vile innovations" and "reprehensible practices" (including occultism, mysticism, and the charlatanry of pseudo-saints) that alienate them and those they influence from the norms of healthy social intercourse. He goes so far as to issue a *fatwa* in his capacity as religious judge calling on "the public authority" to destroy their books by fire and water.[74]

Ibn Khaldun's stance toward the twin pathologies of Kharijism and Sufism—or more properly "pseudo-Sufis" (*mutaṣawwifa*), since he distinguishes them from earlier "outstanding" Sufis who turned away from supernatural pursuits[75]—leads him to the tools that are available to confront such imbalances. As in military affairs, the starting point is a well-devised blueprint or set of laws that serves as the most reliable guide for the proper functioning of the political order, and that must accordingly be treated with utmost reverence. Beyond the Law, however—and because, again as in the military sphere, fortune is fickle and circumstances change—creative and flexible management is also needed. Ibn Khaldun's discussion of Sufism further illustrates the point. As the interiorized pursuit of spiritual fulfillment, Sufism addresses powerful emotional and psychological needs among the believers. It therefore plays a useful role in shaping sound, well-rounded citizens.[76] It does so, moreover, in very subjective ways, and so requires a certain tolerance for individual idiosyncrasies: "there are as many paths to God as there are souls, each one appropriate for the specific individual."⁷⁷ There is a realm of belief that should remain beyond the reach of legislation. At the same time, it is clear that the private pursuit of religious truth can have subversive public consequences. It is here, at the boundary between the private and the public, that the need for skillful oversight arises. In his treatise on Sufism, *Shifaʾ al-Saʾil*, Ibn Khaldun argues that dangerous deviations can be avoided if its practitioners couple their private heterodoxy with public orthodoxy: by obeying the religious laws strictly; by adhering to the generally accepted moral norms; and—perhaps most decisively—by following the guidance of qualified religious leaders or shaykhs who keep them on the straight path.[78]

Thus, the qualified shaykh plays the same role in this sphere as does the commander in the military sphere. His function is to modulate the Sufi devotee's individual intuitive or ecstatic experience—Ibn Khaldun uses the same word, *wijdān*, he used to describe the effects of war music—in a manner consistent with the requirements of the polity. *Wijdānī* experience properly utilized, in short, denotes the mobilization of individual energies on behalf of the common good.[79] Once again, however, because each devotee requires individual attention and because conditions change constantly and unpredictably over time, such modulation cannot be reduced to a "science" of religious management outlined in clear blueprints any more than it can be reduced to a "science" of war laid out in military manuals. Indeed, Ibn Khaldun draws an explicit parallel between the imprecision of warcraft and the imprecision of religious guidance: "the tricks of the enemy in both are infinite, and books cannot encompass them for the range of their objectives and the obscurity of their intentions and the subtlety of their conceptions."[80]

Ibn Khaldun's performance as religious judge in Cairo has led many commentators to view his outlook as being fundamentally religious, and his ideas as falling squarely within the orthodox Sunni tradition exemplified by jurists such as al-Ghazali and Ibn Taymiyya.[81] It is not in the undoubted orthodoxy of his religious opinions, however, as in his preoccupation with the role religion can play in mobilizing citizens for political ends that Ibn Khaldun stands out from his fellow jurists. Even religious scholars more inclined to sanction discretionary judgment on behalf of the public interest—such as Shihab al-Din al-Qarafi (d. 1285), Ibn Taymiyya (d. 1328), or Abu Ishaq al-Shatibi (d. 1388)—nevertheless still understood that interest primarily in terms of spiritual salvation rather than earthly well-being.[82] Thus, whereas Ibn Khaldun appreciates war primarily as a political instrument for the advancement of civilized culture, Ibn Taymiyya, for example, appreciates it primarily as an expression of religious devotion; whereas Ibn Khaldun focuses on how law can serve the interests of the state, Ibn Taymiyya focuses on how the state can serve the implementation of the law; and whereas Ibn Khaldun worries about the enervating effects of submission to laws, Ibn Taymiyya recognizes no such ambivalence.[83] The farther religious scholars went in the direction of ascetic idealism—with its disregard of or even hostility to considerations of *raison d'état*—the greater their distance from Ibn Khaldun.

Ibn Khaldun's preoccupation, in short, is with the art of statecraft specifically as it relates to the this-worldly, political, imperative of creating the conditions for civilized life. Military command and shaykhly guidance now being seen as both subsets of and templates for political governance in general, the latter emerges ever more clearly as an art devoted to the regulation of the shifting balances necessary for sustaining civilization. Like the laws of military command and religious guidance, the broader laws of political governance aim at securing the over-arching objective Ibn Khaldun specifies from the start and never loses sight of: "All laws are based on the effort to preserve culture."[84] Because "the conditions of nations and groups change with the change of eras and the passing of days," however, even the most perfect legislation will give rise to "unavoidable" differences of opinion, requiring the mediation of a human statecraft that can discern what is most needful at any given time.[85] Ibn Khaldun's history can thus be read as a catalog of successful and failed statecraft understood in this manner. Statesmen who uphold the law in cognizance of its underlying intent—and therefore flexibly—will be able to construct civilizations adorned with the cities and libraries that are their "most enduring monuments unto the days."[86] States with rulers who do not practice virtuous statecraft, on the other hand, succumb rapidly to the vagaries of fortune and are consigned to the worst fate possible: to disappear without a trace, "as if they never were."[87]

Ibn Khaldun's premier exemplar here is Muʿawiya, reviled by critics as an unprincipled opportunist and usurper who transformed the caliphate into a hereditary tyranny. Yet Ibn Khaldun always refers to him favorably, insisting that there is no essential difference between his rule and that of the first four "rightly-guided" caliphs, and even going out of his way to claim that one of his own ancestors befriended

Mu'awiya after having received the Prophet's blessings.[88] The reason is not hard to discern. Mu'awiya restored order and stability to the Islamic polity; transferred the capital to the cosmopolitan urban center of Damascus; founded the key institutions of a centralized imperial state; laid the groundwork for the translation project of scientific, military, administrative, and eventually philosophical texts from foreign languages into Arabic; built a formidable fleet; and oversaw an unprecedented territorial expansion that took Muslim troops as far as Algeria in the west and Transoxiana in the east. All this, in the context of a relatively tolerant rule that relied on cajolery, guile, and cooptation far more than repression. Ibn al-Zubayr, who would later revolt against Mu'awiya's son, said of him: "He was the most artful of men, more crafty than a thief."[89] Mu'awiya himself said of his statecraft: "I do not use my sword when my whip is sufficient, and I do not use my whip when my tongue is sufficient. If there is only a hair connecting me to the people, it will not be broken. . . . If they pull at it, I will let go; and if they let go of it, I will pull."[90] It is this responsiveness to changing circumstances that underlay Mu'awiya's readiness to break with convention in military affairs as well—both in victory (as in the naval campaigns he undertook despite 'Umar's opposition which led to the conquests of Cyprus and Rhodes), and in defeat (as in his readiness to retreat and sue for peace with the Byzantines after his siege of Constantinople failed).

By praising him so highly, Ibn Khaldun emphasizes that the ambition and cunning and flexibility Mu'awiya displayed are necessary ingredients for constructing the kind of imperial state that can serve as a crucible for civilization. This ultimate objective, in turn, is what grounds Ibn Khaldun's appreciation for the likes of Mu'awiya in a value beyond mere technical efficacy, and leads him to a notion of justice that—in contrast to ascetic idealism—is not conceived in the abstract, but defined by the metrics of concrete progress toward advanced culture.

Just Regimes and Just Wars

Ibn Khaldun's concept of justice is one in which moral and political imperatives converge. Statecraft is just both insofar as it conduces to the general (as opposed to merely the ruler's) well-being, and insofar as it is effective in facilitating the transition from a "natural" mode of rule (*mulk ṭabiʿī*), based on blood kinship and primal "intentions and appetites," to more diverse and complex polities capable of nurturing the development of advanced culture or civilization. Negotiating such a transition and modulating the necessary balances requires legislation, of either divine or human origin, that can counteract the looming threats of citizen alienation and solidarity erosion, and that applies to and is accepted by all members of the polity.[91] It is crucial that such legislation be genuinely solicitous of the general welfare—in short, just—because only then will the ruled, who are treated with consideration by the ruler, in turn be "infused with love for him, and will fight to the death under him against his enemies," and thereby sustain the polity's drive toward advanced civilization.[92]

Unfortunately, the actually prevailing modes of rule, in Muslim and non-Muslim states alike, fall short in this regard because they continue to be based on the interests of rulers who display disdainful arrogance by treating the interests of their subjects as secondary.[93] This is true even of regimes established by intelligent rulers who draw on historical lore and philosophical insights in an effort to maintain their hold over their subjects. As long as the general welfare remains subordinate, even the gratification of material needs will not suffice to stave off the engines of decay that cut short the life spans of such regimes.

Nevertheless, Ibn Khaldun points to two additional—albeit rare—regime types that are capable of securing popular legitimacy, and therefore capable of sustaining, for prolonged periods of time, a broader or "greater" *ʿaṣabiyya* that can bind the populace together effectively in pursuit of common ends and in resistance to common enemies. One is a regime based on legislation formulated by the lawgiver through the exercise of his own reason, attending both "to the common interests in general, and to the interests of the ruler as they relate to the rectitude of his rule in particular."[94] Ibn Khaldun emphasizes that he is speaking now not of the ideal political regime of the philosophers, in which citizens attain a perfection of soul and character that allows them to dispense with rulers altogether—such utopias are presented by the philosophers merely as heuristic hypotheses or suppositions. The type of rational regime (*siyāsa ʿaqliyya*) he has in mind here, in which the interests of the ruled are not subordinate, is not a mere utopia. It can and has been realized in deed. Echoing al-Farabi and Ibn Rushd, he provides an actual example: "This was the regime of the Persians."[95] That is why their empire was so large and long-lasting, and their civilization so advanced.

Ibn Khaldun hastens to add, however, that with the call to Islam God has made this kind of regime "superfluous for us."[96] For whereas the rational politics exemplified by the ancient Persians promotes human welfare in this world, the second type of rare regime—based on legislation of divine origin—promotes welfare both in this world and in the next. Because of the sanctified character of its Law, moreover, Islam is also more effective at securing compliance and countering the iniquitous features of human nature.[97] It acts as an especially potent internal moral force or "restraining influence," neutralizing "mutual envy and competition" and facilitating the establishment of larger and more stable polities as individual "desires converge in the pressing of claims, and hearts unite and harmonize."[98] Powerful new feelings of fraternity engendered by their shared faith bind together people who have no natural (biological or ethnic) connections. An exceptionally formidable "greater ʿaṣabiyya" comes into being. Now it becomes incumbent on the leadership as well to display the requisite piety by heeding the religion's demand for justice, and by upholding this new principle of social solidarity.

Any leadership that succeeds in identifying itself with such a faith consequently augments both its legitimacy and its efficacy. Internally, it acquires additional power on top of the power it already possesses as a result of the number of its supporters.[99] Externally, it is able to mobilize much more formidable resources against its adversaries because the citizens, energized by their greater ʿaṣabiyya, are now willing to die for their cause and so constitute a force "nothing can withstand." They can attack and defeat enemies "many times as numerous as they." As a result, "the state grows greater."[100] Ibn Khaldun gives several examples of how the religion of the Muslims "multiplied the strength of their ʿaṣabiyya"—viewing the point as so noteworthy that he immediately reiterates it[101]—from the first Arab clans to unite under Islam, to the Berber tribes who founded their own Islamic states in the Maghrib, to the great masses of converted Turkish nomads who went on to establish empires of their own. In his "Autobiography" he describes how the adherence to Islam of Salah al-Din, renowned as a paragon of justice, enabled him to establish a dynasty that—despite its origins in a relatively small social group, a Kurdish tribe known as Banu Hadhan—saw its ranks swell to such an extent under the banner of jihad that it was able to defeat the Crusaders.[102] A community integrated and mobilized by the ethos of such a religion, in short, can transcend normal geographical and temporal limitations. Hence the "miraculous" ability of the early Muslims to "take possession of all seven climes" in such a short period—an "extraordinary" (*khāriq al-ʿāda*) feat in comparison to the normal length of time for established states to be overcome by emergent ones.[103]

The distinguishing feature of the two rare non-tyrannical but also non-utopian regimes, then, is justice. A just regime is both "noble and beneficial" in that it attends to the interests of the subjects rather than relying on coercion alone.[104] It does so through legislation that acts as a restraining influence on the iniquitous impulses—the "animalistic nature"[105]—of human beings. Rulers grow milder. Subjects become more tractable in obeying the law and rallying behind their government. The polity thus acquires vigor. Its *ʿaṣabiyya* is built on more solid, healthier ground, and so it is able to attain the levels of size, complexity, and duration necessary for advanced culture. For if "injustice brings about the ruin of culture," just laws and regulations are "concerned with what is good for culture."[106]

The link between justice and civilization is also evident in the polity's external dynamics. Ibn Khaldun presents his most comprehensive discussion of war in a section of the *Muqaddima* entitled "Wars and Their Dispositions in the Doctrines of Various Nations."[107] He begins by asserting the inescapability of the phenomenon, a starting point consonant with both realist and Islamic perspectives: "wars and different kinds of fighting have occurred in the world ever since God created it. . . . It is something natural among human beings; no nation or generation is free from it."[108] As with regimes, however, Ibn Khaldun then goes on to construct a typology predicated on a moral distinction between just and unjust wars. He identifies two types within each category. The two types of unjust wars are those motivated by envy and competitiveness, and those motivated by aggressive hostility. The two types of just wars are those motivated by irascibility on behalf of God and His religion, and those motivated by irascibility on behalf of human rulership (*mulk*). Ibn Khaldun highlights the fundamental distinction he seeks to draw between types of war that are driven by baser human impulses and fail to transcend their natural origins, and types of war that serve nobler political ends, by emphasizing the primitive features of the former pair. Thus: the first kind of war usually occurs between "neighboring tribes and contending clans" and the second between "savage nations living in desolate regions." Neither is motivated by "desire for rank or kingship; their concern and objective is rather to plunder people of what they possess." The latter two war types, by contrast, aim at state building—at establishing a political order of either divine or human inspiration. One is called by the religious law "jihad," while the other consists of wars waged by rulers of states against those who rebel and those who refuse to submit. Ibn Khaldun concludes: "These are the four types of war. The first two are wars of transgression and discord; the other two are wars of jihad and justice."[109] It bears reiterating the crucial distinction: unlike unjust wars, just wars mobilize the fighting spirit of ʿaṣabiyya on behalf of a moral standard and a political dynamic that have the potential to engender large stable states and consequently advanced culture or civilization. The contrast Ibn Khaldun draws between just and unjust wars parallels the contrast he draws between just and unjust regimes.

A just polity, accordingly, is one that combines, internally and externally alike, the necessary use of force with the restraining influence of a legislation that makes it easier to overcome, reconcile, and assimilate former outsiders into an expanded ʿaṣabiyya. Such a conception highlights the principle of voluntary consent.[110] Only a political leadership that demonstrates the required restraint is judged to be legitimate by its subjects; and only a political leadership that successfully wins the hearts and minds of its subjects in this way—and that thereby serves the imperial, civilizing imperative so central to Ibn Khaldun's concerns—is judged to be legitimate by Ibn Khaldun himself.

Despite Ibn Khaldun's emphasis on the religious variant of just regimes so defined, and despite his recognition of Islam's tremendous moral and political potency as a greater ʿaṣabiyya, viewed at least from the perspective of well-being in this world—and in light of the historical example of the rational variant provided by the ancient Persians—it is nevertheless the case that formally speaking, the ideal type of Islamic leadership (khilāfa or caliphate) is a subset of the category "just regimes." Ibn Khaldun underscores the point repeatedly. At the beginning of the Muqaddima, for example, he takes issue with the proposition of certain philosophers that prophecy and religious law are logically (as opposed to doctrinally) necessary for good government. Even though the majority of the world's inhabitants have not been people of the Book (let alone Muslims), he points out, some of them have nevertheless succeeded in transcending primitive politics to produce dynastic states and lasting monuments.[111] He returns to and expands on this faulty proposition in a later discussion:

One of its premises is that the restraining influence comes only from a God-given law to which all submit in faith and conviction. But this is not indisputable, because the restraining influence may come about through the authority of the king or the compulsion of the powerful, even if there is no religious law. . . . Or we might say: it suffices to eliminate strife for everyone to know that iniquity is forbidden by the authority of reason. So their assertion that strife can be eliminated only by the presence of religious law and the appointment of an imam here or there is not correct. Rather, just as that can take place through the appointment of an imam, it can also be due to the presence of powerful [non-religious] leaders, or through the people themselves refraining from strife and iniquity.[112]

Following precisely the same logic, just as *khilāfa* is a subset of the general conceptual category of just regimes, jihad is a subset of the general conceptual category of just wars. On both levels, Ibn Khaldun's method aims at uncovering general truths that transcend particular manifestations—not least that "iniquity is forbidden by the authority of reason." And on both levels, he shows the two elements necessary for successful political praxis operating side by side. The first element is power, or brute coercive capability, which enables *'aṣabiyya* to mobilize effective collective action. Without power there can be no disciplining of anarchic individuals into a cohesive unit, and without power there can be no further expansion of community into a polity of sufficient magnitude to sustain advanced culture. But Ibn Khaldun has shown that power alone does not suffice—brute coercion weakens the collective solidarity of *'aṣabiyya*, undermining civic virtue and martial élan alike. Hence the second crucial element: the conviction on the part of the led that their commanders are just; that they adhere to and uphold the shared *'aṣabiyya* prevailing at any given point in a polity's development—whether it is the blood-based kinship bonds of the primordial clan, or the common defining principle (e.g., Islam) of complex empires. Without such conviction, the leadership becomes vulnerable to violent challenge, either from elements who are better able to associate themselves with the prevailing *'aṣabiyya*, or from elements who represent narrower but more potent *'aṣabiyyas*. In the latter case especially, fragmentation of the polity into smaller units is likely to ensue.

Ibn Khaldun illustrates the indispensability of both power and justice for eliciting the effective consent of the citizenry in his discussion of the debate as to whether the leader of the Islamic polity must belong to the Prophet's tribe, Quraysh.[113] After acknowledging that there was a consensus affirming this condition among the leading Muslims who gathered to select a successor upon the Prophet's death, and after acknowledging that this remained the dominant opinion among religious scholars in his day as well, Ibn Khaldun nevertheless adopts a contrary stance. He begins by reiterating the point that all proper laws must aim at promoting the public interest, which in this case "is nothing else but regard for the ʿaṣabiyya that makes possible protection and the pressing of claims."[114] Because the numerous, wealthy, and cohesive Quraysh wielded the greatest power in the region, the selection of a Qurayshi successor would facilitate the promotion of this interest: "Had the rule been entrusted to anyone else, opposition and refusal to comply would likely have led to dissension."[115] The crucial distinction of the Quraysh, the true basis of their prestige, in other words, lay not in their kinship with the Prophet—a "blessing" though that is—but in the strength of their particular tribal ʿaṣabiyya, which endowed them with the competence to assume leadership. At the same time, had they not put their tribal ʿaṣabiyya in the service of the greater Islamic ʿaṣabiyya, had they not used their rank over the people "under their control . . . in order to repel what is harmful to them and to bring forth what is to their benefit," then their power alone would have translated into an illegitimate and unsustainable tyranny.[116] Unfortunately for the Quraysh, years of luxury and prosperity, coupled with physical dispersion throughout the realms of Islam, eventually eroded their tribal ʿaṣabiyya and consequently their power. They lost their competence, "became too weak to bear the burdens of the caliphate," and thus forfeited their claim to rule.[117] Here, in his insistence on the indissoluble complementarity of power and justice—even in the face of an orthodox consensus on prerequisites for the caliphate—Ibn Khaldun vividly displays his distinctive realism.

Ibn Khaldun's Islamic Realism

In the course of explaining, near the beginning of the *Muqaddima*, why he set out on his study of the rise and fall of civilizations, Ibn Khaldun notes that some of its themes have been addressed before "in scattered statements by the sages of mankind. However, they did not give them full due."[118] He gives two examples: the speech—"in the story of the owl reported by al-Mas'udi"—of a pre-Islamic Persian high priest on the relationship between royal authority, religious law, justice, and cultivation (*'imāra*); and a book on politics "that is ascribed to Aristotle" on similar themes, but which is likewise inadequate and "mixed with other things."[119] Ibn Khaldun's ambiguity about the ascription to Aristotle is apt, because the text he cites is in fact the pseudo-Aristotelian *Sirr al-Asrar* (Secret of Secrets). Then he adds that one can also find in Ibn al-Muqaffa''s "digressions on politics" many of the observations contained "in this book of ours," but instead of "demonstrating them as we have done" he merely "burnished" them in passing, using the style and eloquence of "rhetoric."[120] Even while asserting his originality and superior rigor, therefore, Ibn Khaldun situates his own work within a scholarly tradition that focuses on practical politics—on governance and statecraft as actually practiced in human history.

A better appreciation of this realism may be gained by considering where Ibn Khaldun positions himself between two general methods of gaining knowledge. One comprises the "philosophical sciences" in which intellect is the primary guide, the other "the transmitted, conventional sciences" derived from revelation in which there is "no place for the intellect" except in determining how to apply general religious injunctions to particular circumstances.[121] Ibn Khaldun makes it clear that the latter method is altogether inappropriate for his present purposes. He does draw a contrast within the religious sciences between a "Hijazi" approach which he describes as provincial and particularly reliant on transmitted traditions, and an "Iraqi" approach he associates with "people of judgment and analogical reasoning" (*ahl al-ra'y wa-l-qiyās*) and describes as more reflective of the "refinement" characterizing advanced culture as well as more "occupied with jihad."[122] Beyond noting this contrast, however, he eschews Islamic jurisprudence in his study of political administration and how it relates to the requirements of civilization, explaining that "this is not the intention of our book" and that it is a subject adequately treated elsewhere in the works of al-Mawardi and "other distinguished jurists."[123]

Ibn Khaldun's concern to distinguish between his approach and the religious sciences recalls Ibn Rushd's effort to keep philosophy and theology distinct. He writes, for example, that when Islamic dialectical theology (*kalām*) evolved beyond its earlier articulations and sought to incorporate logic into defensive polemics on matters of faith, it wrongly "mixed up" its methods and concerns with those of philosophy, causing potentially divisive "confusion" among ordinary people.[124] At any rate, since the only benefit of *kalām* is in argumentation with the enemies of orthodoxy, this science is "not necessary for this age . . . as the apostates and innovators have been wiped out." And since *kalām* does not use rational arguments in order to "seek the truth and verify it with proofs," but merely "to bolster the doctrines of faith," it is of no use to the student of philosophy either.[125]

Ibn Khaldun's path toward the truth, then, is the path of intellect or reason. Within this path, however, he also stands apart from those theoretically inclined philosophers who disdain to occupy themselves with questions about the evolution of actual (and therefore imperfect) polities; questions of central importance for Ibn Khaldun.[126] He affirms by contrast that history "is firmly rooted in" and "deserves to be accounted a branch" of philosophy,[127] and in the section of the *Muqaddima* entitled "A Refutation of Philosophy: The Corruption of the Students of Philosophy," in his turn criticizes philosophers who display an excessively abstract and arid intellectualism: "in restricting themselves to affirming the intellect and neglecting everything beyond it, they are like the naturalists who restrict themselves to substantiating material bodies . . . in the conviction that there is nothing beyond the body in God's wise design."[128] Some scholars have been led by such criticisms to identify Ibn Khaldun as an upholder of religious orthodoxy in opposition to the rationalism of the philosophers. They include both those praising him as a faithful Muslim who fought alien influences imported by philosophers in thrall to Plato and Aristotle, and those denigrating him as a parochial dogmatist ignorant of the insights of philosophy.[129] Ibn Khaldun's insistence on describing his chosen field of history as a branch of philosophy, however, and his acknowledgment that more "competent philosophers" recognize the intellect's limitations, suggests a more nuanced conclusion.[130]

To begin with, like Ibn Rushd before him, Ibn Khaldun focuses his criticisms on specific individuals. After naming al-Farabi, Ibn Sina, Ibn Bajja, and Ibn Rushd as "among the greatest" Muslim philosophers, for example, he singles out only al-Farabi and Ibn Sina as the "most famous" of the scholars who were "led astray" in their opinions.[131] Shortly thereafter, he bemoans the time wasted by "skillful" philosophers on the claim ascribed to Aristotle, al-Farabi, and Ibn Sina that "whoever apprehends the Active Intellect and conjoins with it in his lifetime will have attained his portion of happiness."¹³² As Muhsin Mahdi points out, however, Ibn Khaldun takes care to praise Aristotle's logic in this passage, and to distinguish it from "his" faulty metaphysics—a metaphysics which in fact is found in a Neoplatonic work falsely attributed to Aristotle, comprised primarily of translated paraphrases from the *Enneads* of Plotinus (d. 270), but known in the Arabic speaking world as the *Theology of Aristotle*. In contrast to al-Farabi and Ibn Sina at least, Mahdi notes: "It is of crucial importance that Ibn Khaldun never criticizes Averroes or his doctrines on basic philosophic issues."¹³³ In a section on "Physics" where Ibn Khaldun maintains a respectful stance toward Aristotle's writings, for example, he says of Ibn Sina: "It was as though he differed with Aristotle in many of his topics and stated his own opinions concerning them, whereas Ibn Rushd summarized the books of Aristotle in his own commentaries, following him [exactly] without differing with him."¹³⁴

Beyond a shared aversion to Ibn Sina's Neoplatonically-inspired metaphysics, another point on which Ibn Khaldun follows Ibn Rushd is opposition to those—in both the religious and philosophic camps—who aspire to certainty in areas where there can be no certainty. Ibn Khaldun's central criticism of the dialectical theologians in the *Muqaddima*'s chapter on the sciences is that their quest for logical or scientific certainty on matters such as the essence and attributes of God, the resurrection of the dead, heaven and hell, and predestination, is "to crave the impossible" and can lead to loss of faith altogether.¹³⁵ Likewise, Ibn Khaldun attacks Sufis of his time who also aspire to certainty about what lies beyond "the veil of sense perception"—only this time through mystical or ecstatic experience.¹³⁶ An exactly parallel concern underlies his critique of certain pdeudo-philosophers who "claim that the essences, properties, and proximate and distant causes, of all beings, sensible as well as those that are beyond the senses, can be perceived by theoretical investigations and rational syllogisms."¹³⁷ In reality, the essences of extrasensory substances cannot be known or "proven by demonstration, because the abstraction of intelligibles from particular existents" is "possible only in the case of things we can perceive by the senses."¹³⁸

Echoing Ibn Rushd once again, Ibn Khaldun concludes that "if after all the toil and trouble we are left only with conjectures, the [religious] conjectures we had at the beginning may as well suffice us." Here as well, however, Ibn Khaldun emphasizes that he is speaking only of certain wayward philosophers, not of "competent" ones:

"Plato, the greatest among them," for example, "said that no certainty can be achieved regarding the Divine."¹³⁹ With regard to all the other, worldlier, fields of inquiry, by contrast, "the intellect is indeed a correct scale."¹⁴⁰ This is particularly true of the practical wisdom that enables the philosopher to lead the military general, the religious shaykh, and above all the political ruler in turning away from private concerns and looking to maintain the balances necessary for advancing civilization. Philosophy really comes into its own, then, when it recognizes that happiness does not consist merely in the "apprehension of the existents as they are through logical demonstrations;"¹⁴¹ when, in short, it is no longer vain.

Not the least of the ways Ibn Khaldun continues to privilege reason while maintaining an appreciation of its limits is by rejecting too quick an identification of reason with conventional virtue. His recognition that morality alone will not always prevail, and that divine intervention cannot be counted on, lead him to accommodate primordial drives scorned by more idealistic approaches. When discussing the distinction between the consequences as opposed to the motives of the quest for status or leading rank, for example, he describes the former (the establishment of an effective regime) as being "intended by divine providence as something essential," whereas the latter (self-seeking ambition) "enters into it as something accidental, like all evils decreed by God, because the greater good cannot come into being except in conjunction with the existence of a lesser evil, which is the result of matter. The good does not thereby disappear, but comes to pass conjoined with the lesser evil. It should be understood that this is the meaning of the occurrence of iniquity in the world."¹⁴² In such a conception, war, for example, emerges not only as a natural outcome of natural human impulses, but also as a necessary evil *par excellence*—a dangerous undertaking, always of uncertain outcome and sure only to bring, as ʿAbd al-Hamid al-Katib had put it, "hateful calamities . . . and pain," but nevertheless also an indispensable mechanism for the promotion of a very great good: the creation of civilization-sustaining empires. This is a realist conception both in its insistence that virtuous regimes can in fact be realized in this world, if only necessary evils are taken into account, and in its rejection of dogmatic absolutism in favor of a perpetual calibration of balances against the engines of decay so that, for example, war comes to make sense under some circumstances while (as Ibn Rushd pointed out in his commentary on the *Nicomachean Ethics*) peace comes to make sense under others.

For Ibn Khaldun, one of Islam's great virtues is its compatibility with such a conception. In the course of refuting certain Muʿtazilis and Kharijis, for example, he emphasizes that while Islamic law "censures appetite and irascibility in responsible persons, its intention is not that they be relinquished altogether, because necessity calls for their existence. Instead, the intention is that they be put to proper use."[143] More generally, Islam's realism sets it apart from all other religions: "The religions other than Islam did not have a universal mission, and jihad was not prescribed except for self-defense only. The one in charge of their religious affairs is therefore not concerned with power politics [*siyāsat al-mulk*] at all."[144] Islam's attention to "power politics" enables its leaders to prosecute their universal civilizing mission vigorously, just as it enables them to fall back when reason dictates—as with Caliph ʿUmar ibn ʿAbd al-ʿAziz when he advocated evacuating the Muslim community from Spain altogether on the pragmatic calculation that its defense was no longer sustainable.[145]

At the same time, however, Ibn Khaldun's schema rises above mere expediency by bringing to the fore the ethical component that was said, in chapter 2, to have been eclipsed by the advocacy of *raison d'état* in the writings of ʿAbd al-Hamid al-Katib and Ibn al-Muqaffaʿ. This component is justice, which arises from the fact that maintaining the necessary level of *ʿaṣabiyya*—integrating as it does the principles of solidarity, representation, and consent—obliges virtuous leaders to remain true to the communal ethos that binds the polity together, and that provides it with a standard through which to distinguish between noble and base. On the level of ends, justice mandates a political order that attends to the well-being of all, "assigning people to their proper stations" so that each can receive his or her fair due;[146] which in practical terms means creating the conditions under which all individuals can realize their maximum potential in accordance with their natural endowments. On the level of means, justice requires the leadership to uphold the moral conventions that control and channel the primordial drives of human nature—conventions that become more universal as the polity grows in size and complexity—in accordance with the prevailing needs of decent social life. Such conventions regulate the behavior of citizens in their capacity as soldiers as well, enabling them to maintain their stations in closed line formations—the type of deployment Ibn Khaldun describes as more suited to warriors willing to sacrifice themselves for a greater good, more appropriate for the objective of "preserving order," and accordingly more characteristic of advanced as opposed to primitive polities[147]—and disciplining their conduct in war, as Ibn Khaldun indicates when he cites legal injunctions against killing women, children, and other noncombatants.

In this regard as well, Ibn Khaldun considers Islam well suited to the purpose, for Islamic justice aims at the ultimate end of civilization: "Know that . . . what the Lawgiver had in mind when prohibiting iniquity . . . is the corruption and ruin of culture that ensues from it, and which in turn heralds the extinction of the human species."[148] The propagation of enlightenment and culture is coincident with the propagation of Islamic law and morality, in Ibn Khaldun's synthesis, as long as it is directed by a statecraft capable of applying, pragmatically but authoritatively, the spirit of the law in light of whatever exigencies prevail at any given time.

∽

Writing at nearly the same time, the Florentine Dante Alighieri (d. 1321) relied on some of the same sources (e.g., Orosius, Ibn Rushd) to formulate an argument that parallels Ibn Khaldun's in several respects. In his treatise on *Monarchy*, for example, Dante proposed that mankind can only "actualize" its "full intellectual potential" in the context of a global empire.[149] Although some modern commentators "cannot help but wonder whether he was not also concerned to uncover and promote a more virile and militant form of the Christian ethos to counter what he—anticipating Machiavelli—regarded as the corrupting softness of orthodox Christianity," however, the religion he had at his disposal put Dante in a decisively different position.[150] In particular, it appears to have left him with an altogether inadequate foundation for the waspish and warlike ʿaṣabiyya that Ibn Khaldun found so necessary for any successful imperial enterprise. Dante's failure to reconcile religious and imperial imperatives, in turn, led his most consequential successors—Machiavelli (d. 1527) most overtly, Bacon (d. 1626) and Hobbes (d. 1679) more circumspectly—to abandon both Christianity and the notion of imperialism for the propagation of a transcendent good, lowering their sights in favor of more common, and therefore in their view more dependable, human motivations, and thereby inaugurating the transition to modern Western political thought.

As detailed in this chapter, Ibn Khaldun goes to great lengths to show why the actualization of mankind's potential, the advancement of human culture, can best be realized in a large, diverse, differentiated imperial civilization. Precisely because such a civilization is necessarily peopled by individuals of so many different desires, capabilities, and potentially divisive affiliations, he embraces Islam as capable of providing the over-arching principle of political unity, the greater ʿaṣabiyya, needed to bind the imperial polity together, ground it in a shared moral ethos to discipline its diversity and order of rank, and mobilize it against its enemies. One therefore begins to gain a clearer understanding of what animates Ibn Khaldun when one considers what he is up against: the deadly assault on Islamic ʿaṣabiyya—and consequently on the imperial order toward which it drives—by a mode of thought arising from a joyless renunciation of the works of this world, a hatred of all earthly accomplishment and distinction as misguided manifestations of vanity, in favor of a preoccupation with self-abasement and self-obliteration. Such a mode of thought emasculates the most vigorous impulses of human nature to the point that the polity can no longer generate the artistic and scientific creativity that is possible only in life-affirming societies, and can no longer defend itself against tyranny at home or defeat abroad.

Ibn Khaldun's response sets him apart from writers who seek an illusory certainty in political matters, whether al-Turtushi with his excessive reliance on "apparent" factors (such as numerical superiority) in warfare, or Ibn Manjli with his pedantic efforts at combining science and magic, or Ibn Khaldun's other contemporary Ibn al-Nahhas al-Dumyati (d. 1411), author of "the most detailed *jihad* book available from the classical period," who looks to God for guarantees of victory so long as the intentions of the warriors are pure and focused on the afterlife.[151] Ibn Khaldun's response also sets him apart from the Kharijis who, while displaying a worldly engagement lacking among the apolitical ascetic idealists, embrace a revolutionary praxis too unquestioning and intolerant to accommodate the needs of complex imperial civilization.

Ibn Khaldun's own approach is one that acknowledges the messy ambiguities of political affairs. In the course of criticizing excessively abstract theorizing, for example, he singles out religious scholars as being "the furthest of people" from understanding "politics and its ways." This is because, in contrast to practitioners of the intellectual sciences (*al-ʿulūm al-ʿaqliyya*), religious scholars expect the outside world to conform to their postulates rather than the other way around, and because they are accustomed to the method of analogical reasoning (*qiyās*) in religious jurisprudence (*fiqh*), which is inappropriate for variable political circumstances that cannot always be compared to each other. At the same time, Ibn Khaldun also expands his criticism to include other scholars of "intelligence and subtlety" who nevertheless mirror the political incompetence of the religious jurists in their inclination toward abstract logical speculations divorced from practical reality.[152] Instead, he seeks to build on the distinctive insights of the thinkers reviewed in the previous two chapters in order synthesize them into an alternative realist framework that gives practical wisdom its full due—and by doing so refutes the still altogether too widespread notion that he is a "solitary genius" who "does not belong to any definite current of Arabo-Muslim thought."[153]

While acknowledging Ibn Khaldun's realism, the influential Lebanese philosopher Nasif Nassar has consistently criticized it as a "conservative" outlook satisfied with describing "social historical reality" as it is, but never giving any thought to "reforming the ways of society" in order to effect meaningful "progress" in terms of improving the human condition.[154] This chapter has, by contrast, attempted to show that in the face of a reality that promises only perpetual change and perpetual challenge, never perpetual peace, Ibn Khaldun opposes an art of statecraft that takes the lead in mobilizing primal drives such as ambition and pride, acquisitiveness and magnanimity, aggressiveness and courage, on behalf of its ultimate end: an advanced culture housed in an imperial civilization the greatness of which is measured by its magnitude, creativity, and duration. Far from pessimism or resignation, his tone always remains exhortative, whether in cataloging dynamic civilizations of the past as instructive examples (*'ibar*) for future generations, or in rejoicing at the periodic infusions of vigorous new elements to rejuvenate the Islamic polity, or in evoking great victories still to come against the enemies of Islam.[155]

CHAPTER 5

Contemporary Echoes

> And it is He who has made you viceroys of the earth, and has raised some of you above others in degrees. . . .
>
> —Qur'an 6:165

Ibn Khaldun's ideas enjoyed a significant renaissance during the later years of the last and most extensive of the great multicultural Islamic states, the Ottoman Empire. Founded around the turn of the fourteenth century, it had quickly, within a century, developed "an imperial administration in the Perso-Islamic tradition" and a mode of warfare no longer reflecting the *"ghâzî* spirit" of zealous irregular raiders, but the logic of a centralized "conquering state."[1] Ibn Khaldun himself is reported to have noted at this point that the only conceivable challenge to the Mamluk kingdom in which he lived came from "the sons of Osman."[2] And as he might have expected, it was only after the triumphant expansion of those early centuries gave way to a more mature recognition of limits that Ottoman thinkers began in their turn to grapple with the question of how to prevent enervation, and in the process to rediscover the work of Ibn Khaldun, described by one of them as "a marvelous man" who "has surpassed all historians."[3] Perhaps the greatest of these Ottoman thinkers is Katip Çelebi (1609–1657), whose main concern in his political writings is to reject fatalism or panic, and to argue instead that the decline of "this great state" could still be reversed, and its youthful vigor restored, through wise and decisive statecraft.[4] He begins by identifying a primary cause of the crisis, the fact that philosophy lost its share in governance: "Certain judges outlawed the teaching of philosophy, which was replaced with lessons in right guidance in religion, and thus science declined. . . . As Ibn Khaldun . . . said, this was a sign of the collapse of the state."[5] Whereas in the past "scholars who combined the study of the sacred sciences with that of philosophy were held in high renown," their successors condemned philosophy and sought to restrict teaching to religious subjects alone: "But as restriction to these was not reasonable," in the end "neither philosophy nor [proper religious guidance] was left."[6] An important aspect of reforming statecraft, therefore, is a better grasp of the true relationship between religion and politics in order to "protect the State" from such deviations.[7] Katip Çelebi concentrates his fire on dogmatic zealots who try to suppress what they view as sinful innovations originating both abroad and at home. The former include not just scientific advances, but also new ideas about governance, so Katip Çelebi devotes one of his treatises to a description of European forms of government, including democracy.[8]

Domestically as well, Katip Çelebi adopts a pragmatic approach, advocating a certain degree of tolerance for well-established popular customs and practices: "If one goes deeply into such practices and tries to deter people from them, talk and disputation with the tongue leads to battle and fighting with sword and spear, and the result is wars of fanaticism such as our forefathers saw."[9] Like Ibn Khaldun, then, he recognizes that reform at an advanced stage of civilizational maturity requires particular sensitivity to the power of convention.[10] At the same time, and again like Ibn Khaldun, he urges strong action against those whose heterodoxy and lack of concern for order place the state in danger—for example the Sufis, whose contempt for distinction and rank he describes by quoting a poem:

> The man whose worth is high they denigrate,
> That their own paltry value be enhanced.[11]

Katip Çelebi's recognition that people generally "cannot be forced to comply" leads him to what he calls "the first overriding condition" of political and religious reform: "that if right is enjoined and wrong forbidden, the coming forth of the right and the disappearance of the wrong may be reasonably expected"—in other words, that there is a realistic chance of success.[12] On this kind of deft political pragmatism, respectful of the social ethos and therefore capable of winning the citizenry's consent, he rests his hopes for neutralizing the internal engines of decay, and for defeating the empire's external enemies: "In all of this my aim has been the empowerment of Muslims. . . . For the infidels have by means of [their] sciences occupied a great many places on earth, harassing the Muslims and posing as heroes. . . ."[13]

Even though Katip Çelebi's administrative, pedagogic, and fiscal proposals would lay the groundwork for the Ottoman reform programs that followed, they proved insufficient in the end to overcome the resistance of those he called "gibbering fools."[14] Within two and a half centuries, internal pathologies would combine with celestial accidents such as the Industrial Revolution and the rise of nationalism in the West to erode the foundations of Ottoman ʿaṣabiyya, break the empire up into a new system of states governed for the most part by authoritarian secular nationalist regimes, and bring to a climax the general decline that poses the central political challenge confronting the Muslim world today. In the process, the medieval imperial theories of which Katip Çelebi was the last great exponent were forgotten as well. But the wheel of fortune continued to turn, so let us hurry past this barren landscape of tyranny and chauvinism to the point toward the end of the twentieth century when the post-Ottoman state system begins in its turn to experience stress, and faint echoes of the old realism start to reemerge.

ʿAṣabiyya Crisis

Less than a century after the collapse of the Ottoman Empire, the political order imposed on the Near East under the aegis of European hegemony began to show signs of unraveling. In terms of regimes, that dominant order took the form of authoritarian secular nationalism. It was secular and nationalist, because the new ruling elites had for the most part concluded from the prolonged decline of their imperial predecessors—Ottoman, Qajar, and Mughal—that the only way forward was to emulate the political model of the ascendant Western powers. This drive to modernize along Western lines defined Kemalism in Turkey, Baʿthism in many eastern Arab states, Nasserism in Egypt, Bourguibism in Tunisia, and the ideology of the National Liberation Front in Algeria, but it also shaped the political projects of ostensibly more conservative monarchs such as the Arab Hashemites and the Iranian Pahlavis.

It was authoritarian, because the elites' secularist and nationalist agenda ran counter to the mores of their own populations. İsmet İnönü,

Mustafa Kemal Atatürk's deputy and successor, made the point clear when he told a group of officers during Turkey's War of Independence: "I want you to understand the situation you are in. . . . The [Ottoman] Sultan is your enemy; the seven states [the European occupying powers] are your enemies; listen to me, don't let anyone hear—the people are your enemy."[15] Nevertheless, it took some time for this alienation between elites and their subjects to really manifest itself. In the first place, the masses—overwhelmingly rural and illiterate; traumatized by the bloodshed, famine, and disease accompanying the collapse of the old empires; and in large part themselves recently displaced refugees unsure of their standing[16]—were in no position to press coherent or effective political claims. In the second place, the struggle against British and French hegemony eclipsed all others, and lent the nationalist cause further impetus. As more and more states gained independence, however, and as socioeconomic development efforts generated higher rates of urbanization, literacy, and consequently political mobilization as well, integrated civil societies began to take shape, giving rise by the 1970s to populist political movements and parties seeking to articulate the interests and values of ordinary citizens.

For a variety of historical, structural, and contingent reasons, the timing and dynamics of the ensuing struggle between authoritarian secular nationalist elites and populist—hence predominantly Islamist—oppositions varied considerably from country to country.[17] By the time the Arab uprisings broke out in 2010–2011, at any rate, it had become clear that the majority of the region's people would henceforth only consider legitimate regimes that accommodated their demands for political representation and that reflected their predominant cultural and social mores.[18]

In terms of borders, the hitherto dominant order took the form of a partitioning of former imperial domains into a patchwork of nation-states—and for Arabs, of subnation-states—which reflected the interests of the hegemonic European powers, and which was exemplified by the 1916 Sykes-Picot Agreement wherein Britain and France delineated their respective spheres of influence over the remains of the Ottoman Empire. Even before 2011, however, an array of new entities variously described as *"de facto* states," "unrecognized states," "quasi-states" or "semistates" began to proliferate.[19] A few of these (the constituent elements of Bosnia-Herzegovina and Kosovo, for example) went on to achieve some degree of international recognition, others (the Turkish Republic of Northern Cyprus, Nagorno-Karabakh, Chechnya for a time, Abkhazia, South Ossetia, Iraqi Kurdistan, Palestine, Somaliland) remained in various degrees of diplomatic limbo, but all demonstrate the growing strains on the territorial status quo imposed by the great powers. The dismantling of the Iraqi-Syrian border by fighters of the Islamic State of Iraq and al-Sham (the Levant), or ISIS, during the summer of 2014, which they publicized with images sent out under the Twitter hashtag "#SykesPicotOver," is only the most dramatic manifestation of this ongoing upheaval in the regional map.

The intensifying determination of the region's increasingly mobilized populations to withhold consent from unrepresentative regimes, then, seems to be paralleled by a deepening dissatisfaction with the boundaries erected among them a century ago. While it is much more difficult to gauge this second development accurately, as polling data is quite limited and erratic, it might be worth noting that in Turkey at least, the number of respondents identifying themselves primarily as "Muslim" as opposed to "Turkish citizen" or "Turk" rose from 36 percent in 1999 to 45 percent in 2006 to 49 percent in 2011.[20] As for the Arab world, one public opinion survey conducted in five countries found roughly equal percentages for each of the three primary identity categories—nationality (Arab), citizenship (Egyptian, Jordanian, etc.), and religion—albeit with "Muslim" the only one rising between 2009 and 2011 (from 27 to 31 percent).[21]

The suggestion that the regional map is becoming both more dysfunctional and more illegitimate is bolstered by the criticisms increasingly leveled at it, and not just by militant Islamists. Speaking in the predominantly Kurdish city of Diyarbakır on March 15, 2013, Ahmet Davutoğlu (then foreign minister, later prime minister of Turkey) rejected the "nationalist ideologies" with which the European powers had tried "to dismember us" and called for a "new regional order" based on the restoration of an "older conception" of community (*millet*), one that did not differentiate between "Turk and Kurd, Albanian and Bosnian." Working together, he vowed, "Turks, Kurds, Albanians, Bosnians, [and] Arabs" would erase "artificially drawn maps" and "break the mold that Sykes-Picot drew for us."[22] In a statement issued just one week later, Abdullah Öcalan, the imprisoned leader of the Kurdish PKK—a radically secular and nationalist organization—felt compelled to echo Davutoğlu's sentiments, accusing "Western imperialism" of dividing the "Arab, Turkish, Persian and Kurdish communities" into "nation-states and artificial borders," recalling their "common life under the banner of Islam for almost

1000 years," and declaring that "it is time to restore to the concept of 'us' its old spirit and practice."[23]

As ordinary people throughout the Near East gain agency, then, they seem to be finding the regimes and borders governing their lives increasingly incommensurate with who they are and what they believe. This erosion of ties binding them to their governing structures, which first got underway in the late 1970s, constitutes a crisis of identity and legitimacy—in short, a crisis of ʿaṣabiyya. That is why actors on all sides are struggling to articulate alternative visions based on more viable formal expressions of political community.

Responses

Perhaps the most prominent of these alternative visions in recent years is the one proffered by ISIS, which declared itself a caliphate on June 29, 2014, after conquering extensive territories in Iraq and Syria. On the one hand, the very idea of a caliphate proved so resonant that it drew tens of thousands of Muslims from every corner of the globe to come and fight for it under the most difficult conditions. This alone is striking testament to the magnitude of the ʿaṣabiyya crisis across the Muslim world. On the other hand, the extreme dogmatism and violence displayed by the self-styled Islamic State—along with inevitable organizational and personalistic rivalries—led large segments of even the militant Islamist camp to recoil from it. Hence Abu Muhammad al-Maqdisi's denunciations of its leaders as "worse than Kharijis," for example, despite the fact that "we all wish for the return of the caliphate and the breaking of boundaries and the raising of the banners of unity."[24]

As for Muslim populations more broadly, public opinion polls indicate that ISIS is having difficulty translating the resonance of the idea of a caliphate into support for itself. A Pew Research Center survey conducted during the spring of 2015 showed the following percentages of respondents in Muslim-majority countries saying they have a favorable opinion of ISIS: Jordan (3%), Turkey (8%), Pakistan (9%), Indonesia (4%), Senegal (11%).[25] These numbers contrast sharply with the growing support for democratic governance discussed earlier, and would seem to further confirm al-Maqdisi's warnings that reckless extremism will ultimately turn public opinion against the militant approach.

The main rivals of the revolutionary militants, consequently, are those whose claim to legitimacy has rested on both Islamic *and* democratic credentials. They include the various Arab Muslim Brotherhoods as well as Turkey's AK Party. Unlike their less successful Arab counterparts, however, Turkey's elected Islamists saw an opportunity to couple this legitimacy with the power resources of the state they now governed in order to formulate what they hoped would be a truly effective new *'aṣabiyya*. Long before his 2013 speech denouncing the Sykes-Picot borders, Ahmet Davutoğlu, for example, had written of the need for a "new agenda" that can "revitalize traditional concepts such as the Ummah['s] universal brotherhood, *Dar al-Islam* as a world order and the Caliphate as the political institutionalization of this world order. It is not necessary to have the traditional forms of these institutions."[26] Earlier in his career, President Recep Tayyip Erdoğan for his part had called for "something resembling the Ottoman states system" not only to bind Turkey's "27 ethnic groups" together more effectively, but also to serve as the basis for Turkey's leadership of a much broader regional consolidation: "Turkey has the power to sustain an imperial vision. In fact, . . . it is obliged to adopt an imperial vision."[27] İbrahim Kalın, shortly before joining the government in 2009 as a high-ranking policy advisor and spokesman, wrote that Turkey was now moving toward "a post-nation-state strategic outlook."[28]

Such a competing agenda naturally drew intense criticism from Islamist militants. Just two or three years after the AK Party first took office, Abu Muhammad al-Maqdisi charged that the United States, seeking to liberalize the Muslim world, stood behind Turkey's campaign to export "its democratic model and religious moderation!!"[29] As the Turks pressed their Neo-Ottoman argument in the wake of the Arab uprisings, with Erdoğan declaring that his party's victory in the June 2011 national elections was "Sarajevo's victory as much as Istanbul's; Beirut's victory as much as Izmir's; Damascus' victory as much as Ankara's; Ramallah's, the West Bank's, Jerusalem's, Gaza's victory as much as Diyarbakır's," and Davutoğlu asserting the following year that his government intended "to direct the great transformation wave in the Middle East," the militant attacks intensified.[30] An ISIS video released during the summer of 2015 urged Turks to rise against "this treacherous Satan [Erdoğan] and his friends" and to reject "democracy, secularism, human laws, and all types of other evils."[31]

But it is not only the militants who have attacked the AK Party's attempt to promote a new *'aṣabiyya* for the region. Writing from a very different religious perspective, the influential Turkish intellectual Ali Bulaç went right to the heart of the matter by denouncing the AK Party's realist outlook: "An excessive emphasis on realpolitik leads to a surrender of principle and justice to security, and of ideals to prevailing circumstances."[32] Finding fault not only with philosophers such as al-Farabi but even orthodox authorities such as Ibn Taymiyya, al-Ghazali, and al-Mawardi for their willingness to accommodate political realities, Bulaç blamed "historical Islam"—presumably the entirety of Islamic political practice since Muʿawiya—for "abrogating" the religion's "life-giving values" and paving the way for the "Real-Islam" (*Reel İslam*) represented by the AK Party.[33] From Bulaç's apolitical idealist perspective, the core error of the AK Party leaders lay in their eagerness to engage in governance: "Muslim intellectuals suddenly became state bureaucrats. . . . [They] lost their autonomous and civilian character and came to resemble the Ottoman official clergy (*ulema*). . . . This is the first of the greatest disasters to befall the Islamist movement."[34] As a result, all sorts of ultimately corrupting compromises had to be made with political and economic ("big capital") power centers at home and abroad; compromises that caused the AK Party to lose its moral grounding and erased whatever had distinguished its vision "from what the West is offering everyone." If this is the model of reconciling "Islam and democracy" that the AK Party hoped to "market" to other countries, then it would be exporting "the empty and purposeless life style of a nihilistic culture" and thus "dragging . . . the Middle East and neighboring regions to suicide alongside Turkey."[35]

In a series of opinion pieces published in January 2014, Ali Bulaç returned to this critique of the AK Party's political realism, here focusing specifically on its Neo-Ottoman "illusions." He again denounced the necessary accommodations of realpolitik as "un-Islamic," pointing as an example to the AK Party leadership's desire to join the U.S.-led war against Iraq in 2003, and argued that cooperating in the invasion by foreigners of a Muslim country—regardless, apparently, of the character of its regime—is unambiguously a "sin."[36] Bulaç went on to describe the AK Party's true objective, which it had failed to articulate "frankly," as supplanting the "global powers" in order to "dominate the region by ourselves." This objective is "un-Islamic" as well, because it rests on the assumption that Turkey's historical legacies and geographical context "destine us to regional leadership." But "to assign determinative power" to such worldly or material factors is unacceptable "from a doctrinal perspective." Instead, piety is the decisive criterion, so even the least powerful, most humble Muslim may rule. Moreover, leadership in Islam belongs not to a particular nation but to the Islamic community (*ümmet*) as a whole, so a Turkish bid for regional hegemony can only lead to conflict with other Islamic states such as Iran and Egypt.[37]

Bulaç's apolitical idealism represents a serious current in Islamic thought, but as we have seen it is far from the only one. In the alternative tradition he decried as "Real-Islam" in his 2010 book, and detailed in the preceding chapters here, each of Bulaç's main propositions is contested, beginning with the easy confidence with which he designates various options as sinful or un-Islamic. The older Muslim realists argued that any political enterprise, no matter how virtuous, always involves a complex admixture of nobler and baser motivations and means. Indeed, Ibn Khaldun viewed the aggressive quest for dominance—by individuals and by broader political collectives—as the veritable engine of his civilizational project. It is the project itself, the rationale for political action, which undergirds the normative component of Islamic realism.[38]

As the AK Party entered its second decade in power apparently having neutralized its authoritarian secular nationalist foes and consolidated a support base that gave it a string of impressive electoral victories, at any rate, another, entirely new challenge began to crystallize. This new challenge made its first serious appearance in the protests that broke out in May 2013 over plans to raze Istanbul's Gezi Park for urban development. Prime Minister Erdoğan and many of his colleagues interpreted the massive demonstrations that then spread to other cities as a provocation by hardline Kemalists and other adversaries, and reacted harshly, dispersing demonstrators by force and imposing restrictions on news outlets and social media sites. They were half right, because elements not generally known for their sensitivity to environmental concerns or freedom of expression were indeed trying to jump on the Gezi Park bandwagon for their own purposes. But they were also half wrong: large numbers of mostly young protestors were in fact motivated by precisely such liberal concerns. Since those protests, as a result, the AK Party's leaders, like Turkey's citizens in general—and indeed like Muslims all across the region—have found themselves at a fateful junction, between recognizing that mere majoritarianism will no longer suffice and therefore embracing a more comprehensively representative approach on the one side, or drawing back toward repressive rule on the other. As of this writing, it remains to be seen whether the Turkish government's authoritarian and nationalistic turn represents a temporary deviation in response to the post-Gezi subversion campaigns culminating in the July 2016 coup attempt or, as seems increasingly likely with each passing day, a more definitive retreat from the AK Party's original democratizing and multicultural principles.

The latter outcome would mark a sad end to a promising experiment in reconciling Islamic values with political realities. Even in the former case, however, it is apparent that so far at least there has been a failure to grapple constructively with the challenge that first began to take shape through the smoke and tear gas of Gezi Park. Unless equally appealing alternatives are presented to them, more and more members of the elites and masses alike will flee the brutality of authoritarian regimes and the terror of ISIS toward the softer, gentler, altogether more amiable liberalism of Abdolkarim Soroush's "plump guest in the family of humanity." But what are the implications of such a development for the project of constructing an overarching new regional ʿaṣabiyya? There have been individuals within the AK Party well acquainted with the history of Islamic political thought. Ahmet Davutoğlu, for example, has written extensively on the subject, arguing inter alia that far from being utopian, al-Farabi's political ideas were meant to be realizable.[39] İbrahim Kalın is a scholar of Islamic philosophy who wrote his dissertation about Mulla Sadra (d. 1640) on the intellect and the intelligible. But there is no indication that this knowledge has yet been applied in a manner that addresses the emerging liberal challenge seriously. It may be, however, that the broader conditions for such an application are becoming more propitious.

A Rushdian Revival?

Chapter 3 ended by noting the widespread conviction that Ibn Rushd's approach to philosophy—focused on natural causation and human agency, forthright about its theoretical limitations, and politically engaged—came to be eclipsed by Ibn Sina's more easy-going oversight of the boundaries between philosophy and religion, which in turn inspired the further turn toward intuitive knowledge and mysticism displayed by the Illuminationists and others. According to a recent testimonial by Shahab Ahmed, for example, the "Sufi-philosophical amalgam" shaped by Ibn Sina in the first place, and Suhrawardi and the Sufi mystic Ibn ʿArabi secondarily, constituted the dominant "paradigm of life and thought" at least for the geographically and demographically preponderant portion of the Islamic world he calls the "Balkans-to-Bengal Complex" during the half-millennium before the modern era (1350–1850).[40]

At two separate points during the past century, however—coinciding with the ʿaṣabiyya crises that marked first the onset, then the waning, of the region's authoritarian secular nationalist era—revivals of interest in Ibn Rushd among Arab intellectuals have occurred. The first, in the early 1900s, came as the Ottoman order's collapse prompted an embrace of the rationalism that was understood to be the driving force behind the West's undeniable cultural, scientific, and geopolitical ascendance. This embrace paralleled the adoption of apparently superior Western political structures such as nationalism by a large proportion of Muslim elites during this period. The major difference is that whereas nationalism had no precedent in the ʿaṣabiyyas of Islamic lands, rationalism had an indigenous pedigree tracing back to the medieval philosophers. Hence the renewed interest in Ibn Rushd, whom the Syrian Westernizer Farah Antun presented in a 1902 article as a secular materialist whose legacy had been suppressed for centuries by religious reactionaries. The Muslim reformist Muhammad ʿAbduh then responded by defending Ibn Rushd as an exemplar of the compatibility of Islam and reason. Hampered by lack of access to Ibn Rushd's texts—only two of his manuscripts had been published in Arabic editions by the turn of the twentieth century—and also by the rise of a "progressive" modernizing ethos that too often disdained past traditions, however, this initial wave of interest in Ibn Rushd proved evanescent.

The second wave got underway in the late 1970s, when the authoritarian secular nationalist order in its turn began to erode as a result of the ʿaṣabiyya crisis outlined earlier in this chapter. Confronted by the rise of a potent Islamist populism region-wide, Arab intellectuals—many of them former Baʿthists, Nasserists, and socialists—turned back to their intellectual heritage in search of alternative indigenous models; a quest that led them directly to Ibn Rushd and, to a somewhat lesser extent, Ibn Khaldun as well.[41] This turn took a number of different manifestations. Cultural nationalists such as the Moroccan philosopher Muhammad ʿAbid al-Jabiri emphasized the "authenticity" of the Arab rationalist tradition of which Ibn Rushd is the prime exemplar, the better to "employ it" in building a new polity that is "free" and "democratic" and "socialist."[42] The centerpiece of his argument is the fundamental contrast between Ibn Rushd's politically engaged "realist rationalism" (*ʿaqlāniyya wāqiʿiyya*) and Ibn Sina's "mystical" or "gnostic" outlook, which originated in the emanationist metaphysics of the Sabeans, reflected the resentful national consciousness of a defeated Persian aristocracy against the ʿAbbasid Arabs, focused on the management of the individual self (*siyāsat al-marʾ li-nafsihi*) rather than the construction of a virtuous city in the here and now, and paved the way for the "deadly dark irrationalism" propagated by the likes of al-Ghazali and Suhrawardi that plunged the Islamic world into "retreat and decline" for many centuries.[43]

Although Jabiri's attack has been criticized for distorting Ibn Sina's views as well as for its perceived chauvinism,[44] it resonated not just among fellow cultural nationalists, but also within another current of the renewed interest in Ibn Rushd: modernist Westernizers who are less preoccupied with asserting cultural authenticity. One example is Muhammad ʿAtif al-ʿIraqi, an Egyptian philosophy professor associated with the "Enlightenment" (*tanwīr*) movement which has collaborated with Egypt's Ministry of Culture since the early 1990s to publish works—featuring Ibn Rushd in particular—aimed at countering the ideas of the militant Islamist opposition.[45] Like Jabiri, he extolled Ibn Rushd as the greatest of all Arab philosophers, contrasting his unadulterated Aristotelianism with the Neoplatonic and Sufi influences that allegedly lent an occult irrationalism to Ibn Sina's writings.[46] Like Jabiri, he hoped that the rediscovery of Ibn Rushd's thought would spark a renaissance through which Arabs could finally overcome their "backwardness."[47] In line with his Westernizing orientation, however, ʿIraqi presented Ibn Rushd as an "Arab thinker with a Western soul;" a thinker whose ideas would overcome the "errors and lies" of the fundamentalists and militants who "wish us to . . . return to stone-age life," inaugurating instead a new age of enlightenment wherein "our Arab world will become as if a piece of Europe."[48]

Finally, Ibn Rushd's stock also rose among religiously inclined reformists such as Muhammad ʿImara, who likewise lauded him in contrast to Ibn Sina's inadequately rational methodology, while nevertheless defending him as an unimpeachably mainstream Muslim theologian and jurist as well.[49] On a more official level, Mahmud Hamdi Zaqzuq, who served as Egypt's Minister of Religious Endowments from 1995 to 2011, similarly denied any contradiction between

Ibn Rushd's philosophy and his orthodoxy, and placed him at the apex of the contemporary "enlightenment" movement opposing those extremists who wish "to drag us back blindly."[50]

On the one hand, then, the mere fact that even religious thinkers today can find Ibn Rushd more congenial than Ibn Sina suggests a tectonic shift in the receptivity to his approach. Advances in scientific understanding have rendered obsolete many of the metaphysical problems—the nature of the emanationist hierarchy of celestial beings, for example, or the relation between the human mind and the Active Intellect—which diverted so much of his energy as he tried to tread a viable path between philosophical inquiry and religious orthodoxy, and which for so long gave Ibn Sina and his followers the upper hand. The current ʿaṣabiyya crisis has also increased the appeal of Ibn Rushd's activist reformism relative to Ibn Sina's more politically apathetic stance. Even in Iran, Ali Shariʾati (d. 1977), whose writings were very influential in the build-up to the Iranian Revolution, criticized Ibn Sina as someone who "never showed any concern with the destiny of man and the fate of his society. He saw no connection between his own fate and that of others."[51] No wonder, then, that Jabiri came to see Ibn Rushd as "closer to us today than at any time in the past."[52]

As the current ʿaṣabiyya crisis deepened, on the other hand, and demands for political representation intensified, the tension between democratic principles of equality and freedom and Ibn Rushd's views on hierarchy and governance grew increasingly apparent. This became all the more true as greater access to Ibn Rushd's writings—the first two translations into Arabic of his commentary on Plato's *Republic* (the original text having long been lost), for example, both came out only in 1998—generated more sophisticated understandings of his political philosophy. The early enthusiasts consequently either ignored his critique of democratic egalitarianism, or quietly moved on to other concerns, or joined Muhammad ʿAbid al-Jabiri in concluding that the medieval realists no longer had much to offer by way of practical prescription after all: "while Ibn Rushd and Ibn Khaldun were necessary in seeking the answer to our first question 'whence?' the answer to our second question 'whither?' requires us to depart from their horizons and to fixate instead on the horizon of modernity and its political, economic, social, cultural, and scientific accomplishments."[53]

Others were more direct. ʿAli Mabruk in Egypt and Mustafa Bin Tamassak in Tunisia both denounced Ibn Rushd's assertion of a natural basis for his hierarchical ranking of human beings as inimical to democracy, and indeed supportive of tyranny.⁵⁴ Nasif Nassar in Lebanon agreed, further criticizing Ibn Rushd for failing to articulate a sufficiently secular political philosophy, and concluded that a "kind of rupture" with Ibn Rushd is now required.⁵⁵ A specialist on Ibn Khaldun, Nassar reached the same conclusion with regard to the latter philosopher as well, for likewise remaining trapped in a medieval conception of human nature that "obliterates" the possibility of freedom and equality, and denies the prospect of any polity embarking on a permanently "open progressive path."⁵⁶

Perhaps the most wide-ranging critique from this newer cohort of Arab scholars, however, is by the Moroccan philosophy professor Muhammad al-Misbahi. The problem, according to Misbahi, is not only that the modern understanding of freedom is incompatible with an obsolete "hierarchical model of order" that divides people into "elites and multitudes."⁵⁷ It is that "the modern mind" has become "completely un-Rushdian": "the end of the era of truths that are fixed and that transcend the individual and society and history" has left human beings with a "relativistic view" according to which "what is true in one society may not be true in another, and what is correct today may not be so tomorrow."⁵⁸ Ibn Rushd's "ahistorical" commitment to absolute and eternal truths therefore estranges him from this modern way of thought for which demonstration (*burhān*), causality (*'illiyya*), and necessity (*ḍarūra*) "no longer have the same value they once did," leading Misbahi to reverse Jabiri's judgment: "Our present age is therefore much closer to al-Ghazali and Ibn Sina and Ibn 'Arabi than to Ibn Rushd."⁵⁹

While Misbahi's conclusion may be premature—the region is only just entering its liberal age, after all—his take on the Ibn Rushd revival does highlight, once again, how intellectual developments here may be recapitulating parallel trajectories in the West. Just like the jihad modernists reviewed in chapter 1, the partisans of rationalist modernism set out to counter their militant adversaries by affirming an alternative indigenous tradition they argued is more in line with contemporary international norms. Just like the jihad modernists, the counterattacks of their opponents, coupled with the democratizing pressures of the *'aṣabiyya* crisis, have led them to a critical crossroads. Some are maintaining their alliances with authoritarian regimes against the Islamist revolutionaries, as in the ongoing collaboration between the Egyptian government and the Enlightenment Association. Others, probably the dominant tendency, are embracing democratic liberalism more fully. And a few, judging by Misbahi's comments, are already following the evolution of Western liberalism into its post-modern stage.

Again as in the debate on jihad, there are as yet few signs of a distinctive realist current here seeking to apply the insights of the medieval tradition in order to grapple with the opportunities and challenges of the unfolding liberal age. Nevertheless, it is at least possible that the recent revival of interest in Ibn Rushd and Ibn Khaldun will lead to a deeper reading of their work that may yet allow their realism to find its place in the emerging intellectual constellation, alongside the revolutionary militants and the apolitical idealists as well as the liberal newcomers.

∽

A few years after the September 11 attacks I met a Pakistani doctor on a visiting fellowship in Boston. As we chatted about the challenges of educating our children, she remarked that her greatest worry regarding American schools was that her boys would "lose their ferocity." Ibn Khaldun would have rejoiced at her spirit, but there was no dismissing her concern. One need not conjure up foreign cabals to recognize the magnitude of the effects wrought on beliefs and behaviors by the liberalizing revolution already underway in the Muslim world. It is illustrated by the Islamic modernists' ideas about defensive war and permanent peace discussed in chapter 1. Caught between the desire to conform to norms that are becoming increasingly hegemonic worldwide on the one hand, and the stinging criticisms of Abu Muhammad al-Maqdisi and his fellow militants on the other, contemporary modernists and rationalists find themselves pushed either toward a neoliberalism so utilitarian that it loses sight of the distinction between noble and ignoble ends, or toward an idealism oblivious to the realities of human nature and its aggressive predispositions.

But the militants offer no acceptable alternative. Their refusal to accommodate the less sublime aspects of human nature, and their confidence that those aspects can be overcome through a law that is clearly and easily accessible to all, tend to lead to two dangerous consequences spelled out by Ibn Rushd. One is a certainty about the interpretation of the Law that privileges dogmatic uniformity over nuanced deliberation. The other is the factionalism, conflict, and repression which intolerance of conflicting interpretations inevitably generates. When the egalitarian spirit so often characterizing such revolutionary idealisms is also factored in, the resulting vector force is a pull toward the lowest common denominator in both theory and practice. The excesses of ignorance and cruelty al-Maqdisi decries among some of his fellow militants are thus not merely incidental aberrations: it is rarely the cultured, witty, or forbearing types who rise to the top of such movements, but the narrow-minded, dour, and ruthless ones. The consequences of such coarsening for civic virtue are evident today for all to see.

The consequences of the liberal alternative are more ambiguous. Freedom and equality greatly expand the range of human creativity, but they can also devolve into a self-centered narcissism that erodes *'aṣabiyya*, and a leveling that erases distinctions between high and low, until the polity is enfeebled to the point where it can no longer defend or press its claims against more vigorous enemies. These dangers entailed in the arrival of Soroush's "plump guest" do not stem primarily from the modern reliance on science per se, which after all has tremendously enhanced the conditions for the flourishing of civilization—although excessive faith in certain applications of science can indeed obscure the need for a more artful kind of political expertise. Nor is the central problem democracy as such. Already almost a millennium ago, pace the recent Arab scholars reviewed above, Muslim thinkers such as Ibn Rushd recognized the virtues of democracy. Its strength lies in its diversity: for all the multitudes of slavish conformists and grasping hedonists it nurtures, it also allows the emergence of other types who can contribute something more to their communities. Since democracy will remain *the* characteristic regime of our times, it falls to these other types, realistic and civic-minded, to attend to its needs in order to preserve wisdom's share in governance so that the Ibn Khaldunian balances are maintained, the democratic polity continues to exhibit the fortitude needed to prevail against its domestic and foreign enemies, and the desire for distinction is not debased into a brutal drive for domination.

In the view of the tradition extending from Ibn al-Muqaffaʿ to Katip Çelebi surveyed here, Islam, in accord with nature's exemplary order, recognizes and marshals the full range of human types. It therefore proves exceptionally well suited for the practitioners of artful statecraft, allowing them to take advantage of lesser "natural evils" such as selfish ambition and aggressive acquisitiveness, while still keeping sight of the higher good. If virtuous intent is too unrealistic a criterion to apply to everyone, after all, the same cannot be said of those responsible for steering the polity and maintaining its healthy balances. Islamic realism aims at a convergence of intellectual and moral hierarchies as it seeks to reestablish the link between self and state within an effective greater *'aṣabiyya*.

It can only do so, however, by insisting on the autonomy of its own domain; the domain of politics, where the operating logic is, in Ibn Khaldun's terms, post-prophetic or post-miraculous, and the necessary art is that of the statesman rather than the spiritual guide. A domain, in other words, ordered according to degrees of excellence in statecraft, defined not just in terms of its technical proficiency but also its end: creating the optimum political and cultural conditions for the realization of every citizen's potential according to his or her capabilities. This should be, in the view of the Muslim realists, an agenda capable of attracting those with the necessary skill, spirit, and virtue into serving as its vanguard.

Notes

Introduction

1. Cheryl Benard, *Civil Democratic Islam: Partners, Resources, and Strategies* (Santa Monica: RAND Corporation, 2003), p. 3.
2. Ibid., pp. iii, 49 (note 1).
3. Ibid., pp. xii, 46, 11, 13.
4. Ibid., p. 47.
5. Hans J. Morgenthau, *Scientific Man vs. Power Politics* (Chicago: The University of Chicago Press, 1946), p. 194; *Politics Among Nations: The Struggle for Power and Peace* (New York: Alfred A. Knopf, 1978), pp. 560, 529, 557–58. See James P. Speer II, "Hans Morgenthau and the World State," *World Politics*, vol. 20, no. 2 (January 1968): 207–27; Craig Campbell, "Hans Morgenthau and the World State Revisited" in Michael C. Williams, ed., *Realism Reconsidered: The Legacy of Hans J. Morgenthau in International Relations* (Oxford: Oxford University Press, 2007): 195–215; William E. Scheuerman, "Carl Schmitt and Hans Morgenthau: Realism and Beyond" in ibid.: 62–92. On similar features in the thought of other prominent realists such as E. H. Carr, see Ken Booth, "Security in Anarchy: Utopian Realism in Theory and Practice," *International Affairs*, vol. 67, no. 3 (July 1991): 527–45; Paul Howe, "The Utopian Realism of E. H. Carr," *Review of International Studies*, vol. 20, no. 3 (July 1994): 277–97.
6. Kenneth N. Waltz, *Theory of International Politics* (Boston: McGraw-Hill, 1979), p. 176.
7. Robert Gilpin, *War and Change in World Politics* (Cambridge, UK: Cambridge University Press, 1981), p. 210.
8. Ibid., p. 226.
9. Robert O. Keohane (p. 189), "Theory of World Politics: Structural Realism and Beyond" in Robert O. Keohane, ed., *Neorealism and Its Critics* (New York: Columbia University Press, 1986): 158–203; *After Hegemony: Cooperation and Discord in the World Political Economy* (Princeton, NJ: Princeton University Press, 1984), p. 14. See also Robert Jervis, "Realism, Neoliberalism, and Cooperation: Understanding the Debate," *International Security*, vol. 24, no. 1 (Summer 1999): 42–63.

10. Gilpin, *War and Change*, p. 227. See Steven Forde (p. 155), "International Realism and the Science of Politics: Thucydides, Machiavelli, and Neorealism," *International Studies Quarterly*, vol. 39, no. 2 (June 1995): 141–60.

11. Philip Rieff, *The Triumph of the Therapeutic: Uses of Faith after Freud* (New York: Harper Torchbooks, 1968), p. 27.

12. Francis Fukuyama, "The End of History?," *The National Interest*, no. 16 (Summer 1989): 3–18.

13. See, for example, Harold Bloom, *The American Religion: The Emergence of the Post-Christian Nation* (New York: Touchstone, 1993); Alan Wolfe, *The Transformation of American Religion: How We Actually Live Our Faith* (New York: Free Press, 2003).

14. For an account of how Turkish and Arab Islamist political parties have come to embrace core elements of democracy, see Malik Mufti, "The Many-Colored Cloak: Evolving Conceptions of Democracy in Islamic Political Thought," *American Journal of Islamic Social Sciences*, vol. 27, no. 2 (Spring 2010): 1–27.

15. Abdolkarim Soroush (p. 28), "Livelihood and Virtue," originally published in *Kiyan*, vol. 5 (June–July 1995): 2–11; translated into English by the Foreign Broadcast Information Service in FBIS-NES-95-241-S (15 December 1995): 19–31. Another version, authorized by Soroush himself, later appeared as "Life and Virtue: The Relationship between Socioeconomic Development and Ethics" in *Reason, Freedom, and Democracy in Islam: Essential Writings of Abdolkarim Soroush*, translated and edited by Mahmoud Sadri and Ahmad Sadri (New York: Oxford University Press, 2000): 39–53. I have relied on the earlier translation because it is more explicit on key issues such as the debasement—as opposed to mere "transformation"—of values in the modern age, as well as on other more minor but telling points (see note 21 of this chapter).

16. Ibid., pp. 20, 22.
17. Ibid., p. 20.
18. Ibid., p. 24.
19. Ibid., pp. 29, 27–28, 25.
20. Ibid., p. 28.

21. In the original FBIS translation of the piece just cited, Soroush says that those who view liberal development as a package deal "consider pornography, homosexuality, the new and old imperialism, biological and chemical warfare, and destruction of the environment to be the inevitable effects and values of development, and in this way they pursue the false life of animal existence, which has these predecessors and successors. Consequently, they terrify the religious people who have stood in astonishment against the modern world, and they seek with fearful yearning to eat the poisoned sugar cube of development" (ibid., p. 20). In the later translation (*Reason*, p. 40), however, the same list of vices excludes homosexuality, suggesting that conventions of morality may not be so impervious to the pressures of the new age after all.

22. Quoted in Niyazi Berkes, *The Development of Secularism in Turkey* (Montreal: McGill University Press, 1964), pp. 298–99.

23. Quoted in Bernard Lewis, *The Emergence of Modern Turkey* (London: Oxford University Press, 1968), p. 277.

24. Quoted in Linda G. Jones (p. 20), "Portrait of Rashid al-Ghannoushi," *Middle East Report*, no. 153 (July-August 1988): 19–22.

25. Recognizing, of course, that there is a great deal in Ibn Rushd's work, and that of the other Islamic philosophers, that does not relate to politics. For a critique of approaches charged with reducing all philosophy in Islamic civilization either to a non-rational mysticism or to a preoccupation with politics, see Dimitri Gutas, "The Study of Arabic Philosophy in the Twentieth Century: An Essay on the Historiography of Arabic Philosophy," *British Journal of Middle Eastern Studies*, vol. 29, no. 1 (May 2002): 5–25.

26. Mohamed Talbi, "Ibn Khaldūn," *Encyclopaedia of Islam, Second Edition* (http://www.brillonline.nl/ subscriber/entry?entry=islam_SIM-0753; henceforth Brill Online); T. J. de Boer, quoted in Mohammad Abdullah Enan, *Ibn Khaldun: His Life and Works* (Kuala Lumpur: The Other Press, 2007), p. 123. Another recent commentator writes of "the total otherness of Ibn Khaldun with respect to the world of today"—Aziz Al-Azmeh, *Ibn Khaldun in Modern Scholarship: A Study in Orientalism* (London: Third World Centre for Research and Publishing, 1981), pp. vi–vii. Accordingly, the occasional references to, or discussions of, the realism of various aspects of Ibn Khaldun's thought generally fail to situate him within a broader Islamic tradition of political realism.

Chapter 1

1. See, for example, Rudolph Peters, *Islam and Colonialism: The Doctrine of Jihad in Modern History* (The Hague: Moulton Publishers, 1979); Sohail H. Hashmi, "Interpreting the Islamic Ethics of War and Peace" in Sohail H. Hashmi, ed., *Islamic Political Ethics: Civil Society, Pluralism, and Conflict* (Princeton, NJ: Princeton University Press, 2002): 194–216; John Kelsay, *Arguing the Just War in Islam* (Cambridge, MA: Harvard University Press, 2007); Maher al-Sharif, *Tatawwur Mafhum al-Jihad fi al-Fikr al-Islami* (Damascus: Al-Mada Publishing Company, 2008).

2. Thus: "the modernist interpretation that underscores the defensive character of jihad is now widely accepted and is being taught in schools as a generally received theory" (Peters, *Islam and Colonialism*, pp. 163–64).

3. Mahmud Shaltut, *Al-Islam wa-l-ʿAlaqat al-Dawliyya (fi al-Silm wa-l-Harb)* (Cairo: Matbaʿat al-Azhar, 1951), p. 35; see also p. 24.

4. Muhammad Abu Zahra, *Concept of War in Islam*, trans. Muhammad al-Hady and Taha Omar (Cairo: Ministry of Waqf, 1961), p. 18.

5. See for example Shaltut, *Al-Islam*, pp. 34–35; ʿAbd al-Khaliq al-Nawawi, *Al-ʿAlaqat al-Dawliyya wa-l-Nuzum al-Qadaʾiyya fi al-Shariʿa al-Islamiyya*

(Beirut: Dar al-Kitab al-ʿArabi, 1974), p. 105. On the modernists' "contextual exegesis" see Peters, *Islam and Colonialism*, pp. 128–30.

  6. Mohammad Talaat al-Ghunaimi, *The Muslim Conception of International Law and the Western Approach* (The Hague: Martinus Nijhoff, 1968), pp. 135, 163. Al-Ghunaimi's list of classical doctrine exemplars includes figures such as Abu Hanifa (d. 767), al-Awzaʿi, Abu Yusuf, al-Shaybani, al-Shafiʿi, and the much later Ibn Taymiyya (d. 1328).

  7. Sherman A. Jackson (p. 15), "Jihad and the Modern World," *Journal of Islamic Law and Culture*, vol. 7, no. 1 (Spring/Summer 2002): 1–26.

  8. By one reckoning, for example, "the majority of [classical] jurists" held "that the Qurʾanic *casus belli* are restricted to aggression against Muslims and *fitnah*, that is, persecution of Muslims because of their religious belief." Ahmed Al-Dawoody, *The Islamic Law of War: Justifications and Regulations* (New York: Palgrave Macmillan, 2011), p. 78. On how medieval jurisprudence can support modernist arguments, see also Asma Afsaruddin, *Striving in the Path of God: Jihad and Martyrdom in Islamic Thought* (New York: Oxford University Press, 2013).

  9. Muhammad Abu Zahra, *Al-ʿAlaqat al-Dawliyya fi al-Islam* (Cairo: Al-Dar al-Qawmiyya li-l-Tibaʿa wa-l-Nashr, 1964), pp. 51–52, 78. Among those jurists Abu Zahra mentions by name (p. 78) are al-Awzaʿi (d. 774), Abu Yusuf (d. 798), al-Shaybani (d. 805), al-Shafiʿi (d. 820), and Ibn Hanbal (d. 855). On the characterization as "temporally contingent" of the classical view that war is the norm in relations with non-Muslims, see also Wahba al-Zuhayli, *Athar al-Harb fi al-Fiqh al-Islami: Dirasa Muqarina* (Damascus: Dar al-Fikr, 1962), p. 119.

  10. Abu Zahra, *ʿAlaqat*, pp. 47, 89.

  11. Wahba al-Zuhayli (p. 278), "Islam and International Law," *International Review of the Red Cross*, vol. 87, no. 858 (June 2005): 269–83.

  12. Sobhi Mahmassani, *Al-Qanun wa-l-ʿAlaqat al-Dawliyya fi al-Islam* (Beirut: Dar al-ʿIlm li-l-Malayeen, 1972), p. 77. See also Ghunaimi, *Muslim Conception*, p. 184: "We object to including this division in the Muslim legal theory as one of its principles. . . . The terms *dar al-Islam* and *dar al-Harb* are an innovation of the Abbassid legists."

  13. Shaltut, *Islam*, pp. 7–13, 40–42. See also Abu Zahra, *ʿAlaqat*, pp. 48, 79; Zuhayli, *Athar*, p. 116; Ghunaimi, *Muslim Conception*, p. 198; Mahmassani, *Qanun*, pp. 49, 51, 178; Nawawi, *ʿAlaqat*, pp. 56, 104; Jackson, "Jihad," p. 14.

  14. Shaltut, *Islam*, p. 38. A nearly identical formulation is found in Abu Zahra, *ʿAlaqat*, p. 92. See also Nawawi, *ʿAlaqat* (p. 108): "war in Islam can only be defensive."

  15. Shaltut, *Islam*, p. 44. See also Abu Zahra, *ʿAlaqat*, pp. 34, 35.

  16. Wahba al-Zuhayli, *Al-ʿAlaqat al-Dawliyya fi al-Islam: Muqarana bi-l-Qanun al-Dawli al-Hadith* (Beirut: Muʾassasat al-Risala, 1981), p. 32. See also Zuhayli, *Athar*, pp. 27, 77.

  17. Mahmassani, *Qanun*, p. 205; also pp. 191, 196.

  18. For example Zuhayli, *Athar*, p. 761.

19. Ibid., p. 763.
20. Abu Zahra, ʿAlaqat, pp. 38, 95; Zuhayli, Athar, pp. 584–85.
21. Zuhayli, Athar, pp. 480, 482.
22. Ibid., p. 662.
23. Ibid., p. 612.
24. Shaltut, Islam, p. 58; Zuhayli, Athar, pp. 398, 406, 415, 419, 426, 437; Ghunaimi, Muslim Conception, pp. 190–91; Mahmassani, Qanun, pp. 256, 258. Elsewhere, Mahmassani flatly asserts that Islam has "forbidden the killing and enslavement of prisoners"—Fi Durub al-ʿAdala: Dirasat fi al-Shariʿa wa-l-Qanun wa-l-ʿAlaqat al-Dawliyya (Beirut: Dar al-ʿIlm li-l-Malayeen, 1982), p. 106.
25. Ghunaimi, Muslim Conception, p. 186. See also Zuhayli, Athar, pp. 688–704.
26. See Zuhayli, Athar, pp. 668, 675–76, 686; Mahmassani, Fi Durub al-ʿAdala, p. 91; Yusuf Qaradawi, Nahnu wa-l-Gharb: Asʾila Shaʾika wa-Ajwiba Hasima (Cairo: Dar al-Tawziʿ wa-l-Nashr al-Islamiyya, 2006), p. 26.
27. Qaradawi, Nahnu wa-l-Gharb, pp. 27, 39.
28. Mahmassani, Qanun, p. 113. See also Qaradawi, Nahnu wa-l-Gharb, p. 30.
29. On the dār al-ʿahd: Abu Zahra, ʿAlaqat, pp. 55–56; Zuhayli, Athar, pp. 159–60; Zuhayli, ʿAlaqat, pp. 107–08, 168. On neutrality: Abu Zahra, ʿAlaqat, p. 83; Zuhayli, Athar, pp. 181–203; Ghunaimi, Muslim Conception, pp. 218–19. Here, in this evocation of al-Shafiʿi, is an instance of how modernists do occasionally look to the medieval jurists for doctrinal support (see especially Zuhayli, Athar, pp. 160, 202–03).
30. Zuhayli, Athar, pp. 125, 325.
31. Abu Zahra, ʿAlaqat, pp. 78–79.
32. Abu Zahra, ʿAlaqat, p. 80; Zuhayli, Athar, pp. 337, 339; Ghunaimi, Muslim Conception, pp. 184–85; Mahmassani, Qanun, p. 139.
33. Abu Zahra, ʿAlaqat, p. 57; Zuhayli, Athar, pp. 330.
34. Mahmassani, Qanun, pp. 62, 190.
35. Zuhayli, Athar, pp. 45–46, 203. According to Sobhi Mahmassani (Fi Durub al-ʿAdala, p. 119), Islam mandates "a permanent peace" (silm dāʾim) built on social justice, cooperation, and the "unity of humankind." However see also Zuhayli, ʿAlaqat, p. 23. Sohail Hashmi seeks to reconcile Islam's quest for peace with its recognition of conflict by describing the "Qurʾan's attitude toward war and peace . . . as an idealistic realism" ("Interpreting," p. 199). Ibn Khaldun's views are discussed in chapter 4 below.
36. Nawawi, ʿAlaqat, pp. 34–35, also 56, 68. See also Mahmassani, Qanun, p. 238.
37. Jackson, "Jihad," p. 19.
38. Qaradawi, Nahnu wa-l-Gharb, p. 41. On the inability of "anachronistic" medieval "Islamic law to address contemporary political concerns," see also Hashmi, "Interpreting," pp. 195–96. Al-Qaradawi indicates his own intellectual affiliations by citing the authority of "our shaykh the most learned Mahmud

Shaltut" (p. 73). See, however, Sami E. Baroudi, "The Islamic Realism of Sheikh Yusuf Qaradawi (1926–) and Sayyid Mohammad Hussein Fadlallah (1935–2010)," *British Journal of Middle Eastern Studies*, vol. 43, no. 1 (January 2016): 94–114, for an interesting analysis of al-Qaradawi as an "Islamic realist," albeit of a "defensive" (p. 108) orientation.

39. Zuhayli, *Athar*, pp. 82–85. Nawawi (*'Alaqat*, p. 105) adds that the injunction exempts all "the peaceable of the non-Muslims."

40. 'Abdulhamid A. Abu Sulayman, *The Islamic Theory of International Relations: New Directions for Islamic Methodology and Thought* (Herndon, VA: International Institute of Islamic Thought, 1987), p. 104. Yusuf al-Qaradawi among others also draws a distinction between apostasy in one's "heart"—into which "we do not delve"—and apostasy in the form of public rebellion against Islam, which is "treason" and which must be punished in a manner left to the discretion of the ruler (*Nahnu wa-l-Gharb*, pp. 57–67, 134–35).

41. Nawawi, *'Alaqat*, p. 104. See also Qaradawi, *Nahnu wa-l-Gharb*, pp. 20–21.

42. Zuhayli, *Athar*, pp. 412, 433.

43. Nawawi, *'Alaqat*, pp. 121–23. See also Abu Sulayman, *Islamic Theory*, p. 96. According to historical accounts, the women and children of Banu Qurayza were consigned to captivity. Some commentators distance the Prophet himself from the incident (Ghunaimi, *Muslim Conception*, p. 60); others shift the focus of blame to the Jews in Medina (Shaltut, *Islam*, p. 64; Zuhayli, *Athar*, p. 249); and still others question the veracity of the story altogether, e.g., W. N. Arafat, "New Light on the Story of Banu Qurayza and the Jews of Medina," *Royal Asiatic Society of Great Britain and Ireland*, no. 2 (1976): 100–07.

44. See for example Shaltut, *Islam*, p. 61; Abu Zahra, *'Alaqat*, pp. 105–06; Mahmassani, *Qanun*, p. 123.

45. Sayyid Qutb, chapter on "Jihad in the Cause of God" in *Ma'alim fi al-Tariq* (Beirut: Dar al-Shuruq, 1980), p. 69. Qutb was executed by Jamal 'Abd al-Nasser's regime in 1966.

46. Qutb, *Ma'alim*, p. 67.

47. Ibid., pp. 66, 71.

48. Ibid., p. 71.

49. Ibid., p. 76.

50. Ibid., p. 68.

51. Ibid., pp. 77–80. For the contrasting view that the Meccan period "is absolutely fundamental in the construction of an Islamic ethical system," see Hashmi, "Interpreting," pp. 201–02. For a broader attempt to explain the evolution of the concept of jihad during this early stage, see Reuven Firestone, *Jihad: The Origin of Holy War in Islam* (New York: Oxford University Press, 1999).

52. Qutb, *Ma'alim*, p. 75. See Peters, *Islam and Colonialism*, p. 132.

53. Qutb, *Ma'alim*, pp. 86–87.

54. Ibid., pp. 74, 76.

55. ʿAbd al-Malik al-Barrak, *Rudud ʿala Abatil wa-Shubuhat hawl al-Jihad* (Amman: Al-Nur li-l-Iʿlam al-Islami, 1997), pp. 7–8.

56. Muhammad Saʿid Ramadan al-Buti, *Al-Jihad fi al-Islam: Kayfa Nafhamuhu? Wa-Kayfa Numarisuhu?* (Damascus: Dar al-Fikr, 1993), p. 229. Al-Buti accordingly also argued that only aggression and brigandage, not unbelief, justify war (pp. 54, 57, 94–111); that religious texts seeming to imply otherwise are being misinterpreted (pp. 52–63); that jihad in the form of combat is therefore legitimate only insofar as it aims to defend the Islamic territory, community, and political order, not to expand them (pp. 79, 93, 196–99); and that peace can and should be the norm between Muslims and non-Muslims (pp. 118, 229).

57. Barrak, *Rudud*, p. 132; see also pp. 61, 140.

58. Ibid., p. 152.

59. Ibid., pp. 197, 89, 202.

60. Ibid., pp. 128, 317.

61. Ibid., p. 41.

62. Ibid., p. 300.

63. Ibid., pp. 298, 299.

64. Ibid., pp. 78–79.

65. Ibid., p. 232; also pp. 173–75, 209, 234–40.

66. Ibid., pp. 239–40.

67. Ibid., p. 203.

68. Muhammad ʿAbd al-Salam Faraj, *Al-Farida al-Ghaʾiba*, translated in Johannes J. G. Jansen, *The Neglected Duty: The Creed of Sadat's Assassins and Islamic Resurgence in the Middle East* (New York: Macmillan, 1986), pp. 159–234. For a comprehensive treatment of this shift in focus, see Fawaz A. Gerges, *The Far Enemy: Why Jihad Went Global* (Cambridge, UK: Cambridge University Press, 2005).

69. Faraj, *Farida*, p. 189.

70. Ibid., pp. 190, 202.

71. See Daniel Lav, *Radical Islam and the Revival of Medieval Theology* (New York: Cambridge University Press, 2012); Simon Wolfgang Fuchs, "Do Excellent Surgeons Make Miserable Exegetes? Negotiating the Sunni Tradition in the *ğihādī* Camps," *Die Welt des Islams*, vol. 53, no. 2 (2013): 192–237. For a reading that emphasizes the militants' break with the medieval tradition, by contrast, see Gilles Kepel, *The Roots of Radical Islam*, translated from the French by Jon Rothschild (London: Saqi, 2005).

72. William McCants, ed., *Militant Ideology Atlas: Executive Report* (West Point: Combating Terrorism Center, 2006; http://ctc.usma.edu/atlas/Atlas-ExecutiveReport.pdf), p. 8.

73. Abu Muhammad ʿAsim al-Maqdisi, *Waqafat maʿ Thamarat al-Jihad: Bayn al Jahl fi al-Sharʿ wa-l-Jahl bi-l-Waqiʿ*, 2007 expanded edition, posted on al-Maqdisi's Minbar al-Tawhid wa-l-Jihad website (http://www.ilmway.com/site/maqdis/index.html), p. 99.

74. Ibid., pp. 98–99, 52.

75. Ibid., p. 6; also pp. 7, 15, 18, 20, 30. The tension between these twin imperatives is not discussed in Joas Wagemakers, *A Quietist Jihadi: The Ideology and Influence of Abu Muhammad al-Maqdisi* (Cambridge, UK: Cambridge University Press, 2012). Instead, al-Maqdisi's aversion to terrorist excesses leads Wagemakers, at least in part (p. 75), to describe him as a "quietist jihadi."

76. Maqdisi, *Waqafat*, p. 46. See Faraj, *Farida*, p. 165.

77. Maqdisi, *Waqafat*, p. 50.

78. Abu Muhammad ʿAsim al-Maqdisi, "Husn al-Rifaqa fi Ajwibat Suʾalat Suwaqa" (1995), posted on al-Maqdisi's website (http://www.ilmway.com/site/maqdis/index.html), p. 31.

79. Maqdisi, *Waqafat*, pp. 19–20, 57.

80. Ibid., p. 133 and more generally pp. 130–36.

81. Maqdisi, "Husn al-Rifaqa," pp. 36–37; *Waqafat*, pp. 2–3.

82. Maqdisi, *Waqafat*, p. 2.

83. Ibid., p. 86; "Husn al-Rifaqa," p. 37.

84. Maqdisi, *Waqafat*, pp. 48, 121–22.

85. "Abu Muhammad al-Maqdisi: Al-Salafiyya al-Jihadiyya," interview with Yasir Abu Hilala, *Al-Jazeera*, 10 July 2005 (www.aljazeera.net/channel/archive/archive?ArchiveId=129776).

86. Maqdisi, *Waqafat*, pp. 52, 69. Similar criticisms of al-Qaʿida by other Islamists are cited by Gerges, *Far Enemy*, e.g., pp. 198, 207, 201. See also Fawaz A. Gerges, *Journey of the Jihadist: Inside Muslim Militancy* (Orlando: Harcourt, 2006), pp. 202–29, 256–61.

87. Abu Muhammad ʿAsim al-Maqdisi, *Al-Dimuqratiyya Din* (no date), posted on al-Maqdisi's website (http://www.ilmway.com/site/maqdis/index.html), p. 3.

88. Maqdisi, *Waqafat*, p. 46; *Al-Dimuqratiyya Din*, p. 12.

89. Abu Muhammad ʿAsim al-Maqdisi, *Mashruʿ al-Sharq al-Awsat al-Kabir* (2005), posted on al-Maqdisi's website (http://www.ilmway.com/site/maqdis/index.html), pp. 1, 2.

90. Maqdisi, *Al-Dimuqratiyya Din*, pp. 3, 5.

91. Maqdisi, *Waqafat*, pp. 46–47.

92. Ibid., p. 49, and more generally pp. 46–50.

93. Interview with Yasir Abu Hilala, *Al-Jazeera*, 10 July 2005.

94. Abu Muhammad ʿAsim al-Maqdisi, "Limadha Lam Usammihim Hatta al-An Khawarij Raghm anna fi-him Man Hum Aswaʾ min al-Khawarij" (June 2015), posted on al-Maqdisi's website (http://www.ilmway.com/site/maqdis/MS_14487.html).

95. Buti, *Jihad*, pp. 115, 116.

96. Ibid., pp. 49, 117.

97. Ibid., p. 153.

98. Ibid., pp. 169–73.

99. See video and commentary on Joshua Landis' *Syria Comment*, July 27, 2011 (http://www.joshualandis.com/blog/?p=10989&cp=all).

100. See Afsaruddin's assessments in *Striving in the Path of God*, pp. 245–56, 295.

101. When Turkey's president criticized these events, Jumʿa denounced him as an "ape" and a "criminal" who rose to power with the support of prostitutes, adding: "He is dissolute (*dāʾir*) and his country is dissolute" (http://www.memritv.org/clip/en/4844.htm).

102. Thomas L. Pangle and Peter J. Ahrensdorf, *Justice Among Nations: On the Moral Basis of Power and Peace* (Lawrence: University Press of Kansas, 1999), pp. 73, 80–81, 97.

103. Thomas quoted in ibid., pp. 86–87, 113.

104. Vitoria quoted in ibid., pp. 94, 96.

105. Vitoria quoted in ibid., pp. 104–05.

106. Ibid., p. 111.

107. Ibid., pp. 87–88, 111.

108. Ibid., p. 169.

109. Pew Global Attitudes Project, "Iraqi Vote Mirrors Desire for Democracy in the Muslim World" (February 3, 2005), at http://people-press.org/commentary/?analysisid=107; Mark Tessler and Eleanor Gao, "Gauging Arab Support for Democracy," *Journal of Democracy*, vol. 16, no. 3 (July 2005): 83–97.

110. Fares Braizat, "Post Amman Attacks: Jordanian Public Opinion and Terrorism," Public Opinion Polling Unit, Center for Strategic Studies, University of Jordan (January 2006); Pew Global Attitudes Project 47-Nation Survey, "Global Opinion Trends 2002–2007: Sharp Decline in Support for Suicide Bombing in Muslim Countries" (Washington, DC: July 24, 2007), at http://pewglobal.org/reports/pdf/257.pdf.

111. Ismaʿil al-Faruqi, "Introduction" in Abu Sulayman, *Islamic Theory*, p. xxv.

112. Fred M. Donner (pp. 69n112; 58), "The Sources of Islamic Conceptions of War" in John Kelsay and James Turner Johnson, eds., *Just War and Jihad: Historical and Theoretical Perspectives on War and Peace in Western and Islamic Traditions* (New York: Greenwood Press, 1991): 31–69. See also James Turner Johnson, *The Holy War Idea in Western and Islamic Traditions* (University Park: The Pennsylvania State University Press, 1997), pp. 72–75.

Chapter 2

1. Quoted in Abu al-Hasan al-ʿAmiri, *Al-Saʿada wa-l-Isʿad fi al-Sira al-Insaniyya*, ed. Mojtaba Minovi (Wiesbaden: Franz Steiner Verlag, 1957–1958), pp. 188–89.

2. For illustrative approaches to this question see, on the one side, Fred M. Donner, "Centralized Authority and Military Autonomy in the Early Islamic Conquests" in Averil Cameron, ed., *The Byzantine and Early Islamic Near East, Volume 3: States, Resources, and Armies* (Princeton, NJ: Darwin Press, 1995): 337–60, and Jürgen Paul, *The State and the Military: The Samanid Case* (Bloomington: Indiana University Research Institute for Inner Asian Studies, 1994); and on the other side, Elie Kedourie, "The Nation-State in the Middle East," *The Jerusalem Journal of International Relations*, vol. 9, no. 3 (1987): 1–9, and Wael B. Hallaq, *The Impossible State: Islam, Politics, and Modernity's Predicament* (New York: Columbia University Press, 2013).

3. Patricia Crone, *God's Rule: Government and Islam* (New York: Columbia University Press, 2004), p. 389.

4. The quotations are from Gibb's 1953 essay "An Interpretation of Islamic History" reprinted in Hamilton A. R. Gibb, *Studies on the Civilization of Islam* (Boston: Beacon Press, 1962), pp. 13–14.

5. From Gibb's 1939 essay "Some Considerations on the Sunni Theory of the Caliphate" in ibid., p. 143.

6. See ibid., p. 145.

7. Patricia Crone and Martin Hinds, *God's Caliph: Religious Authority in the First Centuries of Islam* (Cambridge, UK: Cambridge University Press, 1986), p. 115.

8. Ibid., p. 86.

9. Ibid., p. 98.

10. Ibid., pp. 97, 21.

11. Ibid., p. 109.

12. Muhammad Qasim Zaman, *Religion and Politics under the Early 'Abbasids: The Emergence of the Proto-Sunni Elite* (Leiden: E. J. Brill, 1997), p. 209; also pp. 7, 11, 103. See also Roy P. Mottahedeh, *Loyalty and Leadership in an Early Islamic Society* (Princeton, NJ: Princeton University Press, 1980), p. 137. For two more recent critiques, see in Mehrzad Boroujerdi, ed., *Mirror for the Muslim Prince: Islam and the Theory of Statecraft* (Syracuse, NY: Syracuse University Press, 2013): Saïd Amir Arjomand, "Perso-Islamicate Political Ethic in Relation to the Sources of Islamic Law" (pp. 82–106); Aziz Al-Azmeh, "God's Caravan: Topoi and Schemata in the History of Muslim Political Thought" (pp. 326–97).

13. Khaled Abou El Fadl, *Rebellion and Violence in Islamic Law* (Cambridge, UK: Cambridge University Press, 2001), pp. ix, 28–29; Noah Feldman, *The Fall and Rise of the Islamic State* (Princeton, NJ: Princeton University Press, 2008), pp. 6, 40.

14. Zaman, *Religion and Politics*, pp. 121, 127.

15. Ibid., pp. 79, 83–84.

16. Gustave E. von Grunebaum, *Islam: Essays in the Nature and Growth of a Cultural Tradition* (Westport, CT: Greenwood Press, 1981), p. 8.

17. Ihsan ʿAbbas, *Al-Hasan al-Basri: Siratuhu, Shakhsiyyatuhu, Taʿalimuhu wa-Araʾuhu* (Cairo: Dar al-Fikr al-ʿArabi, 1952), pp. 21–22. See also Suleiman Ali Mourad, *Early Islam Between Myth and History: Al-Hasan al-Basri (d. 110 H/728 CE) and the Formation of His Legacy in Classical Islamic Scholarship* (Leiden, Boston: E. J. Brill, 2006), pp. 20–21.

18. ʿAbbas, *Al-Hasan al-Basri*, p. 24.

19. Ibid., p. 32.

20. Ibid., pp. 113 (and more generally 112–15), 107.

21. Quoted in Christopher Melchert, "Asceticism," *Encyclopaedia of Islam, Third Edition* (Brill Online).

22. ʿAbbas, *Al-Hasan al-Basri*, pp. 156, 65.

23. Ibid., pp. 5, 47, 55–59, 60–61. However see Mourad, *Early Islam*, whose analysis of the evolving depictions of al-Hasan over time (pp. 1, 94, 240) leads him to question his political pacifism (p. 40); and Thomas Sizgorich, *Violence and Belief in Late Antiquity: Militant Devotion in Christianity and Islam* (Philadelphia: University of Pennsylvania Press, 2009), who conflates the apolitical and revolutionary (Khariji) idealist perspectives on jihad into an undifferentiated asceticism (pp. 168, 208, 212).

24. For a review of the sometimes conflicting accounts of his life and thought, see Steven C. Judd, "Competitive Hagiography in Biographies of al-Awzaʿi and Sufyan al-Thawri," *Journal of the American Oriental Society*, vol. 122, no. 1 (January-March 2002): 25–37.

25. Melchert, "Asceticism."

26. Emile Tyan, "Djihād," *Encyclopaedia of Islam, Second Edition* (Brill Online). See also Roy Parviz Mottahedeh and Ridwan al-Sayyid (pp. 23, 25, 26), "The Idea of Jihad in Islam before the Crusades" in Angeliki E. Laiou and Roy Parviz Mottahedeh, eds., *The Crusades from the Perspective of Byzantium and the Muslim World* (Washington, DC: Dumbarton Oaks Research Library and Collection, 2001): 23–29; and, for an appreciative reference by a contemporary modernist, Wahba al-Zuhayli, *Al-ʿAlaqat al-Dawliyya fi al-Islam*, p. 94.

27. Jacqueline Chabbi, "Ribāṭ," *Encyclopaedia of Islam, Second Edition* (Brill Online). See also Faruq Hamada, editor's introduction, in Abu Ishaq al-Fazari, *Kitab al-Siyar* (Beirut: Muʾassasat al-Risala, 1987), pp. 35, 36, 26.

28. Michael Bonner, *Jihad in Islamic History: Doctrines and Practice* (Princeton, NJ: Princeton University Press, 2006), pp. 99–100.

29. Ibid., p. 101.

30. Deborah Tor (p. 565), "Privatized Jihad and Public Order in the Pre-Seljuq Period: The Role of the Mutatawwiʿa," *Iranian Studies*, vol. 38, no. 4 (December 2005): 555–73; Michael Bonner, *Aristocratic Violence and Holy War: Studies in the Jihad and the Arab-Byzantine Frontier* (New Haven, CT: American Oriental Society, 1996), p. 73.

31. Bonner, *Aristocratic Violence*, pp. 118, 147.

32. Bonner, *Jihad*, p. 76.

33. Bonner, *Aristocratic Violence*, p. 110; *Jihad*, p. 100.

34. Michael Bonner (p. 25), "Some Observations Concerning the Early Development of Jihad on the Arab-Byzantine Frontier," *Studia Islamica*, no. 75 (1992): 5–31.

35. ʿAbdallah ibn al-Mubarak, *Kitab al-Jihad* (Beirut: Dar al-Nur, 1971), p. 32.

36. Ibid., pp. 109, 110–11, 112, and 114.

37. Bonner, *Jihad*, p. 100.

38. See, for example, ibid., pp. 103, 109.

39. Dimitri Gutas (p. 61), "Classical Arabic Wisdom Literature: Nature and Scope," *Journal of the American Oriental Society*, vol. 101, no. 1 (January-March 1981): 49–86.

40. Steven C. Judd (p. 17), "Al-Awzaʿi and Sufyan al-Thawri: The Umayyad Madhhab?" in Peri Bearman, Rudolph Peters, Frank E. Vogel, eds., *The Islamic School of Law: Evolution, Devolution, and Progress* (Cambridge, MA: Harvard University Press, 2005): 10–25, 208–11.

41. Louise Marlow, "Advice and Advice Literature," *Encyclopaedia of Islam, Third Edition* (Brill Online); Andras Hamori (pp. 164–65), "Prudence, Virtue, and Self-Respect in Ibn al-Muqaffaʿ" in Angelika Neuwirth and Andreas Christian Islebe, eds., *Reflections on Reflections: Near Eastern Writers Reading Literature. Dedicated to Renata Jacobi* (Wiesbaden, Germany: Reichert Verlag, 2006): 161–79.

42. Ibn al-Muqaffaʿ, "Al-Adab al-Kabir" (pp. 40–41) in Muhammad Kurd ʿAli, ed., *Rasaʾil al-Bulaghaʾ* (Cairo: Matbaʿat Lajnat al-Taʾlif wa-l-Tarjama wa-l Nashr, 1954): 40–106.

43. "Muntakhab min ʿAhd Azdashir bin Babak al-Malik: Fi al-Siyasa" (p. 382) in Kurd ʿAli, ed., *Rasaʾil al-Bulaghaʾ*, pp. 382–84. See Said Amir Arjomand (pp. 18–19), "ʿAbd Allah Ibn al-Muqaffaʿ and the ʿAbbasid Revolution," *Iranian Studies*, vol. 27, nos. 1–4 (1994): 9–36.

44. Ibn al-Muqaffaʿ, "Risala fi al-Sahaba" (pp. 119–20) in Kurd ʿAli, ed., *Rasaʾil al-Bulaghaʾ*, pp. 117–34.

45. Ibn al-Muqaffaʿ, "Risala fi al-Sahaba," p. 120; Arjomand "ʿAbd Allah Ibn al-Muqaffaʿ," p. 32. See also Muhammad Qasim Zaman, "The Caliphs, the ʿUlamaʾ, and the Law: Defining the Role and Function of the Caliph in the Early ʿAbbasid Period" in Wael B. Hallaq, ed., *The Formation of Islamic Law* (Aldershot, UK: Ashgate Variorum, 2004): 367–402; Joseph E. Lowry, "The First Islamic Legal Theory: Ibn al-Muqaffaʿ on Interpretation, Authority, and the Structure of the Law," *Journal of the American Oriental Society*, vol. 128, no. 1 (January-March 2008): 25–40; Najm al-Din Yousefi, "Islam without Fuqahāʾ: Ibn al-Muqaffaʿ and His Perso-Islamic Solution to the Caliphate's Crisis of Legitimacy (70–142 AH/690–760 CE)," *Iranian Studies*, vol. 50, no. 1 (2017): 9–44.

46. Ibn al-Muqaffaʿ, "Risala fi al-Sahaba," pp. 126–27. See Shelomo Dov Goitein, "A Turning Point in the History of the Muslim State (Apropos of the

Kitab al-Sahaba of Ibn al-Muqaffaʿ)" reprinted in Goitein, *Studies in Islamic History and Institutions* (Leiden and Boston: E. J. Brill, 2010), p. 163; Zaman, "Caliphs," p. 371; Arjomand "ʿAbd Allah Ibn al-Muqaffaʿ," pp. 32–33. On the attempt, described in the Zoroastrian compendium *Denkard*, by the first Sasanian king Ardashir I to codify "all the scattered teachings" of that religion into one authoritative canon, see Parvaneh Pourshariati, *Decline and Fall of the Sasanian Empire: The Sasanian-Parthian Confederacy and the Arab Conquest of Iran* (London & New York: I. B. Tauris, 2008), pp. 337–38. Pourshariati argues that centralization and codification were Sasanian ideological tropes that reflected imperial aspiration more than reality (pp. 2, 325, 337–38). See also Shaul Shaked (esp. pp. 40, 59), "From Iran to Islam: Notes on Some Themes in Transmission," *Jerusalem Studies in Arabic and Islam*, vol. 4 (1984): 31–67.

47. Ibn al-Muqaffaʿ, "Risala fi al-Sahaba," p. 127.

48. Ibid., p. 121.

49. Ibid., p. 122.

50. Ibid., pp. 122–24, 128, 132.

51. Ibid., p. 133. See Zaman, *Religion and Politics*, pp. 83–84.

52. Goitein, *Studies in Islamic History*, p. 160; see "Risala fi al-Sahaba," pp. 124–25; Arjomand, "ʿAbd Allah Ibn al-Muqaffaʿ," p. 31.

53. Louise Marlow, *Hierarchy and Egalitarianism in Islamic Thought* (Cambridge, UK: Cambridge University Press, 1997), p. 101.

54. Ibn al-Muqaffaʿ, "Risala fi al-Sahaba," p. 130; translation in Marlow, *Hierarchy*, p. 60.

55. Ibn al-Muqaffaʿ, "Risala fi al-Sahaba," pp. 133–34.

56. Ihsan ʿAbbas, editor's introduction (pp. 25–49), *ʿAbd al-Hamid ibn Yahya al-Katib wa-ma Tabaqqa min Rasaʾilihi wa-Rasaʾili Salim Abi al-ʿAlaʾ* (Amman: Dar al-Shuruq, 1988).

57. See Epistles # 8 (pp. 198–201) and # 17 (p. 212) in ʿAbbas, ed., *ʿAbd al-Hamid*; Wadad al-Qadi (pp. 303–04), "The Impact of the Qurʾan on the Epistolography of ʿAbd al-Hamid" in G. R. Hawting and Abdul-Kader A. Shareef, eds., *Approaches to the Qurʾan* (London: Routledge, 1993): 285–313.

58. See Wadad al-Qadi (p. 250), "The Religious Foundation of Late Umayyad Ideology and Practice" in *Saber religioso y poder politico en el Islam: actas del simposio internacional, Granada, 15–18 octubre 1991* (Madrid: Agencia Española de Cooperación Internacional, 1994): 231–73.

59. For example in his "Risala fi Nasihat Wali al-ʿAhd" (pp. 217–19), Epistle # 21 in ʿAbbas, ed., *ʿAbd al-Hamid*, pp. 215–65.

60. "Risala fi Nasihat Wali al-ʿAhd," pp. 223–24; quote translated in Aziz Al-Azmeh, *Muslim Kingship: Power and the Sacred in Muslim, Christian, and Pagan Polities* (London: I. B. Tauris, 1997), p. 78.

61. "Risala fi Nasihat Wali al-ʿAhd," p. 226.

62. On the main foreign and indigenous influences in evidence here, see ʿAbbas, *ʿAbd al-Hamid*, p. 93. On caution, stratagem, and subterfuge as

prominent motifs in the Byzantine tactics manuals of the time, see the section "Statecraft" later in this chapter.

63. ʿAbbas, ʿAbd al-Hamid, pp. 142, 94, 92, 99.

64. Al-Qadi, "Religious Foundation," p. 258.

65. Ibid., p. 72.

66. Ibid., p. 258.

67. "Risala fi Nasihat Wali al-ʿAhd," p. 246.

68. Ibid., pp. 237, 263.

69. Dimitri Gutas, *Greek Thought, Arabic Culture: The Graeco-Arabic Translation Movement in Baghdad and Early ʿAbbasid Society (2nd–4th/8th–10th Centuries)* (London: Routledge, 1999), pp. 77 (al-Masʿudi quotation), 80.

70. Irit Abramski-Bligh (p. 181), "The Judiciary (*Qadis*) as a Governmental-Administrative Tool in Early Islam" in Wael B. Hallaq, ed., *The Formation of Islamic Law* (Aldershot: Ashgate Variorum, 2004): 179–210; Gutas, *Greek Thought*, pp. 82–83.

71. Gutas, *Greek Thought*, pp. 82, 84–85, 93–94.

72. Charles Pellat, "Al-Djāḥiẓ," *Encyclopaedia of Islam, Second Edition* (Brill Online).

73. Josef van Ess (pp. 12–13, 14), "Al-Jāḥiẓ and Early Muʿtazili Theology" in Armin Heinemann, John L. Meloy, Tarif Khalidi, Manfred Kropp, eds., *Al-Jāḥiẓ: A Muslim Humanist for our Time* (Würzburg: Ergon Verlag in Kommission; Beirut: Orient-Institut, 2009): 3–15.

74. Pellat, "Al-Djāḥiẓ;" Charles Pellat, *The Life and Works of Jahiz: Translations of Selected Texts*, translated from the French by D. M. Hawke (Berkeley: University of California Press, 1969), pp. 5–7.

75. Al-Jahiz (pp. 284–85), "Risala fi Nafy al-Tashbih" in *Rasaʾil al-Jahiz*, 4 vols., ed. ʿAbd al-Salam Muhammad Harun (Cairo: Maktabat al-Khanji, 1964–1979), vol. 1, pp. 283–308. See Wadad al-Qadi (pp. 48–53), "The Earliest 'Nābita' and the Paradigmatic 'Nawābit,'" *Studia Islamica*, no. 78 (1993): 27–61; Nimrod Hurvitz (pp. 97–102, 109), "Miḥna as Self-Defense," *Studia Islamica*, no. 92 (2001): 93–111; Michael Cooperson (pp. 200, 204), "Al-Jāḥiẓ, the Misers, and the Proto-Sunni Ascetics" in Heinemann et al., eds., *Al-Jahiz*, pp. 197–219. Al-Qadi defines the *nawābit* as "contemptible, suddenly powerful, irritating sprouters on the scene" (p. 58).

76. Al-Jahiz, "Kitab ma bayn al-ʿAdawa wa-l-Hasad" (p. 339) in *Rasaʾil*, vol. 1, pp. 333–73.

77. Ibid., pp. 345–47.

78. Ibid., p. 339.

79. Michael Cooperson points out that al-Jahiz drew parallels between the asceticism of his doctrinal adversaries and the mean-spirited stinginess of the misers he pilloried in *Kitab al-Bukhalaʾ*: "To judge by his comments in the *Bukhalāʾ*, he considered renunciation of any kind to be a perverse refusal to enjoy the 'good things' (*al-ṭayyibāt*) provided for humankind" ("Al-Jāḥiẓ, the Misers, and the Proto-Sunni Ascetics," p. 201).

80. For example in a (now lost) work entitled "The Necessity of the Imamate" and in the extract "Al-Jawabat wa-Istihqaq al-Imama" in *Rasaʾil*, vol. 4, pp. 283–307. See Jamal F. El-ʿAttar, "The Political Thought of Al-Jāḥiẓ with Special Reference to the Question of Khilāfa (Imāmate): A Chronological Approach" (PhD dissertation, University of Edinburgh, 1996), pp. 53, 75.

81. Al-Jahiz, "Risala fi Nafy al-Tashbih," p. 283.

82. Al-Jahiz, "Fi Hujaj al-Nubuwwa" (p. 242) in *Rasaʾil*, vol. 3, pp. 221–81.

83. Al-Jahiz, *Kitab al-ʿUthmaniyya*, ed. ʿAbd al-Salam Muhammad Harun (Beirut: Dar al-Jil, 1991), p. 186.

84. Ibid., p. 257.

85. Ibid., pp. 250–51.

86. See Gutas, *Greek Thought*, pp. 85–88.

87. Al-Jahiz quoted in Marlow, *Hierarchy and Egalitarianism*, pp. 64–65.

88. Al-Jahiz, "Al-Radd ʿala al-Nasara" (p. 322) in *Rasaʾil*, vol. 3, pp. 200–51.

89. Al-Jahiz, "Al-Awtan wa-l-Buldan" (pp. 126–27) in *Rasaʾil*, vol. 4, pp. 107–47.

90. Ibid.

91. Al-Jahiz, "Risala ila al-Fath ibn Khaqan fi Manaqib al-Turk wa-ʿAmmat Jund al-Khilafa" (p. 71) in *Rasaʾil*, vol. 1, pp. 1–86.

92. Al-Jahiz, passage from *Kitab al-Hayawan*, translated by H. T. Norris (pp. 35–36), "*Shuʿubiyyah* in Arabic Literature" in Julia Ashtiany, T. M. Johnstone, J. D. Latham, R. B. Serjeant, and G. Rex Smith, eds., *ʿAbbasid Belles-Lettres* (Cambridge, UK: Cambridge University Press, 1990): 31–47.

93. Al-Jahiz, "Risala fi al-Nabita" (pp. 20–21) in *Rasaʾil*, vol. 2, pp. 3–23.

94. Al-Jahiz, *Kitab al-ʿUthmaniyya*, pp. 29–30.

95. Al-Jahiz, "Kitab Dhamm Akhlaq al-Kuttab" (p. 193) in *Rasaʾil*, vol. 2, pp. 183–208.

96. Ibid., p. 194.

97. Al-Jahiz, "Manaqib al-Turk," pp. 74, 35, 29.

98. Al-Jahiz, "Al-Nubul wa-l-Tanabbul wa-Dhamm al-Kibr" (p. 182) in *Rasaʾil*, vol. 4, pp. 167–88.

99. El-ʿAttar, *Political Thought of Al-Jahiz*, p. 133.

100. Al-Jahiz (pp. 219–20), "Mufakharat al-Sudan ʿala al-Baydan" in *Rasaʾil*, vol. 1, pp. 173–226.

101. Al-Jahiz, "Manaqib al-Turk," p. 67.

102. Ibid., p. 73.

103. Ibid., p. 34.

104. Al-Jahiz, *Kitab al-ʿUthmaniyya*, p. 257.

105. Al-Jahiz, Part III (Kitab al-ʿAsaʾ) of *Kitab al-Bayan wa-l-Tabyin*, ed. ʿAbd al-Salam Muhammad Harun (Cairo: Maktabat al-Khanji, 1968), vol. 3, pp. 5–6.

106. Norris, "*Shuʿubiyyah*," p. 37. Roy P. Mottahedeh, "The *Shuʿūbiyah* Controversy and the Social History of Early Islamic Iran," *International Journal*

of Middle East Studies, vol. 7, no. 2 (April 1976): 161–82, writes: "The *shuʿūbīs* and some of their opponents continued to use a rhetoric that has been mistaken for egalitarianism, but on closer examination has no such meaning. . . . A society of degrees, a hierarchy in which points of honor gave each man a rank on the ladder which extended from the lowest to the noblest of men, was an idea that many Iranians (and Arabs), whether *shuʿūbī* or anti-*shuʿūbī*, strongly supported" (pp. 176–77).

107. English translation by Hawke in Pellat, *Life and Works*, pp. 123–24.

108. Ibn Qutayba, *ʿUyun al-Akhbar*, vol. 1 (Cairo: Al-Muʾassasa al-Masriyya al-ʿAmma li-l-Taʾlif wa-l-Tarjama wa-l-Tibaʿa wa-l-Nashr, 1964), pp. ḥ–ṭ [v–vi]; *Taʾwil Mukhtalaf al-Hadith*, ed. Muhammad Nafiʿ al-Mustafa (Beirut: Muʾassasat al-Risala, 2004), pp. 408, 417–18.

109. Ishaq Musa Huseini, *The Life and Works of Ibn Qutayba* (Beirut: American Press, 1950), p. 29.

110. Ibn Qutayba, *Taʾwil*, p. 189.

111. Ibn Qutayba, "Kitab al-ʿArab, aw al-Radd ʿala al-Shuʿubiyya," in *Rasaʾil al-Bulaghaʾ*, ed. Muhammad Kurd ʿAli (Cairo: Matbaʿat Lajnat al-Taʾlif wa-l-Tarjama wa-l-Nashr, 1954): 344–77; Huseini, *Life and Works*, p. 51.

112. Ibn Qutayba, "Kitab al-ʿArab," p. 375.

113. Ibid., p. 345.

114. Ibid., p. 350.

115. Ibid., pp. 354–55.

116. Ibid., pp. 356, 360.

117. There are two modern editions: ʿAbd al-Raʾuf ʿAwn, ed., *Mukhtasar Siyasat al-Hurub li-l-Harthami Sahib al-Maʾmun* (Cairo: Al-Muʾassasa al-Misriyya al-ʿAmma li-l-Taʾlif wa-l-Tarjama wa-l-Tibaʿa wa-l-Nashr, 1964); and ʿArif Ahmad ʿAbd al-Ghani, ed., *Mukhtasar fi Siyasat al-Hurub* (Damascus: Dar Kinan, 1995). The discussion of the treatise that follows is derived from Malik Mufti, "The Art of Jihad," *History of Political Thought*, vol. 28, no. 2 (Summer 2007): 189–207.

118. Abu al-Hussein ʿAli al-Masʿudi, *Muruj al-Dhahab wa-Maʿadin al-Jawhar*, ed. Yusuf Asʿad Daghir, 4 vols. (Beirut: Dar al-Andalus li-l-Tibaʿa wa-l-Nashr, 1965–1966), vol. 1, p. 21.

119. Ibn al-Nadim, *Al-Fihrist*, ed. Yusuf ʿAli Tawil (Beirut: Dar al-Kutub al-ʿIlmiyya, 1996), p. 490.

120. Mufti, "Art of Jihad," p. 191. On the *shākiriyya*, see Hugh Kennedy, *The Armies of the Caliphs: Military and Society in the Early Islamic State* (London: Routledge: 2001), pp. 199–204.

121. Aelian, *The Tactics of Aelian, Comprising the Military System of the Grecians*, translated and edited by Henry Augustus Viscount Dillon (London: Cox & Baylis, 1814), pp. li, 162; Maurice, *Maurice's Strategikon: Handbook of Byzantine Military Strategy*, translated and edited by George T. Dennis (Philadelphia: University of Pennsylvania Press, 1984), p. 88; see also p. 9.

122. Walter E. Kaegi, *Some Thoughts on Byzantine Military Strategy* (Brookline, MA: Hellenic College Press, 1983), p. 14.

123. John Haldon, *Warfare, State and Society in the Byzantine World, 565–1204* (London: UCL Press, 1999), p. 8.

124. Maurice, *Strategikon*, pp. 65–66, 102–05, 81, 106.

125. Ibid., p. 65.

126. Ibid., pp. 87, 88. Note the invocations of "peace" on pp. 22, 82, 85, 87, 88, 94.

127. These quotations are appended at the end of ʿAbd al-Ghani's edition of the *Mukhtasar*, pp. 71, 75–77.

128. See Maurice's *Strategikon*, p. 21; Onosander (p. 399), *Strategikos*, translated by William A. Oldfather, in *Aeneas Tacticus, Asclepiodotus, Onosander*, Loeb Classical Library (London: William Heinemann, 1923): 368–527. On the 12,000 man army as a Sasanian trope, see Shapur Shahbazi, "Army: I. Pre-Islamic Iran" in Ehsan Yarshater, ed., *Encyclopaedia Iranica* (New York, 1991): 489–99.

129. Compare Xenophon, *Cyropedia* (5.3.46), translated by Walter Miller, Loeb Classical Library (Cambridge, MA: Harvard University Press, 1994), vol. 2, p. 63; Arrian, *The Campaigns of Alexander*, translated by Aubrey de Sélincourt (London: Penguin, 1971), p. 118; Flavius Vegetius Renatus, *Epitoma Rei Militaris*, edited and translated by Leo F. Stelten (New York: Peter Lang, 1990), pp. 163–65; Maurice, *Strategikon*, p. 88. On the necessity of knowing one's soldiers and their abilities, see also the *Denkard* (8.25.15), vol. 16, translated by D. D. P. Sanjana (London: Kegan Paul, Trench, Trübner & Co., 1917), p. 8.

130. Compare Aelian, *Tactics*, pp. 65, 68; Asclepiodotus (p. 265), *Tactics*, translated by William A. Oldfather, in *Aeneas Tacticus, Asclepiodotus, Onosander*, Loeb Classical Library (London: William Heinemann, 1923): 244–333; Anonymous, *Treatise on Strategy* (p. 51) in George T. Dennis, translator and editor, *Three Byzantine Military Treatises* (Washington, DC: Dumbarton Oaks Research Library and Collection, 1985): 1–136. However see also Xenophon, *Memorabilia* (3.1.8–9 and 3.1.11), translated by Amy L. Bonnette (Ithaca, NY: Cornell University Press, 1994), pp. 72, 73.

131. Kennedy, *Armies of the Caliphs*, p. 112.

132. See al-Masʿudi, *Muruj al-Dhahab*, vol. 3, p. 419; ʿAwn's footnote 1 in *Mukhtasar Siyasat al-Hurub*, p. 41; and also Ibn Qutayba's reference to what "the Persians said" in the "Kitab al-Harb" (Book of War) of his *ʿUyun al-Akhbar*, vol. 1, p. 122.

133. On deploying defensively on the march (chapters 10, 13, 14), see Maurice's *Strategikon*, pp. 20, 21. On securing one's camp (chapters 15, 30), see ibid., p. 81.

134. On watching for feigned retreats (chapter 25), see ibid., p. 133. On not engaging in premature plunder (chapter 26), see ibid., p. 68. On the need

to keep the sun and wind behind you in battle (chapter 16) and to never block a retreating enemy's escape or access to water (chapter 26), see Ibn Qutayba's citation of the Persian *Kitab al-A'īn* in his *'Uyun al-Akhbar*, vol. 1, pp. 112–13; and also Xenophon, *Cyropedia* (4.1.16), vol. 1, p. 319; Arrian, *Campaigns*, p. 244; Maurice, *Strategikon*, pp. 81, 86, 91. On being wary of a besieged enemy (chapter 34), see Maurice, *Strategikon*, p. 106.

135. Polyaenus, *Stratagems of War*, edited and translated by Peter Krentz and Everett L. Wheeler (Chicago: Ares Publishers, 1994), vol. 1, p. 243. See also Maurice's *Strategikon*, p. 81, and contrast to al-'Amiri, *Al-Sa'ada wa-l-Is'ad*, p. 335.

136. The editor 'Abd al-Ra'uf 'Awn speculates (p. 68n4) that the chapter title may refer to its subject matter's location in the original work of which the *Mukhtasar Siyasat al-Hurub* is said to be an epitome. Of course, the resemblance between error and truth has already been raised in previous chapters of the *Mukhtasar* itself.

137. Muhammad al-Shaybani, *The Islamic Law of Nations: Shaybani's Siyar*, translated by Majid Khadduri (Baltimore, MD: Johns Hopkins Press, 1966), pp. 154–55.

138. Khalid Yahya Blankinship, *The End of the Jihad State: The Reign of Hisham Ibn 'Abd al-Malik, and the Collapse of the Umayyads* (Albany: State University of New York Press, 1994), p. 3.

139. Muhammad ibn Manjli, *Al-Adilla al-Rasmiyya fi al-Ta'abi al-Harbiyya*, ed. Mahmud Sheet Khattab (Baghdad: Matba'at al-Majma' al-'Ilmi al-'Iraqi, 1988), p. 140. For direct quotes from the *Mukhtasar* (with corresponding chapters of the original in parentheses), see pp. 149 (31), 153–54 (33), 181 (18), 216–17 (34), 223 (35), 224 (35).

140. Harold Bowen, and C. E. Bosworth, "Niẓām al-Mulk," *Encyclopaedia of Islam, Second Edition* (Brill Online).

141. Nizam al-Mulk, *The Book of Government or Rules for Kings*, translated from Persian by Hubert Darke (London: Routledge & Kegan, 1978), p. 10. See Neguin Yavari, "Mirrors for Princes or a Hall of Mirrors? Nizam al-Mulk's *Siyar al-Muluk* Reconsidered," *Al-Masaq*, vol. 20, no. 1 (March 2008): 47–69, which describes the work as "in effect expanding the authoritative domain of secular kingship" (p. 67).

142. Nizam al-Mulk, *Book of Government*, p. 60; Omid Safi, *The Politics of Knowledge in Premodern Islam: Negotiating Ideology and Religious Inquiry* (Chapel Hill: The University of North Carolina Press, 2006), pp. xxv, 50 (and more generally 43–81). See also Claude Cahen, "Futuwwa," *Encyclopaedia of Islam, Second Edition* (Brill Online).

143. Nizam al-Mulk, *Book of Government*, pp. 193, 194, 197.

144. Ibid., p. 205.

145. Ibid., pp. 9, 139.

Chapter 3

1. Mas'udi, *Muruj al-Dhahab*, vol. 2, §666, p. 6; Gutas, *Greek Thought*, p. 88.
2. Gutas, *Greek Thought*, p. 104. See also Gerhard Endress (p. 62), "The Circle of al-Kindī: Early Arabic Translations from the Greek and the Rise of Islamic Philosophy" in Gerhard Endress and Remke Kruk, eds., *The Ancient Tradition in Christian and Islamic Hellenism* (Leiden: Research School CNWS, 1997): 43–76; Richard Walzer, "New Studies on al-Kindi" (pp. 180, 187, 199–204) in Richard Walzer, *Greek Into Arabic: Essays on Islamic Philosophy* (Cambridge, MA: Harvard University Press, 1962): 175–205; Muhsin S. Mahdi, *Alfarabi and the Foundation of Islamic Political Philosophy* (Chicago: The University of Chicago Press, 2001), pp. 54–55. On al-Kindi and logic, see Charles E. Butterworth (pp. 12–13), "Al-Kindi and the Beginnings of Islamic Political Philosophy" in Charles E. Butterworth, ed., *The Political Aspects of Islamic Philosophy: Essays in Honor of Muhsin S. Mahdi* (Cambridge, MA: Harvard Center for Middle Eastern Studies, 1992): 11–60; Peter Adamson, *Al-Kindi* (New York: Oxford University Press, 2004), pp. 15, 18.
3. Jean Jolivet and Roshdi Rashed, "Al-Kindī," *Encyclopaedia of Islam, Second Edition* (Brill Online); Adamson, *Al-Kindi*, p. 7. See also Alfred L. Ivry (pp. 121, 123–24), "Al-Kindi as Philosopher: The Aristotelian and Neoplatonic Dimensions" in S. M. Stern, Albert Hourani, Vivian Brown, eds., *Islamic Philosophy and the Classical Tradition* (Columbia: University of South Carolina Press, 1972): 117–39; Butterworth, "Al-Kindi," p. 31.
4. Gutas, *Greek Thought*, p. 120; Adamson, *Al-Kindi*, p. 161.
5. See Al-Kindi's "Risala fi Alfaz Suqrat" published in Majid Fakhry, *Dirasat fi al-Fikr al-'Arabi* (Beirut: Dar al-Nahar li-l-Nashr, 1970), pp. 43–46. See also Butterworth, "Al-Kindi," especially pp. 52–58; Adamson, *Al-Kindi*, p. 145; and, on mathematics as a model for al-Kindi's philosophy, Roshdi Rashed (especially pp. 8, 31), "Al-Kindi's Commentary on Archimedes' 'The Measurement of the Circle,'" *Arabic Sciences and Philosophy*, vol. 3 (1993): 7–53.
6. D. S. Margoliouth (pp. 94/113, 107/126), "The Discussion Between Abu Bishr Matta and Abu Sa'id al-Sirafi on the Merits of Logic and Grammar," *The Journal of the Royal Asiatic Society of Great Britain and Ireland* (January 1905): 79–129. Margoliouth here reproduces a version of the debate, in Arabic as well as English translation, originally reported in al-Tawhidi's *Kitab al-Imta' wa-l-Mu'anasa*.
7. Ibid., pp. 105/124.
8. Ibid., pp. 108–109/127–28. For this quotation I have followed Adamson's translation (*Al-Kindi*, p. 18).
9. Adamson, *Al-Kindi*, pp. 17, 210 (n52). The fact that others have seen in this work a parody of dogmatic Muslim theologians as well (e.g., Cooperson, "Al-Jāḥiẓ, the Misers, and the Proto-Sunni Ascetics," cited in

note 75 of the previous chapter), suggests an interesting parallel between the asceticism of religious idealists, focused on otherworldly well-being, and the asceticism of what may be called scientific idealists like al-Kindi, focused on the natural—but non-political—phenomena of this world.

10. Jahiz, *Kitab al-Bukhala'*, ed. Taha al-Hajiri (Cairo: Dar al-Katib al-Misri, 1948), pp. 79, 73. The translated quote is by R. B. Serjeant in *The Book of Misers: A Translation of al-Bukhala'* (Reading, UK: The Center for Muslim Contribution to Civilization, 1997), p. 79.

11. Kindi, "Risala," pp. 43–44.

12. Al-Kindi, *Fi al-Falsafa al-Ula*, translated by Alfred L. Ivry as *Al-Kindi's Metaphysics* (Albany: State University of New York Press, 1974), p. 59. For different views on al-Kindi's relationship with the Muʿtazila, see Fakhry, *Dirasat*, p. 38; Alfred L. Ivry, "Al-Kindi and the Muʿtazila: A Philosophical and Political Reevaluation," *Oriens*, vol. 25/26 (1976): 69–85; Adamson, *Al-Kindi*, pp. 23–25.

13. Pellat, "Al-Djāḥiẓ;" Adamson, *Al-Kindi*, pp. 11–12.

14. Translated in Franz Rosenthal, *Ahmad b. at-Tayyib as-Sarakhsi* (New Haven, CT: American Oriental Society, 1943), p. 117.

15. Farabi, *Falsafat Aflatun*, §36, translated by Muhsin Mahdi in *Alfarabi's Philosophy of Plato and Aristotle* (New York: The Free Press of Glencoe, 1962), pp. 66–67.

16. Mahdi, *Alfarabi*, p. 29; Dimitri Gutas (pp. 259, 260), "The Meaning of *madanī* in al-Fārābī's 'Political' Philosophy," *Mélanges de l'Université Saint-Joseph*, vol. 57 (2004): 259–82.

17. Soheil M. Afnan, *Philosophical Terminology in Arabic and Persian* (Leiden: E. J. Brill, 1964), p. 40; Kiki Kennedy-Day, *Books of Definition in Islamic Philosophy: The Limits of Words* (New York: Routledge Curzon, 2003), pp. 49, 118; Walzer, "New Studies," pp. 203–04; Dimitri Gutas (p. 25), "Origins in Baghdad" in Robert Pasnau, ed., *The Cambridge History of Medieval Philosophy*, vol. 1 (Cambridge, UK: Cambridge University Press, 2010): 11–25. According to Gerhard Endress, al-Kindi's teachings also resonated among the "Illuminationists" of Isfahan eight centuries later ("Circle of al-Kindī," pp. 74–75).

18. Stephen Menn (p. 168), "Avicenna's Metaphysics" in Peter Adamson, ed., *Interpreting Avicenna: Critical Essays* (New York: Cambridge University Press, 2013): 143–69.

19. Ibn Rushd, *Averroes' Tahafut al-Tahafut*, translated by Simon Van Den Bergh (Cambridge, UK: E. J. W. Gibb Memorial Trust, 1987), Discussion 3, Section 198, p. 118. All subsequent citations refer to this edition [thus: *Tahafut al-Tahafut*, 3.198, p. 118], although occasionally (as here) I modify Van Den Bergh's translations, using the Arabic text in *Tahafut al-Tahafut*, ed. Sulayman Dunya, 2 volumes (Cairo: Dar al-Maʿarif bi-Misr, 1969–1971). On this formulation see Ibn Sina, *Al-Shifa'*: *Ilahiyyat*, Book 1, chapter 6 (especially Section 9), in *The Metaphysics of* The Healing: *A Parallel English-Arabic Text*,

translated by Michael E. Marmura (Provo, UT: Brigham Young University Press, 2005) [henceforth *Shifaʾ: Ilahiyyat*, 1.6.9], pp. 29–34. See also Lenn E. Goodman, *Avicenna* (Ithaca, NY: Cornell University Press, 2006), pp. 61–86; and, on translating *"mumkin"* as "contingent" rather than "possible": Robert Wisnovsky, *Avicenna's Metaphysics in Context* (Ithaca, NY: Cornell University Press, 2003), p. 216; Menn, "Avicenna's Metaphysics," p. 149n14.

20. Ibn Sina, *Shifaʾ: Ilahiyyat*, 9.4.2–4, pp. 326–28. For an argument that the Necessary Existent's creation of the universe reflects a more active "will" (*irāda*) that is distinct both from natural compulsion or necessity on the one hand, and from an intention (*qaṣd*) implying desire to acquire something lacking on the other, see Jon McGinnis, *Avicenna* (New York: Oxford University Press, 2010), pp. 206–08.

21. For a succinct account of Ibn Sina's emanationist scheme, see Ian Richard Netton, *Allah Transcendent: Studies in the Structure and Semiotics of Islamic Philosophy, Theology and Cosmology* (London: Routledge, 1989), pp. 162–72.

22. Robert Wisnovsky (*Avicenna's Metaphysics*, p. 187) notes that partly as a result of a misinterpretation by Ibn Sina's influential commentator Nasir al-Din al-Tusi, scholarly attention has unduly neglected Ibn Sina's emphasis on final causality, pointing for example to *Shifaʾ: Ilahiyyat*, 8.6.1–3, pp. 283–84. See also Goodman, *Avicenna*, p. xiii.

23. Ibn Sina, *Isharat wa-Tanbihat*, Class (*namaṭ*) 3, Chapter 12, translated by Shams C. Inati in *Ibn Sina's* Remarks and Admonitions: Physics and Metaphysics; *An Analysis and Annotated Translation* (New York: Columbia University Press, 2014), p. 103. This volume contains Classes 1–3 (on physics) and 4–7 (on metaphysics); the final three Classes 9–10 are contained in a separate volume, also translated by Shams C. Inati: *Ibn Sina and Mysticism:* Remarks and Admonitions: *Part Four* (London and New York: Kegan Paul International, 1996). Henceforth, citations will indicate title, class, chapter, and page numbers without reference to volume, thus: *Isharat*, 3.12, p. 103. For the Arabic original I have used: *Al-Isharat wa-l-Tanbihat li-Abi ʿAli ibn Sina, maʿ Sharh Nasir al-Din al-Tusi*, ed. Sulayman Dunya, 4 volumes (Cairo: Dar al-Maʿarif bi-Misr, 1960–1968); cited by volume and page number, thus: vol. 2, p. 394. See also Ibn Sina, *Al-Shifaʾ: Kitab al-Nafs*, Discourse (*maqāla*) 5, chapter 6, in *Avicenna's De Anima: Being the Psychological Part of Kitab al-Shifaʾ*, ed. Fazlur Rahman (London: Oxford University Press, 1960) [henceforth *Shifaʾ: Nafs* 5.6], pp. 248–50.

24. Ibn Sina, *Isharat*, 10.9, pp. 95–96 (Arabic: *Al-Isharat wa-l-Tanbihat*, vol. 4, pp. 121–24).

25. Fazlur Rahman, *Prophecy in Islam: Philosophy and Orthodoxy* (London: George Allen & Unwin, 1958), pp. 62–64.

26. For example in *Tahafut al-Tahafut*, 6.347, p. 208.

27. Ibid., 3.198, p. 119; 4.276, pp. 163–64. See also ibid., 5.302, p. 179; 5.304–05, p. 180.

28. Ibid., 8.395, p. 238. See also ibid., 10.418, p. 252.
29. Ibid., 3.239, p. 142.
30. Ibid., 4.270, p. 160. See also ibid., 5.299, p. 177.
31. Ibid., 3.180, p. 108.
32. Ibn Sina, *Shifa': Ilahiyyat*, 9.2.11, p. 312; *Isharat*, 10.9, pp. 95–96.
33. Tusi's commentary in *Al-Isharat wa-l-Tanbihat* (Arabic text, ed. Dunya), vol. 4, p. 122.
34. Ibn Rushd, *Averroes on Aristotle's "Metaphysics": An Annotated Translation of the So-Called "Epitome,"* ed. Rüdiger Arnzen (Berlin: De Gruyter, 2010) [henceforth, *Epitome: Metaphysics*], Chapter 2, p. 71; chapter 4, p. 151. See also *Ibn Rushd's Metaphysics: A Translation with Introduction of Ibn Rushd's Commentary on Aristotle's Metaphysics, Book Lām*, ed. Charles Genequand (Leiden: E. J. Brill, 1986) [henceforth, *Metaphysics (Lām)*], 1499–1500, pp. 109–10.
35. Ibn Sina, *Shifa': Ilahiyyat*, 9.5.9–10, p. 337. See Herbert A. Davidson, *Alfarabi, Avicenna, and Averroes, on Intellect: Their Cosmologies, Theories of the Active Intellect, and Theories of Human Intellect* (New York: Oxford University Press, 1992), pp. 78, 82, and more generally pp. 74–83.
36. Ibn Rushd, *Epitome: Metaphysics*, chapter 4, p. 172 and chapter 2, pp. 68, 71–73; *Tahafut al-Tahafut*, 14.478, p. 291; *Metaphysics (Lām)*, 1501–1502, p. 111. See Barry S. Kogan, *Averroes and the Metaphysics of Causation* (Albany: State University of New York Press, 1985), pp. 170–79.
37. Ibn Sina, *Shifa': Nafs*, 5.5, pp. 234–35; *Isharat*, 3.13, p. 105, and 7.9, p. 170. Ibn Rushd, *Epitome: Metaphysics*, chapter 2, p. 75; *Middle Commentary on Aristotle's De Anima*, Discourse 3, Section 297, translated by Alfred L. Ivry (Provo, UT: Brigham Young University Press, 2002) [henceforth *MC: De Anima*, 3.297], p. 116; *Long Commentary on the De Anima of Aristotle*, Book 3, Section 18, translated by Richard C. Taylor (New Haven, CT: Yale University Press, 2009) [henceforth *LC: De Anima*, 3.18], p. 352. See also Rahman, *Prophecy*, pp. 15, 30; Davidson, *Alfarabi, Avicenna, and Averroes*, pp. 47, 85; Richard C. Taylor (p. 229), "Remarks on Cogitatio in Averroes' *Commentarium Magnum in Aristotelis De Anima Libros*" in Jan A. Aertsen and Gerhard Endress, eds., *Averroes and the Aristotelian Tradition: Sources, Constitution and Reception of the Philosophy of Ibn Rushd (1126–1198)* (Leiden: E. J. Brill, 1999): 217–55; Deborah L. Black, "Psychology: Soul and Intellect" in Peter Adamson and Richard C. Taylor, *The Cambridge Companion to Arabic Philosophy* (Cambridge, UK: Cambridge University Press, 2005): 308–26; McGinnis, *Avicenna*, p. 137.
38. Ibn Rushd in his commentary on the *Parva Naturalia*, quoted in Kogan, *Averroes*, p. 82. He also sarcastically attacks many "sharp-witted" Sufis on this score in *The Epistle on the Possibility of Conjunction with the Active Intellect, by Ibn Rushd with the Commentary of Moses Narboni*, translated by Kalman P. Bland (New York: Jewish Theological Seminary of America, 1982), §11, p. 69; §15, p. 103.

39. Ibn Rushd, *Tahafut al-Tahafut*, 4.280, p. 166; see also 10.419, p. 253. Al-Ghazali's attitude toward philosophy is disputed. For an argument that he "never rejected philosophy as a whole" and that Ibn Rushd was, at least initially, "more or less a follower" (p. 52) of his attempt to apply rational methods to the study of revealed texts, see Frank Griffel, "The Relationship between Averroes and al-Ghazālī as It Presents Itself in Averroes' Early Writings, Especially in His Commentary on al-Ghazālī's *al-Mustaṣfā*" in John Inglis, ed., *Medieval Philosophy and the Classical Tradition in Islam, Judaism, and Christianity* (Richmond, UK: Routledge Curzon, 2002): 51–63. On al-Ghazali's agenda more broadly, see Kenneth Garden, *The First Islamic Reviver: Abu Hamid al-Ghazali and His Revival of the Religious Sciences* (New York: Oxford University Press, 2014).

40. Ibn Rushd, *Tahafut al-Tahafut*, 3.246, pp. 146–47.

41. Ibid., 3.184–86, pp. 111–12.

42. Ibn Rushd, *MC: De Anima*, 3.284, p. 112 and 3.297, p. 116; *LC: De Anima*, 3.18, p. 351. See also Davidson, *Alfarabi, Avicenna, and Averroes*, pp. 250, 339, 354–55; Arnzen (n. 231), *Epitome: Metaphysics*, p. 236.

43. Ivry, Introduction to *MC: De Anima*, p. xix.

44. Ibn Rushd, *Talkhis Kitab al-Nafs* (Short Commentary), ed. Ahmad Fu'ad al-Ahwani (Cairo: Maktabat al-Nahda al-Misriyya, 1950), p. 86; *MC: De Anima*, 3.283–85, pp. 111–12, and more generally 3.276–314, pp. 108–23; *LC: De Anima*, 3.4, p. 303, 3.5 pp. 322, 326, and more generally 3.1–36, pp. 292–401. For helpful accounts of how Ibn Rushd's conception of the Material Intellect evolved, see Davidson, *Alfarabi, Avicenna, and Averroes*, pp. 258–98; Ivry's introduction to *MC: De Anima*, pp. xvi–xxviii; and Taylor's introduction to *LC: De Anima*, pp. xix–lxix. Elsewhere, Taylor notes that Ibn Rushd's characterization of the Material Intellect in his Long Commentary is one he had described as "absurd" in his Middle Commentary: Richard C. Taylor (p. 22), "The Agent Intellect as 'Form for Us' and Averroes' Critique of al-Fârâbi," *Proceedings of the Society for Medieval Logic and Metaphysics*, vol. 5 (2005): 18–32.

45. Davidson, *Alfarabi, Avicenna, and Averroes*, p. 355. See also Arthur Hyman (especially p. 195), "Averroes' Theory of the Intellect and the Ancient Commentators" in Gerhard Endress and Jan A. Aertsen, eds., *Averroes and the Aristotelian Tradition: Sources, Constitution and Reception of the Philosophy of Ibn Rushd (1126–1198): Proceedings of the Fourth Symposium Averroicum, Cologne, 1996* (Leiden: E. J. Brill, 1999): 188–98; and Alfred L. Ivry (especially p. 215), "Averroes' Three Commentaries on *De Anima*" in ibid., pp. 199–216. Ivry, however, questions the proposition that Ibn Rushd's three commentaries on the *De Anima* were written in Short-Middle-Long chronological order: "Averroës' Middle and Long Commentaries on the *De Anima*," *Arabic Sciences and Philosophy*, vol. 5, no. 1 (March 1995): 75–92; "Averroes' *Short Commentary* on Aristotle's *De anima*," *Documenti e studi sulla tradizione filosofica medievale*,

vol. 8 (1997): 511–49, especially pp. 513–19. For a contrary view, see Jamal al-Din ʿAlawi, *Al-Matn al-Rushdi: Madkhal li-Qiraʾa Jadida* (Casablanca: Dar Tobiqal, 1986).

46. Ibn Rushd, *LC: De Anima*, 3.5, p. 314; see Davidson, *Alfarabi, Avicenna, and Averroes*, p. 284.

47. Ibn Rushd, *LC: De Anima*, 3.5, p. 315. See also his *Epistle on the Possibility of Conjunction*, §5, p. 40.

48. Kogan, *Averroes*, pp. 17, 255–56, 264–65.

49. Amos Bertolacci (pp. 159, 171), "The Reception of Book B (*Beta*) of Aristotle's *Metaphysics* in the *Ilahiyat* of Avicenna's *Kitab aš-Šifaʾ*" in Jon McGinnis, ed., *Interpreting Avicenna: Science and Philosophy in Medieval Islam* (Leiden, Boston: E. J. Brill, 2004): 157–74.

50. James W. Morris (p. 197), "The Philosopher-Prophet in Avicenna's Political Philosophy" in Charles E. Butterworth, ed., *The Political Aspects of Islamic Philosophy: Essays in Honor of Muhsin S. Mahdi* (Cambridge, MA: Harvard Center for Middle Eastern Studies, 1992): 152–98.

51. See in particular Ibn Rushd's *Tahafut al-Tahafut*, 1.38, p. 22; 3.157–58, pp. 93–94; 11.426–27, pp. 256–57; 11.439, pp. 264–65; 11.442–43, p. 267; and *Al-Kashf ʿan Manahij al-Adilla fi ʿAqaʾid al-Milla*, translated by Ibrahim Najjar as *Faith and Reason in Islam: Averroes' Exposition of Religious Arguments* (Oxford: Oneworld, 2001) [henceforth, *Kashf*], pp. 119–20, 126. Ibn Rushd's evocation of this Qurʾanic verse is noted by Barry Sherman Kogan (p. 164), "Two Gentlemen of Cordova: Averroes and Maimonides on the Transcendence and Immanence of God" in Y. Tzvi Langermann and Josef Stern, eds., *Adaptations and Innovations: Studies on the Interaction Between Jewish and Islamic Thought and Literature from the Early Middle Ages to the Late Twentieth Century, Dedicated to Professor Joel L. Kraemer* (Paris-Louvain: Peeters, 2007): 157–227. To be fair, Ibn Sina also acknowledges that "the knowledge of the Necessary Existent is neither like our knowledge nor comparable to it." Ibn Sina, *The Metaphysica of Avicenna (Ibn Sina): A Critical Translation-Commentary and Analysis of the Fundamental Arguments in Avicenna's* Metaphysica *in the* Danish Nama-i ʿAlaʾi (The Book of Scientific Knowledge), ed. Parviz Morewedge (New York: Columbia University Press, 1973), Chapter 30, pp. 61–62. See also Ibn Sina, *Shifaʾ: Ilahiyyat*, 8.6.13–22, pp. 287–90.

52. Ibn Rushd, *Tahafut al-Tahafut*, introduction to the Natural Sciences, 514, p. 315.

53. Translation in Dimitri Gutas (p. 226), "Ibn Tufayl on Ibn Sina's Eastern Philosophy," *Oriens*, vol. 34 (1994): 222–41.

54. Ibid., p. 241; Dimitri Gutas (pp. 165–66), "Avicenna's Eastern ("Oriental") Philosophy: Nature, Contents, Transmission," *Arabic Sciences and Philosophy*, vol. 10 (2000): 159–80. For one such mystical reading, see Henry Corbin, *Avicenna and the Visionary Recital*, translated from the French by Willard R. Trask (New York: Pantheon Books, 1969). For a careful review of what remains of Ibn Sina's texts on Eastern philosophy, see Dimitri Gutas, *Avicenna*

and the Aristotelian Tradition: Introduction to Reading Avicenna's Philosophical Works (Leiden: E. J. Brill, 1988), pp. 43–49, 115–30.

55. Gutas, "Avicenna's Eastern ("Oriental") Philosophy," p. 163n14.

56. Dimitri Gutas (p. 46), "Avicenna's Philosophical Project" in Peter Adamson, ed., *Interpreting Avicenna: Critical Essays* (Cambridge, UK: Cambridge University Press, 2013): 28–47. See also Gutas, *Avicenna and the Aristotelian Tradition*, pp. 127–28.

57. Dimitri Gutas (p. 372), "Intellect Without Limits: The Absence of Mysticism in Avicenna" in Maria Cândida Pacheco and José F. Meirinhos, eds., *Intellect et imagination dans la Philosophie Médiévale*, Vol. 1 (Turnhout: Brepols, 2006): 351–72.

58. Translated in Carlos Steel and Guy Guldentops (p. 99), "An Unknown Treatise of Averroes Against the Avicennians on the First Cause," *Recherches de Théologie et Philosophie Médiévales*, vol. 64, no. 1 (1997): 86–135.

59. Quoted in H. C. Tunik, "Averroes *Quaestiones in Physica*" (PhD dissertation, Radcliffe, 1956), reproduced in Gutas, *Avicenna and the Aristotelian Tradition*, pp. 118–19. See also Ibn Rushd, *Averroes' "De Substantia Orbis,"* translated from Hebrew by Arthur Hyman (Cambridge and Jerusalem: Medieval Academy Books, 1986), p. 131.

60. Ibn Rushd, *Tahafut al-Tahafut*, 10.421, p. 254.

61. "The Law of Reason in the *Kuzari*" (pp. 125–26) in Leo Strauss, *Persecution and the Art of Writing* (Chicago: The University of Chicago Press, 1988): 95–141.

62. Ibid., p. 125.

63. Ibid., pp. 139–40, 99.

64. Ibn Rushd, *LC: De Anima*, 3.14, p. 346.

65. Ibid., 1.2, p. 2. A short treatise attributed to Ibn Sina entitled *On Governance* opens by praising God's wisdom in endowing people with different abilities and ranks, but deals primarily with the private management of one's self and household. It is translated in Jon McGinnis and David C. Reisman, *Classical Arabic Philosophy: An Anthology of Sources* (Indianapolis, IN: Hackett Publishing Company, 2007): 224–37.

66. Farabi, *Tahsil al-Sa'ada*, §§54, 61, in *Alfarabi's Philosophy of Plato and Aristotle*, pp. 43, 48.

67. Miriam Galston (especially pp. 576–77), "Realism and Idealism in Avicenna's Political Philosophy," *The Review of Politics*, vol. 41, no. 4 (October 1979): 561–77. By contrast, see Mahdi, *Alfarabi*, especially pp. 60–62.

68. Ibn Rushd, *Tahafut al-Tahafut*, Natural Sciences 1.527, p. 322.

69. Ibid., Natural Sciences 4.582–83, p. 360.

70. Ibn Rushd, *Decisive Treatise and Epistle Dedicatory* [*Kitab Fasl al-Maqal wa-Taqrir ma-bayn al-Shari'a wa-l-Hikma min al-Ittisal & Al-Damima*], translated by Charles E. Butterworth (Provo, UT: Brigham Young University Press, 2001), 2.B.6, p. 4.

71. Ibid., 2.B.10, p. 6.

72. Ibid., 3.A.11, p. 8.
73. Ibid., 3.B.14, p. 9.
74. Ibid., 3.C.29, p. 19; 3.C.35, p. 21.
75. Ibid., 3.B.15, p. 11; 3.C.35, p. 21.
76. Ibid., 4.A.52, p. 30. For a review of how medieval religious scholars incorporated philosophical elements into their theological and mystical (Sufi) investigations, see Ali Humayun Akhtar, *Philosophers, Sufis, and Caliphs: Politics and Authority from Cordoba to Cairo and Baghdad* (New York: Cambridge University Press, 2017). For one Ash'ari's attempt to formulate a rationally based conception of political sovereignty, see Ahmed Abdel Meguid, "Reversing Schmitt: The Sovereign as Guardian of Rational Pluralism and the Peculiarity of the Islamic State of Exception in al-Juwaynī's Dialectical Theology," *European Journal of Political Theory* (print version forthcoming; published online on September 12, 2017).
77. Ibn Rushd, *Kashf*, p. 77.
78. Ibid., pp. 59, 66.
79. Ibid., p. 68.
80. Ibid., p. 69.
81. Ibid., pp. 70–71.
82. Ibid., pp. 27, 87.
83. Ibid., pp. 28, 85, 114.
84. Ibid., p. 29.
85. Ibid., pp. 86–87.
86. Ibid., p. 115.
87. Ibn Rushd, *Averroes on Plato's Republic*, translated by Ralph Lerner (Ithaca, NY: Cornell University Press, 1974), p. 81. See also *Epitome: Metaphysics*, chapter 4, pp. 179–80. See George F. Hourani, "Averroes on Good and Evil," *Studia Islamica*, no. 16 (1962): 13–40.
88. Ibn Rushd, *Kashf*, pp. 118–19.
89. Ibid., p. 119.
90. Ibid., pp. 55, 63.
91. Charles E. Butterworth (pp. 119–20), "New Light on the Political Philosophy of Averroës" in George F. Hourani, ed., *Essays on Islamic Philosophy and Science* (Albany: State University of New York Press, 1975): 118–27; Noah Feldman, "Reading the *Nicomachean Ethics* with Ibn Rushd" (D.Phil. thesis, Oxford University, 1994), pp. 60, 67.
92. Ibn Rushd, *Talkhis al-Khataba*, ed. Muhammad Salim Salem (Cairo: Dar al-Tahrir li-l-Tab' wa-l-Nashr, 1967), pp. 136, 139. In discussing this text, I follow the translations of Charles E. Butterworth in "The Political Teaching of Averroes," *Arabic Science and Philosophy*, vol. 2 (1992): 187–202.
93. Ibn Rushd, *Talkhis al-Khataba*, p. 137.
94. Ibid., pp. 137–38.
95. Butterworth, "Political Teaching," p. 202.

96. Patricia Crone, "What Was Al-Farabi's 'Imamic' Constitution?," *Arabica*, Tome 50, Fasc. 3 (July 2003): 306–21.

97. Ibid. (in turn citing Maroun Aouad and Marwan Rashed), p. 306; E. I. J. Rosenthal, *Averroes' Commentary on Plato's Republic* (Cambridge, UK: Cambridge University Press, 1956), p. 282, endnote [Treatise II] xvii.5; pp. 288–89, endnote [Treatise III] xvii.5. Rosenthal suggests as the source the lost commentary on Aristotle's *Nicomachean Ethics*, where al-Farabi is famously reported to have also said that there is no happiness except political happiness.

98. Farabi, *Fusul Muntaza'a*, ed. Fauzi M. Najjar (Beirut: Dar El-Mashreq Publishers, 1971), §58, pp. 66–67. Translated into English by Charles E. Butterworth (pp. 37–38) in *Alfarabi: The Political Writings: "Selected Aphorisms" and Other Texts* (Ithaca, NY: Cornell University Press, 2001), pp. 11–67.

99. Farabi, *Fusul*, §57, p. 65; Crone, "What Was Al-Farabi's 'Imamic' Constitution?," pp. 313, 306.

100. Crone, "What Was Al-Farabi's 'Imamic' Constitution?," pp. 307, 318–21.

101. Farabi, *On the Perfect State (Mabadi' Ara' Ahl al-Madinat al-Fadilah)*, Arabic original and English translation by Richard Walzer (Chicago: Great Books of the Islamic World, 1998), Section 5, chapter 15, §§11–14 [henceforth 5.15.11–14], pp. 244–53.

102. Ibid., 5.15.14, pp. 252, 253. While acknowledging that this is the "dominant" view in "very numerous" Farabian texts (p. 97; also pp. 123, 126, 135, 143), Miriam Galston in her *Politics and Excellence: The Political Philosophy of Alfarabi* (Princeton, NJ: Princeton University Press, 1990) nonetheless discerns a contrary "strand" in al-Farabi's thought suggesting that an excellent political community might be able to do without philosophy (pp. 97, 108–09, 218).

103. Butterworth, "Political Teaching," pp. 191, 193.

104. Ibid., pp. 191, 192, 202.

105. Ibn Rushd, *Averroes on Plato's Republic* (Lerner translation), pp. 56–57, 102.

106. Ibid., pp. 104–06.

107. Farabi, *Kitab al-Siyasa al-Madaniyya*, translated by Charles E. Butterworth (p. 87) as "The Political Regime" in *Alfarabi: The Political Writings, Volume II* (Ithaca, NY: Cornell University Press, 2015): 27–94.

108. Ibn Rushd, *Averroes on Plato's Republic*, pp. 110, 127.

109. Ibid., pp. 111, 128, 130.

110. Ibid., pp. 127, 128.

111. Ibn Rushd, *Talkhis al-Khataba*, p. 221.

112. Ibn Rushd, *Al-Daruri fi Usul al-Fiqh (aw Mukhtasar al-Mustasfa)*, ed. Jamal al-Din al-ʿAlawi (Beirut: Dar al-Gharb al-Islami, 1994), pp. 144–45.

113. Ibn Rushd, *Decisive Treatise*, 7.B.60, p. 33.

114. Muhsin Mahdi (pp. 124–25), "Averroës on Divine Law and Human Wisdom" in Joseph Cropsey, ed., *Ancients and Moderns: Essays on the Tradition*

of Political Philosophy in Honor of Leo Strauss (New York: Basic Books, 1964): 114–31.

115. Maribel Fierro (p. 247), "The Legal Policies of the Almohad Caliphs and Ibn Rushd's *Bidayat al-Mujtahid*," *Journal of Islamic Studies*, vol. 10, no. 3 (1999): 226–48.

116. Translations from Yasin Dutton (p. 197), "The Introduction to Ibn Rushd's *Bidayat al-Mujtahid*," *Islamic Law and Society*, vol. 1, no. 2 (1994): 188–205.

117. Ibn Rushd, *The Distinguished Jurist's Primer: Bidayat al-Mujtahid wa Nihayat al-Muqtasid*, translated by Imran Ahsan Khan Nyazee, two volumes (Reading, UK: Centre for Muslim Contribution to Civilization; Garnet Publishing, 1994–1996); Volume 1, pp. 454–87.

118. Ibid., p. 460.

119. Ibid., p. 463.

120. Ibid., pp. 478, 479.

121. Ibid., pp. 455, 484.

122. Translation by Lawrence V. Berman (p. 439), "Review: *Averroes' Commentary on Plato's 'Republic'* by E. I. J. Rosenthal," *Oriens*, vol. 21 (1968–1969): 436–39. On Ibn Rushd and rectification in the laws of jihad, see Feldman, "Reading the *Nichomachean* Ethics," pp. 227–57.

123. Josep Puig (p. 257), "Materials on Averroes's Circle," *Journal of Near Eastern Studies*, vol. 51, no. 4 (October 1992): 241–60. See also Noah Feldman (pp. 102–04), "War and Reason in Maimonides and Averroes" in Richard Sorabji and David Rodin, eds., *The Ethics of War: Shared Problems in Different Traditions* (Aldershot, UK: Ashgate, 2006): 92–107.

124. Ibn Rushd, *Bidayat al-Mujtahid*, p. 454.

125. Oliver Leaman (p. 174), "Ibn Rushd on Happiness and Philosophy," *Studia Islamica*, no. 52 (1980): 167–81.

126. Ibn Rushd, *Averroes on Plato's Republic*, p. 13.

127. Ibid., p. 11. For a range of views on Ibn Rushd's attitude toward coercive warfare, see Ralph Lerner's introduction to *Averroes on Plato's Republic*, pp. xvii–xviii; Joel L. Kraemer (p. 319), "The Jihad of the Falasifa," *Jerusalem Studies in Arabic and Islam*, vol. 10 (1987): 288–324; Maroun Aouad (pp. 427, 430–31), "Does Averroes Have a Philosophy of History?," *Mélanges de l'Université Saint-Joseph*, vol. 57 (2004): 411–41; Farid al-ʿUlaybi, *Ruʾyat Ibn Rushd al-Siyasiyya* (Beirut: Markaz Dirasat al-Wahda al-ʿArabiyya, 2007), pp. 207–45; Alfred L. Ivry (p. 121), "Averroes' Understanding of the Philosopher's Role in Society" in Anna Akasoy and Wim Raven, eds., *Islamic Thought in the Middle Ages: Studies in Text, Transmission and Translation, in Honour of Hans Daiber* (Leiden, Boston: E. J. Brill, 2008): 113–22.

128. Ibn Rushd, *Averroes on Plato's Republic*, pp. 45–46.

129. Ibid., p. 28.

130. Ibid., pp. 42–43.

131. Ibid., p. 73.

132. Morris, "Philosopher-Prophet," pp. 196–97; Dimitri Gutas (pp. 81, 85–86, 91), "The Heritage of Avicenna: The Golden Age of Arabic Philosophy, 1000–ca. 1350" in Jules Janssens and Daniel De Smet, eds., *Avicenna and His Heritage: Acts of the International Colloquium, Leuven – Louvain-la-Neuve, September 8–September 11, 1999* (Leuven: Leuven University Press, 2002): 81–97. See also Taha 'Abd al-Rahman, *Al-Haqq al-'Arabi fi al-Ikhtilaf al-Falsafi* (Casablanca: Al-Markaz al-Thaqafi al-'Arabi, 2002), who writes of Ibn Rushd: "He was, in truth, a Western philosopher with an Arabic tongue, not an Arab philosopher with an Arab mind" (p. 141n2).

Chapter 4

1. Kraemer, "Jihad of the Falasifa," p. 291.
2. Ibid., pp. 319, 303–04.
3. Gibb, *Studies*, pp. 13–14, 72.
4. Majid Khadduri, *The Islamic Conception of Justice* (Baltimore, MD: The Johns Hopkins University Press, 1984), p. 173.
5. Kraemer, "Jihad of the Falasifa," p. 312n74; see also the sources in note 81 of this chapter. For a rebuttal see Charles E. Butterworth (pp. 96–97n17), "Al-Farabi's Statecraft: War and the Well-Ordered Regime" in James Turner Johnson and John Kelsay, eds., *Cross, Crescent, and Sword: The Justification and Limitation of War in Western and Islamic Tradition* (New York: Greenwood Press, 1990): 79–100.
6. *Al-Muqaddima*, translated by Franz Rosenthal, 3 vols. (New York: Pantheon Books, 1958), vol. 1, chapter 1, section 1, p. 91. Henceforth I will cite Rosenthal's chapter, section and page number (but not volume), followed by the volume and page numbers of Étienne Marc Quatremère's standard 1858 Paris edition of the Arabic text, as follows: M 1.1: 91 [Q I: 71]. I have also used *Muqaddimat Ibn Khaldun* (Beirut: Dar al-Qalam, 1981). While relying primarily on Rosenthal's translation, I have amended it extensively.
7. M 1.Preface: 84 [Q I: 67]. The point is reiterated in M 6.1: 411 [Q II: 364]; 6.16: 77 [Q III: 60]; and 6.22: 137 [Q III: 108]. See Muhsin Mahdi, *Ibn Khaldun's Philosophy of History: A Study in the Philosophic Foundation of the Science of Culture* (Chicago: University of Chicago Press, 1964), p. 173; Lenn Evan Goodman (p. 252), "Ibn Khaldun and Thucydides," *Journal of the American Oriental Society*, vol. 92, no. 2 (April–June 1972): 250–70; James W. Morris (pp. 242, 285n37), "An Arab Machiavelli? Rhetoric, Philosophy and Politics in Ibn Khaldun's Critique of Sufism," *Harvard Middle Eastern and Islamic Review*, vol. 8 (2009): 242–91.
8. M 4.11: 276 [Q II: 239]. See also M 5.16–17: 347–51 [Q II: 307–11]; 6.8: 434–35 [Q II: 383–84].
9. M 4.5: 247 [Q II: 213].

10. *M* 2.19: 293 [*Q* I: 261].
11. *M* 4.17: 291 [*Q* II: 255].
12. Mahdi, *Ibn Khaldun's Philosophy*, p. 208n1, referring here to *M* 2.21: 296–99 [*Q* I: 264–66]. See also pp. 203, 204 on the centrality of the state for Ibn Khaldun.
13. William R. Polk, "Encounters with Ibn Khaldun," March 7, 2001 (http://www.williampolk.com/assets/encounters-with-ibn-khaldun.pdf); Rashid Rida (p. 76), "Islam and the National Idea," 1933 essay in Sylvia G. Haim, ed., *Arab Nationalism: An Anthology* (Berkeley: University of California Press, 1962): 75–77.
14. Francesco Gabrieli, "ʿAṣabiyya," *Encyclopaedia of Islam, Second Edition* (Brill Online); Richard Walzer (pp. 52–53, 58), "Aspects of Islamic Political Thought: Al-Farabi and Ibn Xaldun," *Oriens*, vol. 16 (December 31, 1963): 40–60. On precedents in al-Farabi, see Mahdi, *Ibn Khaldun's Philosophy*, p. 263n1; Muhsin Mahdi (p. 964), "Ibn Khaldun" in M. M. Sharif, ed., *A History of Muslim Philosophy*, vol. 2 (Wiesbaden: Otto Harrassowitz, 1966): 888–904, 961–84; Joshua Parens, *Metaphysics as Rhetoric: Alfarabi's Summary of Plato's "Laws"* (Albany: State University of New York Press, 1995), p. 171n 9. On precedents in al-Masʿudi, see Lenn E. Goodman, *Islamic Humanism* (New York: Oxford University Press, 2003), p. 209. On precedents in al-Mawardi, see Eltigani Abdulqadir Hamid (pp. 5–6, 8, 14–15), "Al-Mawardi's Theory of State: Some Ignored Dimensions," *American Journal of Islamic Social Sciences*, vol. 18, no. 4 (Fall 2001): 1–18; Seyfi Say, *İbn Haldûn'un Düşünce Sistemi ve Uluslararası İlişkiler Kuramı* (Istanbul: İlk Harf Yayınevi, 2011), pp. 327–29. Ibn Khaldun's more multivalent use of the term may also be traced even further back to the ancient Greek concept of *thumos* (spiritedness).
15. *M* 3.21: 380–81 [*Q* I: 338].
16. *M* 1.1: 90, 91 [*Q* I: 70, 71]; 3.35: 73 [*Q* II: 65].
17. *M* 2.7: 262 [*Q* I: 233].
18. *M* 3.1: 313 [*Q* I: 278].
19. *M* 3.21: 381 [*Q* I: 338]; also 1.1: 89–93 [*Q* I: 68–73]; 2.7: 262 [*Q* I: 233]; 3.50: 137 [*Q* II: 126].
20. *M* 2.8 265; 3.18: 374 [*Q* I: 236, 332].
21. *M* 2.12: 274, 275–76 [*Q* I: 243, 244–45]. ʿAbd al-Rahman Badawi rebutted Ibn Khaldun's criticism of Ibn Rushd on two grounds: first for failing to note that Ibn Rushd is merely conveying Aristotle's views instead of his own; and second for failing to note that Ibn Rushd, or rather Aristotle, ascribes prestige to other factors—such as large numbers—in addition to extended lineage. See Badawi (pp. 158–59), "Ibn Khaldun wa-Aristu" in *Aʿmal Mahrajan Ibn Khaldun al-Munʿaqida fi al-Qahira min 2 ila 6 Yanayir 1962* (Cairo: Manshurat al-Markaz al-Qawmi li-l-Buhuth al-Ijtimaʿiyya wa-l-Jinaʾiyya, 1962): 152–62. For a broader discussion of *ḥasab* and *nasab* (lineage), see Mottahedeh, *Loyalty and Leadership*, pp. 98–104.
22. *M* 2.12: 275; 2.18: 288 [*Q* I: 244, 256–57].

23. *M* 2.16: 284 [*Q* I: 252].
24. *M* 2.7: 263 [*Q* I: 234].
25. *M* 2.20: 295; 2.25: 302–05 [*Q* I: 263, 270–72].
26. *M* 2.16: 285 [*Q* I: 253].
27. Badawi, "Ibn Khaldun wa-Aristu," pp. 160–61; Allen James Fromherz, *Ibn Khaldun: Life and Times* (Edinburgh, UK: Edinburgh University Press, 2010), pp. 67, 128, 139, 140, 159; Nasif Nassar, *Al-Isharat wa-l-Masalik: Min Iwan Ibn Rushd ila Rihab al-'Ilmaniyya* (Beirut: Dar al-Tali'a, 2011), pp. 104–05; Robert Irwin, *Ibn Khaldun: An Intellectual Biography* (Princeton, NJ: Princeton University Press, 2018), pp. 188, 207–08. See also Muhammad 'Abid al-Jabiri, *Fikr Ibn Khaldun: Al-'Asabiyya wa-l-Dawla – Ma'alim Nazariyya Khalduniyya fi al-Tarikh al-Islami* (Casablanca: Dar al-Nashr al-Maghribiyya, 1979), pp. 195–96, 400–31, for a more nuanced view of *'asabiyya* that nevertheless still sees it primarily as a force for division and conflict, and therefore as inimical to political integration, stability, and sustained development.
28. *M* 2.8: 264 [*Q* I: 235].
29. *M* 2.16: 284 [*Q* I: 252]. See Goodman, "Ibn Khaldun and Thucydides," pp. 256, 258.
30. Mahdi, *Ibn Khaldun's Philosophy*, p. 198.
31. *M* 3.17: 372 [*Q* I: 330]. See also *M* 3.15: 353–55 [*Q* I: 314–17]; Muhammad Mahmoud Rabi', *The Political Theory of Ibn Khaldun* (Leiden: E. J. Brill, 1967), p. 63.
32. Mahdi, *Ibn Khaldun's Philosophy*, p. 266.
33. *M* 3.17: 373 [*Q* I: 331].
34. *M* 3.23: 385, 386–87 [*Q* I: 342, 343].
35. *M* 3.22: 383 [*Q* I: 340].
36. *M* 3.23: 386 [*Q* I: 342], with Rosenthal's reading of *ma'siya* (insubordination) instead of *'asabiyya*.
37. *M* 3.35: 74–75 [*Q* II: 66]. See *Mukhtasar Siyasat al-Hurub*, chapter 17.
38. *Kitab al-'Ibar wa-Diwan al-Mubtada' wa-l-Khabar fi Ayyam al-'Arab wa-l-'Ajam wa-l-Barbar wa-man 'Asarahum min Dhawi al-Sultan al-Akbar*, ed. Yusuf As'ad Daghir, 7 vols. (Beirut: Dar al-Kitab al-Lubnani, 1956–1961), vol. 2, section 4, pp. 761, 856–57. Henceforth as follows: *KI* 2.4: 761, 856–57.
39. *KI* 3.2: 360, 435.
40. *KI* 2.4: 894–95, 897, 949. See Khalil 'Athamina (pp. 259–60), "The Appointment and Dismissal of Khalid b. al-Walid from the Supreme Command: A Study of the Political Strategy of the Early Muslim Caliphs in Syria," *Arabica*, Tome 41, Fasc. 2 (July 1994): 253–72.
41. *M* 3.26: 415 [*Q* I: 365].
42. *M* 2.6: 259–60 [*Q* I: 231].
43. *M* 4.8: 268 [*Q* II: 231]; *KI* 2.4: 960.
44. *M* Introduction: 36; 2.15: 282 [*Q* I: 26, 251]. On the antecedents to Ibn Khaldun's distinction between nomadic and sedentary societies, see Solomon Pines, "The Societies Providing for the Bare Necessities of Life According to

Ibn Khaldun and to the Philosophers," *Studia Islamica*, no. 34 (1971): 125–38.

45. *M* 2.4: 254; 2.5: 257 [*Q* I: 226, 228–29]. On rich foods, see *M* 1.5: 177–83 [*Q* I: 157–65].

46. *M* 2.21: 297 [*Q* I: 265].

47. *M* 3.32: 39 [*Q* II: 33]. For more on this topic, including additional details on the debate between 'Umar and Mu'awiya and the subsequent success of naval jihad, see *KI* 2.4: 957; 2.5: 1006–009.

48. *M* 3.7: 327–28; 3.9: 332 [*Q* I: 291, 295–96].

49. On the "natural life span" of dynasties, see *M* 2.14: 278–82; 3.12: 343–46 [*Q* I: 247–50, 305–09].

50. *KI* 4.3: 636–64.

51. *M* 3.7: 327–28; 3.9: 332 [*Q* I: 291–92, 295].

52. *KI* 6.1: 3–7, 206.

53. Hayden V. White (pp. 114, 118), "Ibn Khaldun in World Philosophy of History," *Comparative Studies in Society and History*, vol. 2 (1959–1960): 110–25; Miya Syrier (pp. 265, 267, 300), "Ibn Khaldun and Islamic Mysticism," *Islamic Culture*, vol. 21, no. 3 (July 1947): 264–302; Gibb, "Islamic Background," p. 31; 'Ali Mabruk (pp. 99–101), "Al-Inkisar al-Murawigh li-l-'Aqlaniyya: Min Ibn Rushd ila Ibn Khaldun," *Alif*, no. 16 (1996): 89–115. For contrasting views that emphasize the continuity in Ibn Khaldun's political activism, see Rosenthal, "Translator's Introduction" to the *Muqaddima*, pp. li, lxi; Mahdi, *Ibn Khaldun's Philosophy*, pp. 275, 296; Jabiri, *Fikr Ibn Khaldun*, pp. 69, 123; Nathaniel Schmidt, *Ibn Khaldun: Historian, Sociologist and Philosopher* (New York: Columbia University Press, 1930), pp. 43, 45.

54. *M* 4.8: 268–69 [*Q* II: 232]. See Fuad Baali, *Society, State and Urbanism: Ibn Khaldun's Sociological Thought* (Albany: State University of New York Press, 1988), p. 71.

55. *M* 2.6: 260 [*Q* I: 231].

56. "But the nation did not pass away with the passing of the state, nor were the edifices of the religion annihilated with the annihilation of the landmarks of the kingdom" (*KI* 7.1: 21). See Sati' al-Husri, *Dirasat 'an Muqaddimat Ibn Khaldun* (Cairo: Dar al-Ma'arif bi-Misr, 1953), pp. 358–64; Jabiri, *Fikr Ibn Khaldun*, pp. 328, 329.

57. Rosenthal, "Translator's Introduction," pp. lxxxiii–lxxxiv.

58. *M* 3.35: 85 [*Q* II: 76].

59. *M* Preliminary Remarks: 83 [*Q* I: 66]. On al-Turtushi in this regard, see Tarif Khalidi, *Arabic Historical Thought in the Classical Period* (Cambridge, UK: Cambridge University Press, 1994), pp. 195, 222.

60. *M* 3.35: 87 [*Q* II: 77].

61. *M* 3.35: 86 [*Q* II: 76]; see also 3.48: 130–31 [*Q* II: 120].

62. *M* 3.35: 85, 86 [*Q* II: 76].

63. *M* 3.34: 48–49 [*Q* II: 42–43]. Compare al-Ghazali's chapter on auditory and ecstatic experience in his *Ihya' 'Ulum al-Din*, 5 vols. (Beirut: Dar al-Fikr,

Notes to Chapter 4   173

1994), vol. 2, especially pp. 292, 300–01; Ibn Rushd, *Averroes on Plato's Republic*, p. 28. On al-Farabi's reputedly phenomenal mastery of musical manipulation, see Abu al-Hasan ʿAli ibn Zayd al-Bayhaqi, *Tarikh Hukamaʾ al-Islam* (Cairo: Maktabat al-Thaqafa al-Diniyya, 1996), pp. 42–43.

64. *M* 3.35: 79 [*Q* II: 70].

65. *M* 3.35: 86 and 3.48: 131; 3.48: 130–31 [*Q* II: 76, 120]; see, for example, al-Muhallab's testament in *KI* 3.1: 117.

66. *KI* 2.4: 795, 814, 888; 3.1: 189; 4.2: 373. See Briton Cooper Busch, "Divine Intervention in the *Muqaddimah* of Ibn Khaldun," *History of Religions*, vol. 7, no. 4 (May 1968): 317–29.

67. *KI* 5.4: 802–03. The translation is David Ayalon's (pp. 118–20), "The Great Yasa of Chingiz Khan: A Re-examination—C: The Position of the Yasa in the Mamluk Sultanate," *Studia Islamica*, vol. 36 (1972): 113–58.

68. *KI* 7.3: 544–47.

69. *KI* 2.3: 384. On Ibn Khaldun's alleged "obsession" with the supernatural, see Fromherz, *Ibn Khaldun*, pp. 5, 115, 124–25; Irwin, *Ibn Khaldun*, pp. 119, 125, 206. For a critique of this allegation, see Malik Mufti, "Is Ibn Khaldun 'Obsessed' with the Supernatural?," *Journal of the American Oriental Society* (forthcoming, 2019).

70. *M* 3.35: 85 [*Q* II: 75].

71. *M* 3.35: 88 [*Q* II: 78]. Compare to chapters 1 and 40 of the *Mukhtasar Siyasat al-Hurub*.

72. *M* 3.35: 85 [*Q* II: 75].

73. *KI* 3.2: 310; 4.1: 200. On the two groups generally, see *KI* 2.5: 1118–124; 3.2: 303–63; 4.1: 200–11.

74. The fatwa is translated in Morris, "An Arab Machiavelli?," pp. 249–50. On Sufi excesses in Ibn Khaldun's time: Jabiri, *Fikr Ibn Khaldun*, pp. 40–41. See also *M* 6.16: 101–02 [*Q* III: 79].

75. *M* 6.16: 102 [*Q* III: 79–80]; Morris, "An Arab Machiavelli?," p. 249.

76. *M* 6.16: 100 [*Q* III: 78].

77. *Shifaʾ al-Saʾil li-Tahdhib al-Masaʾil*, ed. Abu Yaʿrub al-Marzuqi (Tunis: Al-Dar al-ʿArabiyya li-l-Kitab, 1991), p. 234. For an English translation see Yumna A. Adal, "Sufism in Ibn Khaldun: An Annotated Translation of the Shifaʾ al-Saʾil li-Tahdhib al-Masaʾil" (PhD dissertation, Indiana University, 1990): 135–296.

78. Ibid., pp. 194–99.

79. On *wijdān* in the Sufi context: *M* 6.16: 83, 85, 89, 101 [*Q* III: 65, 67, 70, 78]. Franz Rosenthal notes Ibn Khaldun's use of the same term in different contexts (p. 198n277)—e.g., *M* 1.6: 198 [*Q* I: 177]; 3.34: 48 [*Q* II: 42]; 5.11: 340 [*Q* II: 300]; 6.16: 77, 83 [*Q* III: 60, 65]; 6.30: 252 [*Q* III: 215]—as does Morris, "An Arab Machiavelli?," p. 270. Morris's account, however, highlights Ibn Khaldun's disapproval of the irrational character of *wijdānī* experience, in contrast to the appreciation for its political uses suggested here.

80. *Shifaʾ al-Saʾil*, p. 231; see also pp. 234, 238, 247.

81. For example: Hamilton A. R. Gibb (pp. 25, 27), "The Islamic Background of Ibn Khaldun's Political Theory," *Bulletin of the School of Oriental Studies*, vol. 7, no. 1 (1933): 23–31; Jabiri, *Fikr Ibn Khaldun*, pp. 201, 203; Mabruk, "Al-Inkisar al-Murawigh," pp. 97, 105; Majid Fakhry, *A History of Islamic Philosophy* (New York: Columbia University Press, 1983), p. 325; Barbara Freyer Stowasser, *Religion and Political Development: Some Comparative Ideas of Ibn Khaldun and Machiavelli* (Washington, DC: Center for Contemporary Arab Studies–Georgetown University, 1983), p. 23; ʿAli Wardi, *Mantiq Ibn Khaldun: Fi Dawʾ Hadaratihi wa-Shakhsiyyatihi* (London: Dar Kufan, 1994), pp. 50, 171, 179.

82. For an argument that al-Qarafi's overall objective is to curtail executive authority and that for him "the state is justified only to the extent that it promotes the efforts of the individual to obey and worship the Creator" (p. 224), see Sherman A. Jackson, *Islamic Law and the State: The Constitutional Jurisprudence of Shihab al-Din al-Qarafi* (Leiden: E. J. Brill, 1996). For an argument that al-Shatibi's notions of benefit and harm "are in no way determined by considerations of secular public good" but aim rather at "preparing" the individual "for life in the hereafter" (p. 170), see Wael B. Hallaq, *A History of Islamic Legal Theories: An Introduction to Sunni Usul al-Fiqh* (Cambridge, UK: Cambridge University Press, 1997), ch. 5. On Ibn Taymiyya's religious or theological—as opposed to "political"—focus, see Abou El Fadl, *Rebellion and Violence*, p. 63; Yahya Michot, *Ibn Taymiyya: Muslims under Non-Muslim Rule* (Oxford: Interface Publications, 2006), p. 19; Tamara Sonn (p. 135), "Irregular Warfare and Terrorism in Islam: Asking the Right Questions" in Johnson and Kelsay, eds., *Cross, Crescent, and Sword*, pp. 129–47.

83. See, for example, Ibn Taymiyya's discussions of jihad in *Al-Siyasa al-Sharʿiyya fi Islah al-Raʿi wa-l-Raʿiyya*, ed. ʿAbd al-Basit ibn Yusuf al-Gharib (Dammam: Dar al-Rawi, 2000); and in *Fiqh al-Jihad li-Shaykh al-Islam al-Imam Ibn Taymiyya*, ed. Zuhayr Shafiq al-Kabi (Beirut: Dar al-Fikr al-ʿArabi, 1992).

84. M Preliminary Remarks: 80 [Q I: 64].

85. M Introduction: 56–57 [Q I: 44]; 6.12: 3 [Q III: 2]; 6.13: 30 [Q III: 23].

86. KI 7.2: 402.

87. KI 7.1: 80, 95.

88. KI 2.5: 1141–142; *Al-Taʿrif bi-Ibn Khaldun wa-Rihlatuhu Gharban wa-Sharqan*, ed. Muhammad ibn Tawit al-Tanji (Cairo: Matbaʿat Lajnat al-Taʾlif wa-l-Tarjama wa-l-Nashr, 1951), pp. 2–3. On the historian al-Masʿudi's celebration of Muʿawiya's politic forbearance, see Goodman, *Islamic Humanism*, p. 208. On the philosopher Ibn Bajja's denunciation of the preference for Muʿawiya over ʿAli, by contrast, see note 126 of this chapter. See also Erling Ladewig Petersen, *ʿAli and Muʿawiya in Early Arabic Tradition: Studies on the Genesis and Growth of Islamic Historical Writing until the End of the Ninth Century* (Copenhagen: Munksgaard, 1964).

89. Quoted in Aisha Bewley, *Muʿawiya: Restorer of the Muslim Faith* (London: Dar al-Taqwa, 2002), p. 37.

90. Ibn ʿAbd Rabbih, *Al-ʿIqd al-Farid* (The Unique Necklace), vol. 1, translated by Issa J. Boullata (Reading, UK: Garnet Publishing, 2006), p. 18.
91. *M* 3.23: 386 [*Q* I: 342–43].
92. *M* 3.22: 383 [*Q* I: 340].
93. *M* 3.50: 138–39 [*Q* II: 127–28].
94. *M* 3.50: 138 [*Q* II: 127].
95. Ibid.
96. Ibid.
97. *M* 2.7: 262 [*Q* I: 233]. Mahdi contrasts rational and religious regimes more sharply than I do by characterizing the end of Ibn Khaldun's rational regime as the attainment of merely sensual well-being, as opposed to philosophical as well as spiritual fulfillment in the case of the religious regime (*Ibn Khaldun's Philosophy*, pp. 278–80, 283). See also Rabiʿ, *Political Theory*, pp. 141–43.
98. *M* 2.26: 305 [*Q* I: 273]; 3.5: 320 [*Q* I: 284–85]; 3.4: 319 [*Q* I: 284].
99. *M* 3.5: 320 [*Q* I: 284].
100. *M* 3.5: 320 [*Q* I: 285]; 3.4: 320 [*Q* I: 284].
101. *M* 3.5: 321, 322 [*Q* I: 285, 286].
102. *Taʿrif*, p. 315. Another example is Abu Bakr's succession to the caliphate after the Prophet despite his origins in a minor branch of the Quraysh tribe. Ibn Khaldun explains that this was due to the lingering effects of the "miraculous advent of Islamic prophecy." Within a few years, when people "forgot prophecy and miracles" and matters resumed their normal course, the Banu Umayya clan with its superior numbers and more powerful solidarity asserted its natural dominance as Muʿawiya seized the caliphate (*KI* 3.1: 3, 6–7).
103. *M* 3.8: 330 [*Q* I: 294]; 3.48: 134–35 [*Q* II: 123–24].
104. *M* 3.22: 383 [*Q* I: 340].
105. *M* 3.21: 381 [*Q* I: 338]; 3.23: 385 [*Q* I: 342].
106. *M* 3.41: 103 [*Q* II: 93]; 2.27: 307 [*Q* I: 275]. In his *Kitab al-ʿIbar*, Ibn Khaldun praises several statesmen for their promotion of culture, including the Barmakids (*KI* 3.2: 472–76); al-Hakam al-Mustansir, the Andalusian Umayyad (*KI* 4.2: 316); Masʿud the Ghaznavid (*KI* 4.4: 823); ʿAbd al-Wahid the Almohad (*KI* 6.3: 553); and Abu Yusuf Yaʿqub the Marinid (*KI* 7.2: 402, 434–35).
107. *M* 3.35: 73–89 [*Q* II: 65–79].
108. *M* 3.35: 73 [*Q* II: 65].
109. *M* 3.35: 74 [*Q* II: 65–66]. In his *Kitab al-ʿIbar*, Ibn Khaldun describes an Indian community that gave offense both through abhorrent practices such as the killing of unwed daughters, and by taking up arms against the Islamic empire. He does not specify to what extent the subsequent punitive expedition was motivated by the defensive imperative of maintaining law and order versus a proactive moral desire to reform the community's practices. He simply cites both considerations before relating with satisfaction that the commander "slaughtered them and sent [back] the heads of their notables

to be displayed . . . so that the condition of the land was set right" (*KI* 4.4: 873). On just war as *mission civilisatrice*, see Farabi, *Tahsil al-Saʿada*, §§41–43, in *Alfarabi's Philosophy of Plato and Aristotle*, pp. 36–37; ʿAmiri, *Kitab al-Iʿlam*, pp. 157, 174–77, 191. See also Paul L. Heck (pp. 104–05), "Jihad Revisited," *Journal of Religious Ethics*, vol. 32, no. 1 (March 2004): 95–128; Say, *İbn Haldûn'un Düşünce Sistemi*, pp. 621–57.

110. Rabiʿ, *Political Theory*, pp. 59, 132.

111. *M* 1.1: 92–93 [*Q* I: 72–73].

112. *M* 3.24: 390 [*Q* I: 345–46].

113. *M* 3.24: 396–402 [*Q* I: 350–54]. See Rabiʿ, *Political Theory*, pp. 122–25.

114. *M* 3.24: 399 [*Q* I: 352].

115. *M* 3.24: 400 [*Q* I: 353]. See also Ibn Khaldun's defense, on the same grounds, of the subsequent practice of succession after Muʿawiya in *M* 3.28: 431–34 [*Q* I: 379–81].

116. *M* 3.24: 399 [*Q* I: 352]; *M* 5.6: 329 [*Q* II: 290].

117. *M* 3.24: 397 [*Q* I: 350].

118. *M* Preliminary Remarks: 80 [*Q* I: 64]. On Ibn Khaldun's predecessors and sources, see Malik Mufti (pp. 389–90, 394–95), "Jihad as Statecraft: Ibn Khaldun on the Conduct of War and Empire," *History of Political Thought*, vol. 30, no. 3 (Autumn 2009): 385–410.

119. *M* Preliminary Remarks: 80–82 [*Q* I: 64–65].

120. *M* Preliminary Remarks: 82–83 [*Q* I: 65].

121. *M* 6.9: 436 [*Q* II: 385]. See also 6.26: 153–54 [*Q* III: 122]. For conflicting interpretations of how highly Ibn Khaldun ultimately ranked his own approach vis-à-vis the religious and philosophical sciences, see Gibb, "Islamic Background," p. 28; and Mahdi, *Ibn Khaldun's Philosophy*, pp. 225, 290.

122. *M* 6.12: 4, 12–13, 32 [*Q* III: 2–3, 9, 25]; 6.11: 461 [*Q* II: 405].

123. *M* 3.32: 5–6 [*Q* II: 3].

124. *M* 6.14: 50–54 [*Q* III: 40–43]; 6.26: 153 [*Q* III: 122].

125. *M* 6.14: 54–55 [*Q* III: 43]; 6.26: 154 [*Q* III: 122].

126. *M* Preliminary Remarks: 78–79 [*Q* I: 62–63]. According to Mahdi (*Ibn Khaldun's Philosophy*, p. 275n1): "This extreme position is represented by Farabi and Ibn Bajja in particular. . . . Ibn Bajja . . . denounces the preference of Muʿawiya over ʿAli . . . [and] delegates the study of actual regimes, a subject which he holds in great contempt, to the historian." Khalidi (*Arabic Historical Thought*, p. 163n93) adds: "A signal exception to this low view of history [among the *falāsifa*] may be found in Abu al-Hasan al-ʿAmiri . . . [and so] Ibn Sina savagely repudiated ʿAmiri's association with philosophy."

127. *M* Foreword: 6 [*Q* I: 2].

128. *M* 6.30: 250–51 [*Q* III: 213].

129. For a review and sharp critique of the praisers by one of the denigrators, see Mohamed Mzoughi, "Ibn Khaldun wa-l-Falsafa: Taqyim Naqdi" in Massimo Campanini, ed., *Studies on Ibn Khaldun* (Milan: Polimetrica, 2005):

145–79. Mzoughi's depiction of Ibn Khaldun as hostile to philosophy (pp. 146, 153, 168) is echoed by Erwin I. J. Rosenthal (especially pp. 80–81, 84), "Ibn Jaldun's Attitude to the Falasifa," *Al-Andalus*, vol. 20, no. 1 (1955): 75–85; Abu al-ʿAlaʾ ʿAfifi (especially pp. 135–36), "Mawqif Ibn Khaldun min al-Falsafa wa-l-Tasawwuf" in *Aʿmal Mahrajan Ibn Khaldun al-Munʿaqida fi al-Qahira min 2 ila 6 Yanayir 1962* (Cairo: Manshurat al-Markaz al-Qawmi li-l-Buhuth al-Ijtimaʿiyya wa-l-Jinaʾiyya, 1962): 135–43; Fakhry, *History of Islamic Philosophy*, p. 325; and Wardi, *Mantiq Ibn Khaldun*, p. 13. Aziz Al-Azmeh, while denying that Ibn Khaldun rejected rationalism as such, nevertheless concludes that "he is not a philosopher and is paradigmatically alien to philosophy"—Al-Azmeh, *Ibn Khaldun: An Essay in Reinterpretation* (Budapest: Central European University Press, 2003), pp. 102–03. See also Al-Azmeh, *Ibn Khaldun in Modern Scholarship*, pp. 90, 99–101, 106.

130. *M* 6.30: 252 [*Q* III: 215]. See Mahdi, *Ibn Khaldun's Philosophy*, pp. 33, 77 (n. 2), 109 (n. 1), 110.

131. *M* 6.18: 116 [*Q* III: 92]; 6.30: 250 [*Q* III: 213].

132. *M* 6.30: 254–55 [*Q* III: 217].

133. Mahdi, *Ibn Khaldun's Philosophy*, pp. 108–09.

134. *M* 6.23: 147 [*Q* III: 117]. See Morris ("An Arab Machiavelli?," p. 286n39), on whose translation of this passage I have relied here.

135. *M* 6.9: 438 [*Q* II: 386]; 6.14: 38 [*Q* III: 30].

136. See the *Muqaddima*'s section on Sufism: *M* 6.16: 76–103 [*Q* III: 59–80], as well as the entirety of the *Shifaʾ al-Saʾil*.

137. *M* 6.30: 246–47 [*Q* III: 210]. The translation here is Mahdi's (*Ibn Khaldun's Philosophy*, p. 109).

138. *M* 6.30: 252 [*Q* III: 214–15].

139. *M* 6.30: 252 [*Q* III: 215].

140. *M* 6.14: 38 [*Q* III: 30].

141. *M* 6.30: 253 [*Q* III: 215].

142. *M* 5.6: 329–30 [*Q* II: 290].

143. *M* 3.24: 391 [*Q* I: 347]; see also 3.26: 415 [*Q* I: 365].

144. *M* 3.31: 473 [*Q* I: 415].

145. *KI* 7.2: 390.

146. *M* 2.19: 294 [*Q* I: 262].

147. *M* 3.35 74–75, 79 [*Q* II: 66–67, 70].

148. *M* 3.41: 107 [*Q* II: 97].

149. Dante, *Monarchia* (1.4, p. 11), translated and edited by Prue Shaw (Cambridge, UK: Cambridge University Press, 1995).

150. Pangle and Ahrensdorf, *Justice Among Nations*, pp. 273–74 (n. 32); see Larry Peterman (esp. pp. 176, 188–89), "An Introduction to Dante's *De Monarchia*," *Interpretation*, vol. 3, nos. 2–3 (Winter 1973): 169–90.

151. Ahmad bin Ibrahim ibn al-Nahhas al-Dumyati, *Mashariʿ al-Ashwaq ila Masariʿ al-ʿUshshaq fi Fadaʾil al-Jihad*, abridged by Salah ʿAbd al-Fattah

al-Khalidi (Amman: Dar al-Nafaʾis li-l-Nashr wa-l-Tawziʿ, 1999), pp. 216, 225–39; characterized by David Cook, *Martyrdom in Islam* (Cambridge, UK: Cambridge University Press, 2007), p. 40.

152. M 6.41: 308–10 [Q III: 268–69]. By contrast note the contention, advanced by some of the authors cited near the beginning of chapter 2, that Ibn Khaldun subordinates political authority to the *sharīʿa* as interpreted by religious scholars.

153. Talbi, "Ibn Khaldun."

154. Nasif Nassar, *Al-Fikr al-Waqiʿi ʿinda Ibn Khaldun: Tafsir Tahlili wa-Jadali li-Fikr Ibn Khaldun fi Bunyatihi wa-Maʿnah* (Beirut: Dar al-Taliʿa, 1981), pp. 99, 101, 107 (on Ibn Khaldun's realism); and pp. 176, 283, 301 (on Ibn Khaldun's conservatism). See also Nassar, *Al-Isharat wa-l-Masalik*, pp. 97, 99.

155. M 3.32: 46 [Q II: 40]. On *ʿibar* see Mahdi, *Ibn Khaldun's Philosophy*, pp. 63–73; Jabiri, *Fikr Ibn Khaldun*, p. 123; Waseem El-Rayes, "The Political Aspects of Ibn Khaldun's Study of Culture and History" (PhD dissertation, University of Maryland, College Park, 2008), pp. 38, 53–58; and—by contrast—Al-Azmeh, *Ibn Khaldun in Modern Scholarship*, p. 36n70; *Ibn Khaldun: An Essay in Reinterpretation*, p. 144.

Chapter 5

1. Linda T. Darling (pp. 162, 161), "Contested Territory: Ottoman Holy War in Comparative Context," *Studia Islamica*, no. 91 (2000): 133–63.

2. According to Ibn Khaldun's contemporary, the historian Ibn Hajar; quoted in Cemal Kafadar, *Between Two Worlds: The Construction of the Ottoman State* (Berkeley: University of California Press, 1995), p. 182n142.

3. Cornell Fleischer, "Royal Authority, Dynastic Cyclism, and 'Ibn Khaldunism' in Sixteenth-Century Ottoman Letters" in Bruce B. Lawrence, ed., *Ibn Khaldun and Islamic Ideology* (Leiden: E. J. Brill, 1984): 46–68. According to Fleischer (pp. 47–48): "The first firm date in the story of the Ottoman adoption of Ibn Khaldun is 1598, when the scholar and poet Veysi (d. 1628) acquired a manuscript of the *Muqaddimah* in Cairo. Not until the middle of the seventeenth century did Ottoman authors begin to make explicit reference to Ibn Khaldun. . . . The early eighteenth century marks the true beginning of Ibn Khaldun's popularity among Ottoman historians." See also Say, *İbn Haldûn'un Düşünce Sistemi*, pp. 34–35. The praise of Ibn Khaldun is by Naima (ca. 1665–1716), quoted in Lewis V. Thomas, *A Study of Naima*, edited by Norman Itzkowitz (New York: New York University Press, 1972), p. 112.

4. Katip Çelebi, *Düsturu'l-Amel li-Islahi'l-Halel (Bozuklukların Düzeltilmesinde Tutulacak Yollar)*, translated into modern Turkish by Ali Can (Ankara: Başbakanlık Basınevi, 1982), pp. 34, 21, 32. In his introduction the translator

suggests that here Katip Çelebi "departs" from Ibn Khaldun's alleged (see chapter 4) fatalism. See also Fleischer, "Royal Authority," p. 48; Thomas, *A Study of Naima*, p. 78.

5. Katip Çelebi, *Kashf al-Zunun 'an Asami al-Kutub wa-l-Funun*, translated and quoted in Bekir Karlıağa, "The Horizon of Katip Çelebi's Thought," article dated June 16, 2009, and posted on the website MuslimHeritage.com [http://muslimheritage.com/article/horizon-katip-celebi%E2%80%99s-thought], p. 6.

6. Katip Çelebi, *The Balance of Truth*, translated by G. L. Lewis (London: George Allen & Unwin, 1957), p. 26.

7. Ibid., p. 42.

8. Karlıağa, "Horizon," p. 15.

9. Katip Çelebi, *Balance of Truth*, p. 48; also pp. 29, 89. See Michael Cook, *Commanding Right and Forbidding Wrong in Islamic Thought* (Cambridge, UK: Cambridge University Press, 2000), p. 330.

10. See *M* 3.44: 117–18 [Q II: 107].

11. Katip Çelebi, *Balance of Truth*, pp. 42, 45.

12. Ibid., pp. 90, 107.

13. Quoted in Karlıağa, "Horizon," p. 12.

14. Katip Çelebi, *Balance of Truth*, p. 29; Karlıağa, "Horizon," p. 4.

15. First quoted in *Ulus* newspaper, May 17, 1968.

16. By one count, for example, 25 percent of Turkey's population at independence in 1923 consisted of immigrant families who arrived during the previous few decades: Berna Pekesen, "Expulsion and Emigration of the Muslims from the Balkans," *European History Online*, March 7, 2012 (www.ieg-ego.eu/pekesenb-2011-en). For an account of how the disasters of this period affected ordinary people throughout the region more generally, see Leila Tarazi Fawaz, *A Land of Aching Hearts: The Middle East in the Great War* (Cambridge, MA: Harvard University Press, 2014).

17. For a comparative analysis of the Turkish and Arab trajectories, see Malik Mufti, "Democratizing Potential of the 'Arab Spring': Some Early Observations," *Government and Opposition*, vol. 50, no. 3 (July 2015): 394–419.

18. See, for example, the sources cited in note 109 of chapter 1 for polling evidence of the growing ascendance of democratic discourse.

19. Scott Pegg, *International Society and the De Facto State* (Brookfield: Ashgate, 1998); Charles King, "The Benefits of Ethnic War: Understanding Eurasia's Unrecognized States," *World Politics*, vol. 53, no. 2 (2001): 524–52; Dov Lynch, *Engaging Eurasia's Separatist States: Unresolved Conflicts and De Facto States* (Washington, DC: USIP, 2004); Pål Kolstø, "The Sustainability and Future of Unrecognized Quasi-States," *Journal of Peace Research*, vol. 43, no. 6 (2006): 723–40.

20. Ali Çarkoğlu and Binnaz Toprak, *Değişen Türkiye'de Din, Toplum ve Siyaset* (Istanbul: TESEV Yayınları, 2006) [http://research.sabanciuniv.edu/5851/1/DegisenTRdeDin-Toplum-Siyaset.pdf], pp. 29–30; Pew Research Center, *Pew*

Global Attitudes Project Spring 2011 Topline (http://www.pewglobal.org/2011/05/15/spring-2011-survey/), p. 42.

21. Shibley Telhami, in conjunction with Zogby International, *2011 Annual Arab Public Opinion Survey*, October 2011 (http://www.brookings.edu/research/reports/2011/11/21-arab-public-opinion-telhami).

22. Ahmet Davutoğlu speech posted on the Turkish Ministry of Foreign Affairs website (http://www.mfa.gov.tr/disisleri-bakani-ahmet-davutoglu_nun-diyarbakir-dicle-universitesinde-verdigi-_buyuk-restorasyon_-kadim_den-kuresellesmeye-yeni.tr.mfa).

23. "Öcalan'ın Nevruz Mesajı," CNNTürk.com news service, March 21, 2013 (http://www.cnnturk.com/2013/guncel/03/21/ocalanin.nevruz.mesaji/701058.0/).

24. Abu Muhammad ʿAsim al-Maqdisi, "Hadha Baʿd ma ʿindi wa-Laisa Kullahu" (July 2014), posted on al-Maqdisi's Minbar al-Tawhid wa-l-Jihad website (http://www.ilmway.com/site/maqdis/MS_14487.html), p. 6. For a broader review of the political uses and abuses to which simplistic assertions of Islamic unity can be put, see Cemil Aydın, *The Idea of the Muslim World: A Global Intellectual History* (Cambridge, MA: Harvard University Press, 2017).

25. Jacob Poushter, "In Nations with Significant Muslim Populations, Much Disdain for ISIS," Pew Research Center *Fact Tank*, November 17, 2015 (http://www.pewresearch.org/fact-tank/2015/11/17/in-nations-with-significant-muslim-populations-much-disdain-for-isis/). However, the percentages of respondents in these five overwhelmingly Muslim countries who replied "I Don't Know" were as follows: Jordan (4%), Turkey (19%), Pakistan (62%), Indonesia (18%), Senegal (29%). See also note 110 of chapter 1.

26. Ahmet Davutoğlu, *Civilizational Transformation and the Muslim World* (Kuala Lumpur: Mahir Publications Sdn. Bhd., 1994), p. 113.

27. Recep Tayyip Erdoğan (pp. 421–22), "Demokrasi Amaç Değil, Araçtır" in Metin Sever and Cem Dizdar, eds., *2. Cumhuriyet Tartışmaları: Yeni Arayışlar, Yeni Yönelimler* (Ankara: Başak Yayınları, 1993): 417–32.

28. İbrahim Kalın (p. 26), "Turkey and the Middle East: Ideology or Geo-Politics?," *Private View*, no. 13 (Autumn 2008): 26–35.

29. Maqdisi, *Mashruʿ al-Sharq al-Awsat al-Kabir*, p. 2.

30. "Başbakan'dan Üçüncü Balkon Konuşması," *Hürriyet* newspaper, June 12, 2011; "Dışişleri Bakanı Sayın Ahmet Davutoğlu'nun TBMM Genel Kurulu'nda Suriye'deki Olaylar Hakkında Yaptığı Konuşma, 26 Nisan 2012," Turkish Ministry of Foreign Affairs website (http://www.mfa.gov.tr/disisleri-bakani-sayin-ahmet-davutoglu_nun-tbmm-genel-kurulu_nda-suriye_deki-olaylar-hakkinda-yaptigi-konusma_-26-nisan-2012.tr.mfa).

31. "ISIS Video Calls on Turks to Conquer Istanbul, Refers to President Erdoğan as 'Satan,'" *Daily Sabah* newspaper, August 18, 2015 (http://www.dailysabah.com/nation/2015/08/18/isis-video-calls-on-turks-to-conquer-istanbul-refers-to-president-erdogan-as-satan).

32. Ali Bulaç, *Göçün ve Kentin İktidarı: Milli Görüş'ten Muhafazakar Demokrasi'ye AK Parti* (Istanbul: Çıra Yayınları, 2010), p. 24.
33. Ibid., pp. 336, 24, 52.
34. Ibid., p. 448.
35. Ibid., pp. 51, 441–42.
36. Ali Bulaç, "Doktrinin Kritiği," *Zaman* newspaper, January 4, 2014.
37. Ali Bulaç, "Kaçan Fırsat," *Zaman* newspaper, January 6, 2014. Bulaç was arrested in the aftermath of the July 15, 2016, coup attempt in Turkey.
38. The reading of Ibn Khaldun offered here accordingly differs from those found in the few discussions of him by international relations scholars, who generally are interested not so much in his overall project as in the utility of some aspects of his thought—for example, his treatments of decline and change, his consideration of unit actors beyond just Westphalian states, and his attention to issues of identity—in refining or transcending contemporary neorealist theory. Thus, Robert W. Cox's "Towards a Post-Hegemonic Conceptualization of World Order: Reflections on the Relevancy of Ibn Khaldun" in James N. Rosenau and Ernst-Otto Czempiel, eds., *Governance Without Government: Order and Change in World Politics* (Cambridge, UK: Cambridge University Press, 1992): 132–59, looks forward to "the possibility of alternative intersubjective worlds coexisting" without the aggression implicit in Ibn Khaldun's concept of *ʿaṣabiyya* (p. 159). See also Jack Kalpakian, "Ibn Khaldun's Influence on Current International Relations Theory," *The Journal of North African Studies*, vol. 13, no. 3 (September 2008): 363–76, who views the *Muqaddima* primarily as a precursor of various neorealist and constructivist ideas. Even a scholar trying to articulate an Islamic alternative to Western international relations theory paradigms such as Amr G. E. Sabet, in "The Islamic Paradigm of Nations: Toward a Neo-Classical Approach," *Peace and Conflict Studies*, vol. 8, no. 2 (January 2001): 23–50, seeks primarily to "expand and reconstruct" Ibn Khaldun's concept of *ʿaṣabiyya* "beyond its . . . narrow Khaldunian meaning in order to apply it to contemporary structures and contingencies"—more specifically, to formulate a "defensive" theory of jihad that can regulate the Islamic world's relations with Western imperialism (pp. 43; 45n4). Likewise, the main focus of Mustapha Kemal Pasha's "Ibn Khaldun and World Order" in Stephen Gill and James H. Mittelman, eds., *Innovation and Transformation in International Studies* (Cambridge, UK: Cambridge University Press, 1997): 56–70, is on the need to "constitute *ʿasabiyya*" so as to challenge globalized neo-liberalism and the neorealist "fiction of permanence or order" that sustains it (pp. 62, 65). Seyfi Say, for his part, identifies the incorporation of moral principles as a feature distinguishing Ibn Khaldun from Western realists, but instead of elaborating is content simply to label Ibn Khaldun's approach a "synthesis of realism and idealism" (*İbn Haldûn'un Düşünce Sistemi*, pp. 684, 709–10). Both Pasha (pp. 63–66) and Sabet (pp. 29–36) note the dysfunctionality of the state structures currently in place in many Muslim lands.

39. Ahmet Davutoğlu (p. 39), "Medeniyetlerin Ben-İdraki," *Divan*, vol. 2, no. 3 (1997): 1–53. See also Davutoğlu, "İslam Düşünce Geleneğinin Temelleri, Oluşum Süreci ve Yeniden Yorumlanması," *Divan*, vol. 1, no. 1 (1996): 1–44.

40. Shahab Ahmed, *What Is Islam? The Importance of Being Islamic* (Princeton, NJ: Princeton University Press, 2016), pp. 26, 31, 32, 80, 82. See also Seyyed Hossein Nasr, *Three Muslim Sages: Avicenna, Suhrawardi, Ibn ʿArabi* (Cambridge, MA: Harvard University Press, 1964).

41. See Anke von Kügelgen, "A Call for Rationalism: 'Arab Averroists' in the Twentieth Century," *Alif*, no. 16 (1996): 97–132; ʿIsmat Nassar, *Al-Ab ʿad al-Tanwiriyya li-l-Falsafa al-Rushdiyya fi al-Fikr al-ʿArabi al-Hadith* (Al-Fayyum: Dar al-ʿIlm bi-l-Fayyum, 2000); Fauzi M. Najjar, "Ibn Rushd (Averroes) and the Egyptian Enlightenment Movement," *British Journal of Middle Eastern Studies*, vol. 31, no. 2 (November 2004): 195–213; ʿAbd al-Nabi Harri, *Surat Ibn Rushd fi al-Fikr al-Maghribi al-Muʿasir* (Casablanca: Al-Markaz al-Thaqafi al-ʿArabi, 2015); and more generally, Ibrahim M. Abu-Rabiʿ, *Contemporary Arab Thought: Studies in Post-1967 Arab Intellectual History* (London: Pluto Press, 2004); Michaelle L. Browers, *Political Ideology in the Arab World: Accommodation and Transformation* (Cambridge, UK: Cambridge University Press, 2009); Elizabeth Suzanne Kassab, *Contemporary Arab Thought: Cultural Critique in Comparative Perspective* (New York: Columbia University Press, 2010).

42. Muhammad ʿAbid al-Jabiri, *Nahnu wa-l-Turath: Qiraʾat Muʿasira fi Turathina al-Falsafi* (Beirut: Dar al-Taliʿa li-l-Tibaʿa wa-l-Nashr, 1980), p. 66.

43. Ibid., pp. 217, 282–83; 167, 188 (on the Sabeans); 41, 208 (on Persian nationalist resentment); 147 (on Ibn Sina's focus on the self); 194 (on Islamic decline). On Ibn Rushd's belief in the actualizability of a virtuous city in his time and place, see also Muhammad ʿAbid al-Jabiri, *Ibn Rushd: Sira wa-Fikr. Dirasa wa-Nusus* (Beirut: Markaz Dirasat al-Wahda al-ʿArabiyya, 1998), p. 247.

44. See, for example, George Tarabishi's two critiques, *Madhbahat al-Turath fi al-Thaqafa al-ʿArabiyya al-Muʿasira* (London: Dar al-Saqi, 1993); and *Wahdat al-ʿAql al-ʿArabi al-Islami: Naqd Naqd al-ʿAql al-ʿArabi* (Beirut: Dar al-Saqi, 2002), especially Chapter 1 on Ibn Sina (pp. 11–126).

45. See Najjar, "Ibn Rushd."

46. Muhammad ʿAtif al-ʿIraqi, *Al-Manhaj al-Naqdi fi Falsafat Ibn Rushd* (Cairo: Dar al-Maʿarif, 1980), pp. 15, 38, 200, 205–06, and more generally pp. 193–228.

47. Muhammad ʿAtif al-ʿIraqi (p. 355), "Ibn Rushd wa-Mustaqbal al-Thaqafa al-ʿArabiyya" in *Al-Ufuq al-Kawni li-Fikr Ibn Rushd: Aʿmal al-Nadwa al-Dawliyya bi-Munasabat Murur Thamaniyat Qurun ʿala Wafat Ibn Rushd, Marrakesh 12–15 Disimbir 1998* (Marrakesh: Al-Jamʿiyya al-Falsafiyya al-Maghribiyya, 2001): 355–75.

48. Ibid., pp 355–56; Muhammad ʿAtif al-ʿIraqi, *Ibn Rushd Faylasufan ʿArabiyyan bi-Ruh Gharbiyya* (Cairo: Al-Majlis al-Aʿla li-l-Thaqafa, 2002), p. 3.

49. Muhammad ʿImara, *Muslimun Thuwwar* (Beirut: Al-Muʾassasa al-ʿArabiyya li-l-Dirasa wa-l-Nashr, 1974), p. 73; *Ibn Rushd bayn al-Gharb wa-l-Islam* (Cairo: Dar Nahdat Misr, 1997), p. 3.

50. Mahmud Hamdi Zaqzuq (pp. 105, 108), "Mafhum al-Tanwir fi Fikr Ibn Rushd" in Mourad Wahba and Mona Abousenna, eds., *Ibn Rushd wa-l-Tanwir* (Cairo: Dar al-Thaqafa al-Jadida, 1997): 105–14.

51. Ali Shariʾati, *On the Sociology of Islam: Lectures by Ali Shariʾati*, translated by Hamid Algar (Berkeley: Mizan Press, 1979), p. 68.

52. Jabiri, *Ibn Rushd: Sira wa-Fikr*, p. 265.

53. Muhammad ʿAbid al-Jabiri (pp. 8, 12, 21), "Al-Intiqal ila al-Dimuqratiyya fi al-Maghrib: Asʾila wa-Afaq," Part 2, *Fikr wa-Naqd*, vol. 4, no. 32 (October 2000): 5–22.

54. Mabruk, "Al-Inkisar al-Murawigh," pp. 92–95; Mustafa Bin Tamassak, *Ibn Rushd: Al-Siyasa wa-l-Din bayn al-Fasl wa-l-Wasl* (Casablanca: Al-Markaz al-Thaqafi al-ʿArabi, 2015), pp. 79–80, 111–12 (however see also p. 90).

55. Nassar, *Al-Isharat wa-l-Masalik*, pp. 7, 20–21, 26, 27, 38.

56. Ibid., pp. 75, 94.

57. Muhammad al-Misbahi, *Maʿ Ibn Rushd* (Casablanca: Dar Tobiqal, 2007), pp. 41, 60, 63.

58. Muhammad al-Misbahi (pp. 403–04), "Bayna Nihayatayn: Nihayat al-ʿAql al-Rushdi wa-Nihayat al-ʿAql al-Hadathi" in *Al-Ufuq al-Kawni li-Fikr Ibn Rushd: Aʿmal al-Nadwa al-Dawliyya bi-Munasabat Murur Thamaniyat Qurun ʿala Wafat Ibn Rushd, Marrakesh 12–15 Disimbir 1998* (Marrakesh: Al-Jamʿiyya al-Falsafiyya al-Maghribiyya, 2001): 395–410.

59. Muhammad al-Misbahi, *Al-Wajh al-Akhar li-Hadathat Ibn Rushd* (Beirut: Dar al-Taliʿa, 1998), pp. 34–35.

Bibliography

ʿAbbas, Ihsan. *Al-Hasan al-Basri: Siratuhu, Shakhsiyyatuhu, Taʿalimuhu wa-Araʾuhu.* Cairo: Dar al-Fikr al-ʿArabi, 1952.

———. *ʿAbd al-Hamid ibn Yahya al-Katib wa-ma Tabaqqa min Rasaʾilihi wa-Rasaʾili Salim Abi al-ʿAlaʾ.* Amman: Dar al-Shuruq, 1988.

ʿAbd al-Rahman, Taha. *Al-Haqq al-ʿArabi fi al-Ikhtilaf al-Falsafi* (Casablanca: Al-Markaz al-Thaqafi al-ʿArabi, 2002.

Abdel Meguid, Ahmed. "Reversing Schmitt: The Sovereign as Guardian of Rational Pluralism and the Peculiarity of the Islamic State of Exception in al-Juwaynī's Dialectical Theology." *European Journal of Political Theory* (print version forthcoming; published online on 12 September 2017).

Abou El Fadl, Khaled. *Rebellion and Violence in Islamic Law.* Cambridge, UK: Cambridge University Press, 2001.

Abramski-Bligh, Irit. "The Judiciary (*Qadis*) as a Governmental-Administrative Tool in Early Islam." In *The Formation of Islamic Law*, edited by Wael B. Hallaq, pp. 179–210. Aldershot: Ashgate Variorum, 2004.

Abu-Rabiʿ, Ibrahim M. *Contemporary Arab Thought: Studies in Post-1967 Arab Intellectual History.* London: Pluto Press, 2004.

Abu Sulayman, ʿAbdulhamid A. *The Islamic Theory of International Relations: New Directions for Islamic Methodology and Thought.* Herndon, Virginia: International Institute of Islamic Thought, 1987.

Abu Zahra, Muhammad. *Concept of War in Islam.* Translated by Muhammad al-Hady and Taha Omar. Cairo: Ministry of Waqf, 1961.

———. *Al-ʿAlaqat al-Dawliyya fi al-Islam.* Cairo: Al-Dar al-Qawmiyya li-l-Tibaʿa wa-l-Nashr, 1964.

Adal, Yumna A. "Sufism in Ibn Khaldun: An Annotated Translation of the Shifaʾ al-Saʾil li-Tahdhib al-Masaʾil." PhD dissertation, Indiana University, 1990.

Adamson, Peter. *Al-Kindi.* New York: Oxford University Press, 2004.

Aelian. *The Tactics of Aelian, Comprising the Military System of the Grecians.* Translated and edited by Henry Augustus Viscount Dillon. London: Cox & Baylis, 1814.

'Afifi, Abu al-'Ala'. "Mawqif Ibn Khaldun min al-Falsafa wa-l-Tasawwuf." In *A'mal Mahrajan Ibn Khaldun al-Mun'aqida fi al-Qahira min 2 ila 6 Yanayir 1962*, pp. 135–43. Cairo: Manshurat al-Markaz al-Qawmi li-l-Buhuth al-Ijtima'iyya wa-l-Jina'iyya, 1962.

Afnan, Soheil M. *Philosophical Terminology in Arabic and Persian*. Leiden: E. J. Brill, 1964.

Afsaruddin, Asma. *Striving in the Path of God: Jihad and Martyrdom in Islamic Thought*. New York: Oxford University Press, 2013.

Ahmed, Shahab. *What Is Islam? The Importance of Being Islamic*. Princeton, NJ: Princeton University Press, 2016.

Akhtar, Ali Humayun. *Philosophers, Sufis, and Caliphs: Politics and Authority from Cordoba to Cairo and Baghdad*. New York: Cambridge University Press, 2017.

'Alawi, Jamal al-Din. *Al-Matn al-Rushdi: Madkhal li-Qira'a Jadida*. Casablanca: Dar Tobiqal, 1986.

Al-Azmeh, Aziz. *Ibn Khaldun in Modern Scholarship: A Study in Orientalism*. London: Third World Centre for Research and Publishing, 1981.

———. *Muslim Kingship: Power and the Sacred in Muslim, Christian, and Pagan Polities*. London: I. B. Tauris, 1997.

———. *Ibn Khaldun: An Essay in Reinterpretation*. Budapest: Central European University Press, 2003.

———. "God's Caravan: Topoi and Schemata in the History of Muslim Political Thought." In *Mirror for the Muslim Prince: Islam and the Theory of Statecraft*, edited by Mehrzad Boroujerdi, pp. 326–97. Syracuse, NY: Syracuse University Press, 2013.

Al-Dawoody, Ahmed. *The Islamic Law of War: Justifications and Regulations*. New York: Palgrave Macmillan, 2011.

'Amiri, Abu al-Hasan al-. *Al-Sa'ada wa-l-Is'ad fi al-Sira al-Insaniyya*. Edited by Mojtaba Minovi. Wiesbaden: Franz Steiner Verlag, 1957–1958.

Aouad, Maroun. "Does Averroes Have a Philosophy of History?" *Mélanges de l'Université Saint-Joseph*, vol. 57 (2004): 411–41.

Arafat, W. N. "New Light on the Story of Banu Qurayza and the Jews of Medina." *Royal Asiatic Society of Great Britain and Ireland*, no. 2 (1976): 100–07.

Arjomand, Said Amir. "'Abd Allah Ibn al-Muqaffa' and the 'Abbasid Revolution." *Iranian Studies*, vol. 27, nos. 1–4 (1994): 9–36.

———. "Perso-Islamicate Political Ethic in Relation to the Sources of Islamic Law." In *Mirror for the Muslim Prince: Islam and the Theory of Statecraft*, edited by Mehrzad Boroujerdi, pp. 82–106. Syracuse, NY: Syracuse University Press, 2013.

Arrian. *The Campaigns of Alexander*. Translated by Aubrey de Sélincourt. London: Penguin, 1971.

Asclepiodotus. *Tactics*. In *Aeneas Tacticus, Asclepiodotus, Onosander*, translated by William A. Oldfather, pp. 244–333. Loeb Classical Library. London: William Heinemann, 1923.

ʿAthamina, Khalil. "The Appointment and Dismissal of Khalid b. al-Walid from the Supreme Command: A Study of the Political Strategy of the Early Muslim Caliphs in Syria." *Arabica*, Tome 41, Fasc. 2 (July 1994): 253–72.

Ayalon, David. "The Great Yasa of Chingiz Khan: A Re-examination—C: The Position of the Yasa in the Mamluk Sultanate." *Studia Islamica*, vol. 36 (1972): 113–58.

Aydın, Cemil. *The Idea of the Muslim World: A Global Intellectual History*. Cambridge, MA: Harvard University Press, 2017.

Baali, Fuad. *Society, State and Urbanism: Ibn Khaldun's Sociological Thought*. Albany: State University of New York Press, 1988.

Badawi, ʿAbd al-Rahman. "Ibn Khaldun wa-Aristu." In *Aʿmal Mahrajan Ibn Khaldun al-Munʿaqida fi al-Qahira min 2 ila 6 Yanayir 1962*, pp. 152–62. Cairo: Manshurat al-Markaz al-Qawmi li-l-Buhuth al-Ijtimaʿiyya wa-l-Jinaʾiyya, 1962.

Baroudi, Sami E. "The Islamic Realism of Sheikh Yusuf Qaradawi (1926–) and Sayyid Mohammad Hussein Fadlallah (1935–2010)." *British Journal of Middle Eastern Studies*, vol. 43, no. 1 (January 2016): 94–114.

Barrak, ʿAbd al-Malik al-. *Rudud ʿala Abatil wa-Shubuhat hawl al-Jihad*. Amman: Al-Nur li-l-Iʿlam al-Islami, 1997.

Bayhaqi, Abu al-Hasan ʿAli ibn Zayd al-. *Tarikh Hukamaʾ al-Islam*. Cairo: Maktabat al-Thaqafa al-Diniyya, 1996.

Benard, Cheryl. *Civil Democratic Islam: Partners, Resources, and Strategies*. Santa Monica, CA: RAND Corporation, 2003.

Berkes, Niyazi. *The Development of Secularism in Turkey*. Montreal: McGill University Press, 1964.

Berman, Lawrence V. "Review: *Averroes' Commentary on Plato's 'Republic'* by E. I. J. Rosenthal." *Oriens*, vol. 21 (1968–1969): 436–39.

Bertolacci, Amos. "The Reception of Book B (*Beta*) of Aristotle's *Metaphysics* in the *Ilahiyat* of Avicenna's *Kitab aš-Šifaʾ*." In *Interpreting Avicenna: Science and Philosophy in Medieval Islam*, edited by Jon McGinnis, pp. 157–74. Leiden, Boston: Brill, 2004.

Bewley, Aisha. *Muʿawiya: Restorer of the Muslim Faith*. London: Dar al-Taqwa, 2002.

Bin Tamassak, Mustafa. *Ibn Rushd: Al-Siyasa wa-l-Din bayn al-Fasl wa-l-Asl*. Casablanca: Al-Markaz al-Thaqafi al-ʿArabi, 2015.

Black, Deborah L. "Psychology: Soul and Intellect." In *The Cambridge Companion to Arabic Philosophy*, edited by Peter Adamson and Richard C. Taylor, pp. 308–26. Cambridge, UK: Cambridge University Press, 2005.

Blankinship, Khalid Yahya. *The End of the Jihad State: The Reign of Hisham Ibn ʿAbd al-Malik, and the Collapse of the Umayyads*. Albany: State University of New York Press, 1994.

Bloom, Harold. *The American Religion: The Emergence of the Post-Christian Nation*. New York: Touchstone, 1993.

Bonner, Michael. "Some Observations Concerning the Early Development of Jihad on the Arab-Byzantine Frontier." *Studia Islamica*, no. 75 (1992): 5–31.

———. *Aristocratic Violence and Holy War: Studies in the Jihad and the Arab-Byzantine Frontier*. New Haven, CT: American Oriental Society, 1996.

———. *Jihad in Islamic History: Doctrines and Practice*. Princeton, NJ: Princeton University Press, 2006.

Booth, Ken. "Security in Anarchy: Utopian Realism in Theory and Practice." *International Affairs*, vol. 67, no. 3 (July 1991): 527–45.

Bowen, Harold, and C. E. Bosworth. "Niẓām al-Mulk." *Encyclopaedia of Islam, Second Edition*. http://referenceworks.brillonline.com/entries/encyclopaedia-of-islam-2/nizam-al-mulk-SIM_5942?s.num=0&s.f.s2_parent=s.f.book.encyclopaedia-of-islam-2&s.q=Nizam+al-Mulk (accessed 21 May 2016).

Braizat, Fares. "Post Amman Attacks: Jordanian Public Opinion and Terrorism." Public Opinion Polling Unit, Center for Strategic Studies, University of Jordan (January 2006).

Browers, Michaelle L. *Political Ideology in the Arab World: Accommodation and Transformation*. Cambridge: Cambridge University Press, 2009.

Bulaç, Ali. *Göçün ve Kentin İktidarı: Milli Görüş'ten Muhafazakar Demokrasi'ye AK Parti*. Istanbul: Çıra Yayınları, 2010.

———. "Doktrinin Kritiği." *Zaman* newspaper, 4 January 2014.

———. "Kaçan Fırsat." *Zaman* newspaper, 6 January 2014.

Busch, Briton Cooper. "Divine Intervention in the *Muqaddimah* of Ibn Khaldun." *History of Religions*, vol. 7, no. 4 (May 1968): 317–29.

Buti, Muhammad Saʿid Ramadan al-. *Al-Jihad fi al-Islam: Kayfa Nafhamuhu? Wa-Kayfa Numarisuhu?* Damascus: Dar al-Fikr, 1993.

Butterworth, Charles E. "New Light on the Political Philosophy of Averroës." In *Essays on Islamic Philosophy and Science*, edited by George F. Hourani, pp. 118–27. Albany: State University of New York Press, 1975.

———. "Al-Farabi's Statecraft: War and the Well-Ordered Regime." In *Cross, Crescent, and Sword: The Justification and Limitation of War in Western and Islamic Tradition*, edited by James Turner Johnson and John Kelsay, pp. 79–100. New York: Greenwood Press, 1990.

———. "The Political Teaching of Averroes." *Arabic Science and Philosophy*, vol. 2 (1992): 187–202.

———. "Al-Kindi and the Beginnings of Islamic Political Philosophy." In *The Political Aspects of Islamic Philosophy: Essays in Honor of Muhsin S. Mahdi*, edited by Charles E. Butterworth, pp. 11–60. Cambridge, MA: Harvard Center for Middle Eastern Studies, 1992.

Cahen, Claude. "Futuwwa." *Encyclopaedia of Islam, Second Edition*. http://referenceworks.brillonline.com/entries/encyclopaedia-of-islam-2/futuwwa-COM_0228?s.num=0&s.f.s2_parent=s.f.book.encyclopaedia-of-islam-2&s.q=Futuwwa (accessed 21 May 2016).

Campbell, Craig. "Hans Morgenthau and the World State Revisited." In *Realism Reconsidered: The Legacy of Hans J. Morgenthau in International Relations*, edited by Michael C. Williams, pp. 195–215. Oxford: Oxford University Press, 2007.

Çarkoğlu, Ali, and Binnaz Toprak. *Değişen Türkiye'de Din, Toplum ve Siyaset*. Istanbul: TESEV Yayınları, 2006. http://research.sabanciuniv.edu/5851/1/DegisenTRdeDin-Toplum-Siyaset.pdf (accessed 22 May 2016).

Chabbi, Jacqueline. "Ribāṭ." *Encyclopaedia of Islam, Second Edition*. http://referenceworks.brillonline.com/entries/encyclopaedia-of-islam-2/ribat-COM_0919?s.num=0&s.q=Rib%C4%81t (accessed 21 May 2016).

Cook, David. *Martyrdom in Islam*. Cambridge, UK: Cambridge University Press, 2007.

Cook, Michael. *Commanding Right and Forbidding Wrong in Islamic Thought*. Cambridge, UK: Cambridge University Press, 2000.

Cooperson, Michael. "Al-Jāḥiẓ, the Misers, and the Proto-Sunni Ascetics." In *Al-Jāḥiẓ: A Muslim Humanist for our Time*, edited by Armin Heinemann, John L. Meloy, Tarif Khalidi, and Manfred Kropp, pp. 197–219. Würzburg: Ergon Verlag in Kommission; Beirut: Orient-Institut, 2009.

Corbin, Henry. *Avicenna and the Visionary Recital*. Translated by Willard R. Trask. New York: Pantheon Books, 1969.

Cox, Robert W. "Towards a Post-Hegemonic Conceptualization of World Order: Reflections on the Relevancy of Ibn Khaldun." In *Governance Without Government: Order and Change in World Politics*, edited by James N. Rosenau & Ernst-Otto Czempiel, pp. 132–59. Cambridge, UK: Cambridge University Press, 1992.

Crone, Patricia. "What Was Al-Farabi's 'Imamic' Constitution?" *Arabica*, Tome. 50, Fasc. 3 (July 2003): 306–21.

———. *God's Rule: Government and Islam*. New York: Columbia University Press, 2004.

Crone, Patricia, and Martin Hinds. *God's Caliph: Religious Authority in the First Centuries of Islam*. Cambridge, UK: Cambridge University Press, 1986.

Dante. *Monarchia*. Translated and edited by Prue Shaw. Cambridge, UK: Cambridge University Press, 1995.

Darling, Linda T. "Contested Territory: Ottoman Holy War in Comparative Context." *Studia Islamica*, no. 91 (2000): 133–63.

Davidson, Herbert A. *Alfarabi, Avicenna, and Averroes, on Intellect: Their Cosmologies, Theories of the Active Intellect, and Theories of Human Intellect*. New York: Oxford University Press, 1992.

Davutoğlu, Ahmet. *Civilizational Transformation and the Muslim World*. Kuala Lumpur: Mahir Publications Sdn. Bhd., 1994.

———. "İslam Düşünce Geleneğinin Temelleri, Oluşum Süreci ve Yeniden Yorumlanması." *Divan*, vol. 1, no. 1 (1996): 1–44.

———. "Medeniyetlerin Ben-İdraki." *Divan*, vol. 2, no. 3 (1997): 1–53.

———. 26 April 2012 speech. Turkish Ministry of Foreign Affairs website. http://www.mfa.gov.tr/disisleri-bakani-sayin-ahmet-davutoglu_nun-tbmm-genel-kurulu_nda-suriye_deki-olaylar-hakkinda-yaptigi-konusma_-26-nisan-2012.tr.mfa (accessed 23 May 2016).

———. 15 March 2013 speech. Turkish Ministry of Foreign Affairs website. http://www.mfa.gov.tr/disisleri-bakani-ahmet-davutoglu_nun-diyarbakir-dicle-universitesinde-verdigi-_buyuk-restorasyon_-kadim_den-kuresellesmeye-yeni.tr.mfa (accessed 23 May 2016).

Denkard. Vol. 16. Translated by D. D. P. Sanjana. London: Kegan Paul, Trench, Trübner & Co., 1917.

Donner, Fred M. "The Sources of Islamic Conceptions of War." In *Just War and Jihad: Historical and Theoretical Perspectives on War and Peace in Western and Islamic Traditions*, edited by John Kelsay and James Turner Johnson, pp. 31–69. New York: Greenwood Press, 1991.

———. "Centralized Authority and Military Autonomy in the Early Islamic Conquests." In *The Byzantine and Early Islamic Near East, Volume 3: States, Resources, and Armies*, edited by Averil Cameron, pp. 337–60. Princeton, NJ: Darwin Press, 1995.

Dumyati, Ahmad bin Ibrahim ibn al-Nahhas al-. *Mashariʿ al-Ashwaq ila Masariʿ al-ʿUshshaq fi Fadaʾil al-Jihad*. Abridged and edited by Salah ʿAbd al-Fattah al-Khalidi. Amman: Dar al-Nafaʾis li-l-Nashr wa-l-Tawziʿ, 1999.

Dutton, Yasin. "The Introduction to Ibn Rushd's *Bidayat al-Mujtahid*." *Islamic Law and Society*, vol. 1, no. 2 (1994): 188–205.

El-ʿAttar, Jamal F. "The Political Thought of Al-Jāḥiẓ with Special Reference to the Question of Khilāfa (Imāmate): A Chronological Approach." PhD dissertation, University of Edinburgh, 1996.

El-Rayes, Waseem. "The Political Aspects of Ibn Khaldun's Study of Culture and History." PhD dissertation, University of Maryland, College Park, 2008.

Enan, Mohammad Abdullah. *Ibn Khaldun: His Life and Works*. Kuala Lumpur: The Other Press, 2007.

Endress, Gerhard. "The Circle of al-Kindī: Early Arabic Translations from the Greek and the Rise of Islamic Philosophy." In *The Ancient Tradition in Christian and Islamic Hellenism*, edited by Gerhard Endress and Remke Kruk, pp. 43–76. Leiden: Research School CNWS, 1997.

Erdoğan, Recep Tayyip. "Demokrasi Amaç Değil, Araçtır." In *2. Cumhuriyet Tartışmaları: Yeni Arayışlar, Yeni Yönelimler*, edited by Metin Sever and Cem Dizdar, pp. 417–32. Ankara: Başak Yayınları, 1993.

Ess, Josef van. "Al-Jāḥiẓ and Early Muʿtazili Theology." In *Al-Jāḥiẓ: A Muslim Humanist for our Time*, edited by Armin Heinemann, John L. Meloy, Tarif Khalidi, and Manfred Kropp, pp. 3–15. Würzburg: Ergon Verlag in Kommission; Beirut: Orient-Institut, 2009.

Fakhry, Majid. *A History of Islamic Philosophy*. New York: Columbia University Press, 1983.

Farabi, Abu Nasr al-. *Alfarabi's Philosophy of Plato and Aristotle*. Translated by Muhsin Mahdi. New York: The Free Press of Glencoe, 1962.

———. *Fusul Muntazaʿa*. Edited by Fauzi M. Najjar. Beirut: Dar El-Mashreq Publishers, 1971. English translation by Charles E. Butterworth in *Alfarabi:*

The Political Writings: "Selected Aphorisms" and Other Texts, pp. 11–67. Ithaca, NY: Cornell University Press, 2001.

———. *Kitab al-Siyasa al-Madaniyya*. English translation by Charles E. Butterworth as "The Political Regime" in *Alfarabi: The Political Writings, Volume II*, pp. 27–94. Ithaca, NY: Cornell University Press, 2015.

———. *On the Perfect State (Mabadi' Ara' Ahl al-Madinat al-Fadilah)*. Arabic original and English translation edited by Richard Walzer. Chicago: Great Books of the Islamic World, 1998.

Faraj, Muhammad ʿAbd al-Salam. *Al-Farida al-Ghaʾiba*. Translated in Johannes J. G. Jansen, *The Neglected Duty: The Creed of Sadat's Assassins and Islamic Resurgence in the Middle East*, pp. 159–234. New York: Macmillan, 1986.

Faruqi, Ismaʿil al-. Introduction to *The Islamic Theory of International Relations: New Directions for Islamic Methodology and Thought*, by ʿAbdulhamid A. Abu Sulayman. Herndon, VA: International Institute of Islamic Thought, 1987.

Fawaz, Leila Tarazi. *A Land of Aching Hearts: The Middle East in the Great War*. Cambridge, MA: Harvard University Press, 2014.

Fazari, Abu Ishaq al-. *Kitab al-Siyar*. Edited by Faruq Hamada. Beirut: Muʾassasat al-Risala, 1987.

Feldman, Noah. "Reading the *Nicomachean Ethics* with Ibn Rushd." D.Phil. thesis, Oxford University, 1994.

———. "War and Reason in Maimonides and Averroes." In *The Ethics of War: Shared Problems in Different Traditions*, edited by Richard Sorabji and David Rodin, pp. 92–107. Aldershot, UK: Ashgate, 2006.

———. *The Fall and Rise of the Islamic State*. Princeton, NJ: Princeton University Press, 2008.

Fierro, Maribel. "The Legal Policies of the Almohad Caliphs and Ibn Rushd's *Bidayat al-Mujtahid*." *Journal of Islamic Studies*, vol. 10, no. 3 (1999): 226–48.

Firestone, Reuven. *Jihad: The Origin of Holy War in Islam*. New York: Oxford University Press, 1999.

Fleischer, Cornell. "Royal Authority, Dynastic Cyclism, and 'Ibn Khaldunism' in Sixteenth-Century Ottoman Letters." In *Ibn Khaldun and Islamic Ideology*, edited by Bruce B. Lawrence, pp. 46–68. Leiden: E. J. Brill, 1984.

Forde, Steven. "International Realism and the Science of Politics: Thucydides, Machiavelli, and Neorealism." *International Studies Quarterly*, vol. 39, no. 2 (June 1995): 141–60.

Fromherz, Allen James. *Ibn Khaldun: Life and Times*. Edinburgh, UK: Edinburgh University Press, 2010.

Fuchs, Simon Wolfgang. "Do Excellent Surgeons Make Miserable Exegetes? Negotiating the Sunni Tradition in the *ğihādī* Camps." *Die Welt des Islams*, vol. 53, no. 2 (2013): 192–237.

Fukuyama, Francis. "The End of History?" *The National Interest*, no. 16 (Summer 1989): 3–18.

Gabrieli, Francesco. "ʿAṣabiyya." *Encyclopaedia of Islam, Second Edition.* http://referenceworks.brillonline.com/entries/encyclopaedia-of-islam-2/asabiyya-SIM_0753?s.num=0&s.f.s2_parent=s.f.book.encyclopaedia-of-islam-2&s.q=A%E1%B9%A3abiyya (accessed 22 May 2016).

Galston, Miriam. "Realism and Idealism in Avicenna's Political Philosophy." *The Review of Politics*, vol. 41, no. 4 (October 1979): 561–77.

———. *Politics and Excellence: The Political Philosophy of Alfarabi.* Princeton, NJ: Princeton University Press, 1990.

Garden, Kenneth. *The First Islamic Reviver: Abu Hamid al-Ghazali and His Revival of the Religious Sciences.* New York: Oxford University Press, 2014.

Gerges, Fawaz A. *The Far Enemy: Why Jihad Went Global.* Cambridge, UK: Cambridge University Press, 2005.

———. *Journey of the Jihadist: Inside Muslim Militancy.* Orlando, FL: Harcourt, 2006.

Ghazali, Abu Hamid al-. *Ihyaʾ ʿUlum al-Din.* 5 vols. Beirut: Dar al-Fikr, 1994.

Ghunaimi, Mohammad Talaat al-. *The Muslim Conception of International Law and the Western Approach.* The Hague: Martinus Nijhoff, 1968.

Gibb, Hamilton A. R. "The Islamic Background of Ibn Khaldun's Political Theory." *Bulletin of the School of Oriental Studies*, vol. 7, no. 1 (1933): 23–31.

———. *Studies on the Civilization of Islam.* Boston: Beacon Press, 1962.

Gilpin, Robert. *War and Change in World Politics.* Cambridge, UK: Cambridge University Press, 1981.

Goitein, Shelomo Dov. *Studies in Islamic History and Institutions.* Leiden and Boston: E. J. Brill, 2010.

Goodman, Lenn Evan. "Ibn Khaldun and Thucydides." *Journal of the American Oriental Society*, vol. 92, no. 2 (April-June 1972): 250–70.

———. *Islamic Humanism.* New York: Oxford University Press, 2003.

———. *Avicenna.* Ithaca, NY: Cornell University Press, 2006.

Griffel, Frank. "The Relationship between Averroes and al-Ghazālī as It Presents Itself in Averroes' Early Writings, Especially in His Commentary on al-Ghazālī's *al-Mustaṣfā*." In *Medieval Philosophy and the Classical Tradition in Islam, Judaism, and Christianity*, edited by John Inglis, pp. 51–63. Richmond, UK: Routledge Curzon, 2002.

Grunebaum, Gustave E. von. *Islam: Essays in the Nature and Growth of a Cultural Tradition.* Westport, CT: Greenwood Press, 1981.

Gutas, Dimitri. "Classical Arabic Wisdom Literature: Nature and Scope." *Journal of the American Oriental Society*, vol. 101, no. 1 (January-March 1981): 49–86.

———. *Avicenna and the Aristotelian Tradition: Introduction to Reading Avicenna's Philosophical Works.* Leiden: E. J. Brill, 1988.

———. "Ibn Tufayl on Ibn Sina's Eastern Philosophy." *Oriens*, vol. 34 (1994): 222–41.

———. *Greek Thought, Arabic Culture: The Graeco-Arabic Translation Movement in Baghdad and Early ʿAbbasid Society (2nd–4th/8th–10th Centuries)*. London: Routledge, 1999.

———. "Avicenna's Eastern ("Oriental") Philosophy: Nature, Contents, Transmission." *Arabic Sciences and Philosophy*, vol. 10 (2000): 159–80.

———. "The Heritage of Avicenna: The Golden Age of Arabic Philosophy, 1000–ca. 1350." In *Avicenna and His Heritage: Acts of the International Colloquium, Leuven–Louvain-la-Neuve, September 8–September 11, 1999*, edited by Jules Janssens and Daniel De Smet, pp. 81–97. Leuven: Leuven University Press, 2002.

———. "The Study of Arabic Philosophy in the Twentieth Century: An Essay on the Historiography of Arabic Philosophy." *British Journal of Middle Eastern Studies*, vol. 29, no. 1 (May 2002): 5–25.

———. "The Meaning of *madanī* in al-Fārābī's 'Political' Philosophy." *Mélanges de l'Université Saint-Joseph*, vol. 57 (2004): 259–82.

———. "Intellect Without Limits: The Absence of Mysticism in Avicenna." In *Intellect et imagination dans la Philosophie Médiévale*, vol. 1, edited by Maria Cândida Pacheco and José F. Meirinhos, pp. 351–72. Turnhout: Brepols, 2006.

———. "Origins in Baghdad." In *The Cambridge History of Medieval Philosophy*, vol. 1, edited by Robert Pasnau, pp. 11–25. Cambridge, UK: Cambridge University Press, 2010.

———. "Avicenna's Philosophical Project." In *Interpreting Avicenna: Critical Essays*, edited by Peter Adamson, pp. 28–47. Cambridge, UK: Cambridge University Press, 2013.

Haldon, John. *Warfare, State and Society in the Byzantine World, 565–1204*. London: UCL Press, 1999.

Hallaq, Wael B. *A History of Islamic Legal Theories: An Introduction to Sunni Usul al-Fiqh*. Cambridge, UK: Cambridge University Press, 1997.

———. *The Impossible State: Islam, Politics, and Modernity's Predicament*. New York: Columbia University Press, 2013.

Hamada, Faruq. Introduction to *Kitab al-Siyar* by Abu Ishaq al-Fazari. Beirut: Muʾassasat al-Risala, 1987.

Hamid, Eltigani Abdulqadir. "Al-Mawardi's Theory of State: Some Ignored Dimensions." *American Journal of Islamic Social Sciences*, vol. 18, no. 4 (Fall 2001): 1–18.

Hamori, Andras. "Prudence, Virtue, and Self-Respect in Ibn al-Muqaffaʿ." In *Reflections on Reflections: Near Eastern Writers Reading Literature. Dedicated to Renata Jacobi*, edited by Angelika Neuwirth and Andreas Christian Islebe, pp. 161–79. Wiesbaden, Germany: Reichert Verlag, 2006.

Harri, ʿAbd al-Nabi al-. *Surat Ibn Rushd fi al-Fikr al-Maghribi al-Muʿasir*. Casablanca: Al-Markaz al-Thaqafi al-ʿArabi, 2015.

Hashmi, Sohail H. "Interpreting the Islamic Ethics of War and Peace." In *Islamic Political Ethics: Civil Society, Pluralism, and Conflict*, edited by Sohail H. Hashmi, pp. 194–216. Princeton, NJ: Princeton University Press, 2002.
Heck, Paul L. "*Jihad* Revisited." *Journal of Religious Ethics*, vol. 32, no. 1 (March 2004): 95–128.
Hourani, George F. "Averroes on Good and Evil." *Studia Islamica*, no. 16 (1962): 13–40.
Howe, Paul. "The Utopian Realism of E. H. Carr." *Review of International Studies*, vol. 20, no. 3 (July 1994): 277–97.
Hurvitz, Nimrod. "Miḥna as Self-Defense." *Studia Islamica*, no. 92 (2001): 93–111.
Huseini, Ishaq Musa. *The Life and Works of Ibn Qutayba*. Beirut: American Press, 1950.
Husri, Satiʿ al-. *Dirasat ʿan Muqaddimat Ibn Khaldun*. Cairo: Dar al-Maʿarif bi-Misr, 1953.
Hyman, Arthur. "Averroes' Theory of the Intellect and the Ancient Commentators." In *Averroes and the Aristotelian Tradition: Sources, Constitution, and Reception of the Philosophy of Ibn Rushd (1126–1198): Proceedings of the Fourth Symposium Averroicum, Cologne, 1996*, edited by Gerhard Endress and Jan A. Aertsen, pp. 188–98. Leiden: E. J. Brill, 1999.
Ibn ʿAbd Rabbih. *Al-ʿIqd al-Farid*. Vol. 1. Translated by Issa J. Boullata. Reading, UK: Garnet Publishing, 2006.
Ibn al-Mubarak, ʿAbdallah. *Kitab al-Jihad*. Beirut: Dar al-Nur, 1971.
Ibn al-Muqaffaʿ. "Al-Adab al-Kabir." In *Rasaʾil al-Bulaghaʾ*, edited by Muhammad Kurd ʿAli, pp. 40–106. Cairo: Matbaʿat Lajnat al-Taʾlif wa-l-Tarjama wa-l-Nashr, 1954.
———. "Risala fi al-Sahaba." In *Rasaʾil al-Bulaghaʾ*, edited by Muhammad Kurd ʿAli, pp. 117–34. Cairo: Matbaʿat Lajnat al-Taʾlif wa-l-Tarjama wa-l-Nashr, 1954.
Ibn al-Nadim. *Al-Fihrist*. Edited by Yusuf ʿAli Tawil. Beirut: Dar al-Kutub al-ʿIlmiyya, 1996.
Ibn Khaldun. *Al-Taʿrif bi-Ibn Khaldun wa-Rihlatuhu Gharban wa-Sharqan*. Edited by Muhammad ibn Tawit al-Tanji. Cairo: Matbaʿat Lajnat al-Taʾlif wa-l-Tarjama wa-l-Nashr, 1951.
———. *Kitab al-ʿIbar wa-Diwan al-Mubtadaʾ wa-l-Khabar fi Ayyam al-ʿArab wa-l-ʿAjam wa-l-Barbar wa-man ʿAsarahum min Dhawi al-Sultan al-Akbar*. 7 vols. Edited by Yusuf Asʿad Daghir. Beirut: Dar al-Kitab al-Lubnani, 1956–1961.
———. *Muqaddimat Ibn Khaldun (Prolégomènes d' Ebn-Khaldoun)*. 3 vols. Edited by Étienne Marc Quatremère. Paris: Academie des Inscriptions et Belles-Lettres, 1858.
———. *Al-Muqaddima*. 3 vols. Translated by Franz Rosenthal. New York: Pantheon Books, 1958.
———. *Muqaddimat Ibn Khaldun*. Beirut: Dar al-Qalam, 1981.
———. *Shifaʾ al-Saʾil li-Tahdhib al-Masaʾil*. Edited by Abu Yaʿrub al-Marzuqi. Tunis: Al-Dar al-ʿArabiyya li-l-Kitab, 1991.

Ibn Manjli, Muhammad. *Al-Adilla al-Rasmiyya fi al-Taʿabi al-Harbiyya*. Edited by Mahmud Sheet Khattab. Baghdad: Matbaʿat al-Majmaʿ al-ʿIlmi al-ʿIraqi, 1988.

Ibn Qutayba. "Kitab al-ʿArab, aw al-Radd ʿala al-Shuʿubiyya." In *Rasaʾil al-Bulaghaʾ*, edited by Muhammad Kurd ʿAli, pp. 344–77. Cairo: Matbaʿat Lajnat al-Taʾlif wa-l-Tarjama wa-l-Nashr, 1954.

———. *ʿUyun al-Akhbar*. Vol. 1. Cairo: Al-Muʾassasa al-Masriyya al-ʿAmma li-l-Taʾlif wa-l-Tarjama wa-l-Tibaʿa wa-l-Nashr, 1964.

———. *Taʾwil Mukhtalaf al-Hadith*. Edited by Muhammad Nafiʿ al-Mustafa. Beirut: Muʾassasat al-Risala, 2004.

Ibn Rushd. *Talkhis Kitab al-Nafs*. Edited by Ahmad Fuʾad al-Ahwani. Cairo: Maktabat al-Nahda al-Misriyya, 1950.

———. *Averroes' Commentary on Plato's Republic*. Translated by E. I. J. Rosenthal, Cambridge, UK: Cambridge University Press, 1956.

———. *Talkhis al-Khataba*. Edited by Muhammad Salim Salem. Cairo: Dar al-Tahrir li-l-Tabʿ wa-l-Nashr, 1967.

———. *Tahafut al-Tahafut*. Edited by Sulayman Dunya. 2 vols. Cairo: Dar al-Maʿarif bi-Misr, 1969–1971.

———. *Averroes on Plato's Republic*. Translated by Ralph Lerner. Ithaca, NY: Cornell University Press, 1974.

———. *The Epistle on the Possibility of Conjunction with the Active Intellect, by Ibn Rushd with the Commentary of Moses Narboni*, translated by Kalman P. Bland. New York: The Jewish Theological Seminary of America, 1982.

———. *Averroes' "De Substantia Orbis."* Translated by Arthur Hyman. Cambridge and Jerusalem: Medieval Academy Books, 1986.

———. *Ibn Rushd's Metaphysics: A Translation with Introduction of Ibn Rushd's Commentary on Aristotle's Metaphysics, Book Lām*. Translated and edited by Charles Genequand. Leiden: E. J. Brill, 1986.

———. *Averroes' Tahafut al-Tahafut*. Translated by Simon Van Den Bergh. Cambridge, UK: E. J. W. Gibb Memorial Trust, 1987.

———. *Al-Daruri fi Usul al-Fiqh (aw Mukhtasar al-Mustasfa)*. Edited by Jamal al-Din al-ʿAlawi. Beirut: Dar al-Gharb al-Islami, 1994.

———. *The Distinguished Jurist's Primer: Bidayat al-Mujtahid wa Nihayat al-Muqtasid*. 2 vols. Translated by Imran Ahsan Khan Nyazee. Reading, UK: Centre for Muslim Contribution to Civilization; Garnet Publishing, 1994–1996.

———. "An Unknown Treatise of Averroes Against the Avicennians on the First Cause." Translated by Carlos Steel and Guy Guldentops. *Recherches de Théologie et Philosophie Médiévales*, vol. 64, no. 1 (1997): 86–135.

———. *Faith and Reason in Islam: Averroes' Exposition of Religious Arguments*. Translated by Ibrahim Najjar. Oxford: Oneworld, 2001.

———. *Decisive Treatise and Epistle Dedicatory* [*Kitab Fasl al-Maqal wa-Taqrir ma bayn al-Shariʿa wa-l-Hikma min al-Ittisal & Al-Damima*]. Translated by Charles E. Butterworth. Provo, UT: Brigham Young University Press, 2001.

———. *Middle Commentary on Aristotle's De Anima*. Translated by Alfred L. Ivry. Provo, UT: Brigham Young University Press, 2002.

———. *Long Commentary on the De Anima of Aristotle*. Translated by Richard C. Taylor. New Haven, CT: Yale University Press, 2009.

———. *Averroes on Aristotle's "Metaphysics": An Annotated Translation of the So-Called "Epitome."* Translated and edited by Rüdiger Arnzen. Berlin: De Gruyter, 2010.

Ibn Sina. *Avicenna's De Anima: Being the Psychological Part of Kitab al-Shifaʾ*. Edited by Fazlur Rahman. London: Oxford University Press, 1960.

———. *Al-Isharat wa-l-Tanbihat li-Abi ʿAli ibn Sina, maʿ Sharh Nasir al-Din al-Tusi*. 4 vols. Edited by Sulayman Dunya. Cairo: Dar al-Maʿarif bi-Misr, 1960–1968.

———. *The* Metaphysica *of Avicenna (Ibn Sina): A Critical Translation-Commentary and Analysis of the Fundamental Arguments in Avicenna's* Metaphysica *in the* Danish Nama-i ʿAlaʾi *(The Book of Scientific Knowledge)*. Edited by Parviz Morewedge. New York: Columbia University Press, 1973.

———. *Ibn Sina and Mysticism:* Remarks and Admonitions: *Part Four*. Translated by Shams C. Inati. London and New York: Kegan Paul International, 1996.

———. *The Metaphysics of* The Healing: *A Parallel English-Arabic Text*. Translated by Michael E. Marmura. Provo, UT: Brigham Young University Press, 2005.

———. *On Governance*. Translated in Jon McGinnis and David C. Reisman, *Classical Arabic Philosophy: An Anthology of Sources*, pp. 224–37. Indianapolis, IN: Hackett Publishing Company, 2007.

———. *Ibn Sina's* Remarks and Admonitions: Physics and Metaphysics; *An Analysis and Annotated Translation*. Translated by Shams C. Inati. New York: Columbia University Press, 2014.

Ibn Taymiyya. *Fiqh al-Jihad li-Shaykh al-Islam al-Imam Ibn Taymiyya*. Edited by Zuhayr Shafiq al-Kabi. Beirut: Dar al-Fikr al-ʿArabi, 1992.

———. *Al-Siyasa al-Sharʿiyya fi Islah al-Raʿi wa-l-Raʿiyya*. Edited by ʿAbd al-Basit ibn Yusuf al-Gharib. Dammam: Dar al-Rawi, 2000.

ʿImara, Muhammad. *Muslimun Thuwwar*. Beirut: Al-Muʾassasa al-ʿArabiyya li-l-Dirasa wa-l-Nashr, 1974.

———. *Ibn Rushd bayn al-Gharb wa-l-Islam*. Cairo: Dar Nahdat Misr, 1997.

ʿIraqi, Muhammad ʿAtif al-. *Al-Manhaj al-Naqdi fi Falsafat Ibn Rushd*. Cairo: Dar al-Maʿarif, 1980.

———. "Ibn Rushd wa-Mustaqbal al-Thaqafa al-ʿArabiyya." In *Al-Ufuq al-Kawni li-Fikr Ibn Rushd: Aʿmal al-Nadwa al-Dawliyya bi-Munasabat Murur Thamaniyat Qurun ʿala Wafat Ibn Rushd, Marrakesh 12–15 Disimbir 1998*, pp. 355–75. Marrakesh: Al-Jamʿiyya al-Falsafiyya al-Maghribiyya, 2001.

———. *Ibn Rushd Faylasufan ʿArabiyyan bi-Ruh Gharbiyya*. Cairo: Al-Majlis al-Aʿla li-l-Thaqafa, 2002.

Irwin, Robert. *Ibn Khaldun: An Intellectual Biography*. Princeton, NJ: Princeton University Press, 2018.

"ISIS Video Calls on Turks to Conquer Istanbul, Refers to President Erdoğan as 'Satan.'" *Daily Sabah* newspaper, 18 August 2015. http://www.daily sabah.com/nation/2015/08/18/isis-video-calls-on-turks-to-conquer-istanbul-refers-to-president-erdogan-as-satan (accessed 23 May 2016).

Ivry, Alfred L. "Al-Kindi as Philosopher: The Aristotelian and Neoplatonic Dimensions." In *Islamic Philosophy and the Classical Tradition*, edited by S. M. Stern, Albert Hourani, and Vivian Brown, pp. 117–39. Columbia: University of South Carolina Press, 1972.

———. "Al-Kindi and the Muʿtazila: A Philosophical and Political Reevaluation." *Oriens*, vol. 25/26 (1976): 69–85.

———. "Averroës' Middle and Long Commentaries on the *De Anima*." *Arabic Sciences and Philosophy*, vol. 5, no. 1 (March 1995): 75–92.

———. "Averroes' Short Commentary on Aristotle's *De anima*." *Documenti e studi sulla tradizione filosofica medievale*, vol. 8 (1997): 511–49.

———. "Averroes' Three Commentaries on *De Anima*." In *Averroes and the Aristotelian Tradition: Sources, Constitution, and Reception of the Philosophy of Ibn Rushd (1126–1198): Proceedings of the Fourth Symposium Averroicum, Cologne, 1996*, edited by Gerhard Endress and Jan A. Aertsen, pp. 199–216. Leiden: E. J. Brill, 1999.

———. Introduction to *Middle Commentary on Aristotle's De Anima*, by Ibn Rushd. Provo, UT: Brigham Young University Press, 2002.

———. "Averroes' Understanding of the Philosopher's Role in Society." In *Islamic Thought in the Middle Ages: Studies in Text, Transmission and Translation, in Honour of Hans Daiber*, edited by Anna Akasoy and Wim Raven, pp. 113–22. Leiden, Boston: E. J. Brill, 2008.

Jabiri, Muhammad ʿAbid al-. *Fikr Ibn Khaldun: Al-ʿAṣabiyya wa-l-Dawla – Maʿalim Nazariyya Khalduniyya fi al-Tarikh al-Islami*. Casablanca: Dar al-Nashr al-Maghribiyya, 1979.

———. *Nahnu wa-l-Turath: Qiraʾat Muʿasira fi Turathina al-Falsafi*. Beirut: Dar al-Taliʿa li-l-Tibaʿa wa-l-Nashr, 1980.

———. *Ibn Rushd: Sira wa-Fikr. Dirasa wa-Nusus*. Beirut: Markaz Dirasat al-Wahda al-ʿArabiyya, 1998.

———. "Al-Intiqal ila al-Dimuqratiyya fi al-Maghrib: Asʾila wa-Afaq," Part 2. *Fikr wa-Naqd*, vol. 4, no. 32 (October 2000): 5–22.

Jackson, Sherman A. *Islamic Law and the State: The Constitutional Jurisprudence of Shihab al-Din al-Qarafi*. Leiden: E. J. Brill, 1996.

———. "Jihad and the Modern World." *Journal of Islamic Law and Culture*, vol. 7, no. 1 (Spring/Summer 2002): 1–26.

Jahiz. *Kitab al-Bukhalaʾ*. Edited by Taha al-Hajiri. Cairo: Dar al-Katib al-Misri, 1948.

———. *Rasaʾil al-Jahiz*. 4 vols. Edited by ʿAbd al-Salam Muhammad Harun. Cairo: Maktabat al-Khanji, 1964–1979.

———. *Kitab al-Bayan wa-l-Tabyin*. Vol. 3. Edited by ʿAbd al-Salam Muhammad Harun. Cairo: Maktabat al-Khanji, 1968.

———. *Kitab al-'Uthmaniyya*. Edited by 'Abd al-Salam Muhammad Harun. Beirut: Dar al-Jil, 1991.

———. *The Book of Misers: A Translation of al-Bukhala'*. Translated by R. B. Serjeant. Reading, UK: The Center for Muslim Contribution to Civilization, 1997.

Jervis, Robert. "Realism, Neoliberalism, and Cooperation: Understanding the Debate." *International Security*, vol. 24, no. 1 (Summer 1999): 42–63.

Johnson, James Turner. *The Holy War Idea in Western and Islamic Traditions*. University Park: The Pennsylvania State University Press, 1997.

Jolivet, Jean, and Roshdi Rashed. "Al-Kindī." *Encyclopaedia of Islam, Second Edition*. http://referenceworks.brillonline.com/entries/encyclopaedia-of-islam-2/al-kindi-SIM_4380?s.num=0&s.f.s2_parent=s.f.book.encyclopaedia-of-islam-2&s.q=Al-Kind%C4%AB (accessed 22 May 2016).

Jones, Linda G. "Portrait of Rashid al-Ghannoushi." *Middle East Report*, no. 153 (July–August 1988): 19–22.

Judd, Steven C. "Competitive Hagiography in Biographies of al-Awza'i and Sufyan al-Thawri." *Journal of the American Oriental Society*, vol. 122, no. 1 (January–March 2002): 25–37.

———. "Al-Awza'i and Sufyan al-Thawri: The Umayyad Madhhab?" In *The Islamic School of Law: Evolution, Devolution, and Progress*, edited by Peri Bearman, Rudolph Peters, and Frank E. Vogel, pp. 10–25, 208–11. Cambridge, MA: Harvard University Press, 2005.

Kaegi, Walter E. *Some Thoughts on Byzantine Military Strategy*. Brookline: Hellenic College Press, 1983.

Kafadar, Cemal. *Between Two Worlds: The Construction of the Ottoman State*. Berkeley: University of California Press, 1995.

Kalın, İbrahim. "Turkey and the Middle East: Ideology or Geo-Politics?" *Private View*, no. 13 (Autumn 2008): 26–35.

Kalpakian, Jack. "Ibn Khaldun's Influence on Current International Relations Theory." *The Journal of North African Studies*, vol. 13, no. 3 (September 2008): 363–76.

Karlıağa, Bekir. "The Horizon of Katip Çelebi's Thought." Muslim Heritage website. http://muslimheritage.com/article/horizon-katip-celebi%E2%80%99s-thought (accessed 22 May 2016).

Kassab, Elizabeth Suzanne. *Contemporary Arab Thought: Cultural Critique in Comparative Perspective*. New York: Columbia University Press, 2010.

Katip Çelebi. *The Balance of Truth*. Translated by G. L. Lewis. London: George Allen & Unwin, 1957.

———. *Düsturu'l-Amel li-Islahi'l-Halel (Bozuklukların Düzeltilmesinde Tutulacak Yollar)*. Translated into modern Turkish by Ali Can. Ankara: Başbakanlık Basınevi, 1982.

Kedourie, Elie. "The Nation-State in the Middle East." *The Jerusalem Journal of International Relations*, vol. 9, no. 3 (1987): 1–9.

Kelsay, John. *Arguing the Just War in Islam*. Cambridge, MA: Harvard University Press, 2007.
Kennedy, Hugh. *The Armies of the Caliphs: Military and Society in the Early Islamic State*. London: Routledge: 2001.
Kennedy-Day, Kiki. *Books of Definition in Islamic Philosophy: The Limits of Words*. New York: Routledge Curzon, 2003.
Keohane, Robert O. *After Hegemony: Cooperation and Discord in the World Political Economy*. Princeton, NJ: Princeton University Press, 1984.
———. "Theory of World Politics: Structural Realism and Beyond." In *Neorealism and Its Critics*, edited by Robert O. Keohane, pp. 158–203. New York: Columbia University Press, 1986.
Kepel, Gilles. *The Roots of Radical Islam*. Translated by Jon Rothschild. London: Saqi, 2005.
Khadduri, Majid. *The Islamic Conception of Justice*. Baltimore, MD: The Johns Hopkins University Press, 1984.
Khalidi, Tarif. *Arabic Historical Thought in the Classical Period*. Cambridge, UK: Cambridge University Press, 1994.
Kindi, Abu Yusuf al-. "Risala fi Alfaz Suqrat." In Majid Fakhry, *Dirasat fi al-Fikr al-ʿArabi*, pp. 43–46. Beirut: Dar al-Nahar li-l-Nashr, 1970.
———. *Al-Kindi's Metaphysics*. Translated by Alfred L. Ivry. Albany: State University of New York Press, 1974.
King, Charles. "The Benefits of Ethnic War: Understanding Eurasia's Unrecognized States." *World Politics*, vol. 53, no. 2 (2001): 524–52.
Kogan, Barry S. *Averroes and the Metaphysics of Causation*. Albany: State University of New York Press, 1985.
———. "Two Gentlemen of Cordova: Averroes and Maimonides on the Transcendence and Immanence of God." In *Adaptations and Innovations: Studies on the Interaction Between Jewish and Islamic Thought and Literature from the Early Middle Ages to the Late Twentieth Century, Dedicated to Professor Joel L. Kraemer*, edited by Y. Tzvi Langermann and Josef Stern, pp. 157–227. Paris-Louvain: Peeters, 2007.
Kolstø, Pål. "The Sustainability and Future of Unrecognized Quasi-States." *Journal of Peace Research*, vol. 43, no. 6 (2006): 723–40.
Kraemer, Joel L. "The Jihad of the Falasifa." *Jerusalem Studies in Arabic and Islam*, vol. 10 (1987): 288–324.
Kügelgen, Anke von. "A Call for Rationalism: 'Arab Averroists' in the Twentieth Century." *Alif*, no. 16 (1996): 97–132.
Lav, Daniel. *Radical Islam and the Revival of Medieval Theology*. New York: Cambridge University Press, 2012.
Leaman, Oliver. "Ibn Rushd on Happiness and Philosophy." *Studia Islamica*, no. 52 (1980): 167–81.
Lerner, Ralph. Introduction to *Averroes on Plato's Republic*, by Ibn Rushd. Ithaca, NY: Cornell University Press, 1974.

Lewis, Bernard. *The Emergence of Modern Turkey*. London: Oxford University Press, 1968.

Lowry, Joseph E. "The First Islamic Legal Theory: Ibn al-Muqaffaʿ on Interpretation, Authority, and the Structure of the Law." *Journal of the American Oriental Society*, vol. 128, no. 1 (January–March 2008): 25–40.

Lynch, Dov. *Engaging Eurasia's Separatist States: Unresolved Conflicts and De Facto States*. Washington, DC: USIP, 2004.

Mabruk, ʿAli. "Al-Inkisar al-Murawigh li-l-ʿAqlaniyya: Min Ibn Rushd ila Ibn Khaldun." *Alif*, no. 16 (1996): 89–115.

Mahdi, Muhsin. *Ibn Khaldun's Philosophy of History: A Study in the Philosophic Foundation of the Science of Culture*. Chicago: University of Chicago Press, 1964.

———. "Averroës on Divine Law and Human Wisdom." In *Ancients and Moderns: Essays on the Tradition of Political Philosophy in Honor of Leo Strauss*, edited by Joseph Cropsey, pp. 114–31. New York: Basic Books, 1964.

———. "Ibn Khaldun." In *A History of Muslim Philosophy*, vol. 2, edited by M. M. Sharif, pp. 888–904, 961–84. Wiesbaden: Otto Harrassowitz, 1966.

———. *Alfarabi and the Foundation of Islamic Political Philosophy*. Chicago: The University of Chicago Press, 2001.

Mahmassani, Sobhi. *Al-Qanun wa-l-ʿAlaqat al-Dawliyya fi al-Islam*. Beirut: Dar al-ʿIlm li-l-Malayeen, 1972.

———. *Fi Durub al-ʿAdala: Dirasat fi al-Shariʿa wa-l-Qanun wa-l-ʿAlaqat al-Dawliyya*. Beirut: Dar al-ʿIlm li-l-Malayeen, 1982.

Maqdisi, Abu Muhammad ʿAsim al-. *Al-Dimuqratiyya Din*. Minbar al-Tawhid wa-l-Jihad, n.d. http://www.ilmway.com/site/maqdis/index.html (accessed 21 May 2016).

———. "Husn al-Rifaqa fi Ajwibat Suʾalat Suwaqa." Minbar al-Tawhid wa-l-Jihad, 1995. http://www.ilmway.com/site/maqdis/index.html (accessed 21 May 2016).

———. *Mashruʿ al-Sharq al-Awsat al-Kabir*. Minbar al-Tawhid wa-l-Jihad, 2005. http://www.ilmway.com/site/maqdis/index.html (accessed 21 May 2016).

———. "Abu Muhammad al-Maqdisi: Al-Salafiyya al-Jihadiyya." Interview with Yasir Abu Hilala, *Al-Jazeera*, 10 July 2005. www.aljazeera.net/channel/archive/archive?ArchiveId=129776 (accessed 24 May 2016).

———. *Waqafat maʿ Thamarat al-Jihad: Bayn al Jahl fi al-Sharʿ wa-l-Jahl bi-l-Waqiʿ*. Minbar al-Tawhid wa-l-Jihad, 2007. http://www.ilmway.com/site/maqdis/index.html (accessed 21 May 2016).

———. "Hadha Baʿd ma ʿindi wa-Laisa Kullahu." Minbar al-Tawhid wa-l-Jihad, July 2014. http://www.ilmway.com/site/maqdis/MS_14487.html (accessed 21 May 2016).

———. "Limadha Lam Usammihim Hatta al-An Khawarij Raghm anna fihim Man Hum Aswaʾ min al-Khawarij." Minbar al-Tawhid wa-l-Jihad, June 2015. http://www.ilmway.com/site/maqdis/index.html (accessed 21 May 2016).

Margoliouth, D. S. "The Discussion Between Abu Bishr Matta and Abu Saʿid al-Sirafi on the Merits of Logic and Grammar." *The Journal of the Royal Asiatic Society of Great Britain and Ireland* (January 1905): 79–129.

Marlow, Louise. "Advice and Advice Literature." *Encyclopaedia of Islam, Third Edition.* http://referenceworks.brillonline.com/entries/encyclopaedia-of-islam-3/advice-and-advice-literature-COM_0026?s.num=0&s.f.s2_parent=s.f.book.encyclopaedia-of-islam-3&s.q=Advice+and+Advice+Literature (accessed 22 May 2016).

———. *Hierarchy and Egalitarianism in Islamic Thought.* Cambridge, UK: Cambridge University Press, 1997.

Masʿudi, Abu al-Hussein ʿAli al-. *Muruj al-Dhahab wa-Maʿadin al-Jawhar.* 4 vols. Edited by Yusuf Asʿad Daghir. Beirut: Dar al-Andalus li-l-Tibaʿa wa-l-Nashr, 1965–1966.

Maurice. *Maurice's Strategikon: Handbook of Byzantine Military Strategy.* Translated and edited by George T. Dennis. Philadelphia: University of Pennsylvania Press, 1984.

McCants, William, ed. *Militant Ideology Atlas: Executive Report.* West Point: Combating Terrorism Center, 2006. https://www.ctc.usma.edu//wp-content/uploads/2012/04/Atlas-ExecutiveReport.pdf (accessed 21 May 2016).

McGinnis, Jon. *Avicenna.* New York: Oxford University Press, 2010.

Melchert, Christopher. "Asceticism." *Encyclopaedia of Islam, Third Edition.* http://referenceworks.brillonline.com/entries/encyclopaedia-of-islam-3/asceticism-COM_0022?s.num=0&s.f.s2_parent=s.f.book.encyclopaedia-of-islam-3&s.q=Asceticism (accessed 22 May 2016).

Menn, Stephen. "Avicenna's Metaphysics." In *Interpreting Avicenna: Critical Essays,* edited by Peter Adamson, pp. 143–69. New York: Cambridge University Press, 2013.

Michot, Yahya. *Ibn Taymiyya: Muslims under Non-Muslim Rule.* Oxford: Interface Publications, 2006.

Misbahi, Muhammad al-. *Al-Wajh al-Akhar li-Hadathat Ibn Rushd.* Beirut: Dar al-Taliʿa, 1998.

———. "Bayna Nihayatayn: Nihayat al-ʿAql al-Rushdi wa-Nihayat al-ʿAql al-Hadathi." In *Al-Ufuq al-Kawni li-Fikr Ibn Rushd: Aʿmal al-Nadwa al-Dawliyya bi-Munasabat Murur Thamaniyat Qurun ʿala Wafat Ibn Rushd, Marrakesh 12–15 Disimbir 1998,* pp. 395–410. Marrakesh: Al-Jamʿiyya al-Falsafiyya al-Maghribiyya, 2001.

———. *Maʿ Ibn Rushd.* Casablanca: Dar Tobiqal, 2007.

Morgenthau, Hans J. *Scientific Man vs. Power Politics.* Chicago: The University of Chicago Press, 1946.

———. *Politics Among Nations: The Struggle for Power and Peace.* New York: Alfred A. Knopf, 1978.

Morris, James W. "The Philosopher-Prophet in Avicenna's Political Philosophy." In *The Political Aspects of Islamic Philosophy: Essays in Honor of Muhsin S.*

Mahdi, edited by Charles E. Butterworth, pp. 152–98. Cambridge, MA: Harvard Center for Middle Eastern Studies, 1992.

———. "An Arab Machiavelli? Rhetoric, Philosophy and Politics in Ibn Khaldun's Critique of Sufism." *Harvard Middle Eastern and Islamic Review*, vol. 8 (2009): 242–91.

Mottahedeh, Roy P. "The *Shuʿūbiyah* Controversy and the Social History of Early Islamic Iran." *International Journal of Middle East Studies*, vol. 7, no. 2 (April 1976): 161–82.

———. *Loyalty and Leadership in an Early Islamic Society*. Princeton, NJ: Princeton University Press, 1980.

Mottahedeh, Roy Parviz, and Ridwan al-Sayyid. "The Idea of Jihad in Islam before the Crusades." In *The Crusades from the Perspective of Byzantium and the Muslim World*, edited by Angeliki E. Laiou and Roy Parviz Mottahedeh, pp. 23–29. Washington, DC: Dumbarton Oaks Research Library and Collection, 2001.

Mourad, Suleiman Ali. *Early Islam Between Myth and History: Al-Hasan al-Basri (d. 110 H/728 CE) and the Formation of His Legacy in Classical Islamic Scholarship*. Leiden, Boston: Brill, 2006.

Mufti, Malik. "The Art of Jihad." *History of Political Thought*, vol. 28, no. 2 (Summer 2007): 189–207.

———. "Jihad as Statecraft: Ibn Khaldun on the Conduct of War and Empire." *History of Political Thought*, vol. 30, no. 3 (Autumn 2009): 385–410.

———. "The Many-Colored Cloak: Evolving Conceptions of Democracy in Islamic Political Thought." *American Journal of Islamic Social Sciences*, vol. 27, no. 2 (Spring 2010): 1–27.

———. "Democratizing Potential of the 'Arab Spring': Some Early Observations." *Government and Opposition*, vol. 50, no. 3 (July 2015): 394–419.

———. "Is Ibn Khaldun 'Obsessed' with the Supernatural?" *Journal of the American Oriental Society* (forthcoming, 2019).

Mukhtasar fi Siyasat al-Hurub. Edited by ʿArif Ahmad ʿAbd al-Ghani. Damascus: Dar Kinan, 1995.

Mukhtasar Siyasat al-Hurub li-l-Harthami Sahib al-Maʾmun. Edited by ʿAbd al-Raʾuf ʿAwn. Cairo: Al-Muʾassasa al-Misriyya al-ʿAmma li-l-Taʾlif wa-l-Tarjama wa-l-Tibaʿa wa-l-Nashr, 1964.

"Muntakhab min ʿAhd Azdashir bin Babak al-Malik: Fi al-Siyasa." In *Rasaʾil al-Bulaghaʾ*, edited by Muhammad Kurd ʿAli, pp. 382–84. Cairo: Matbaʿat Lajnat al-Taʾlif wa-l-Tarjama wa-l-Nashr, 1954.

Mzoughi, Mohamed. "Ibn Khaldun wa-l-Falsafa: Taqyim Naqdi." In *Studies on Ibn Khaldun*, edited by Massimo Campanini, pp. 145–79. Milan: Polimetrica, 2005.

Najjar, Fauzi M. "Ibn Rushd (Averroes) and the Egyptian Enlightenment Movement." *British Journal of Middle Eastern Studies*, vol. 31, no. 2 (November 2004): 195–213.

Nasr, Seyyed Hossein. *Three Muslim Sages: Avicenna, Suhrawardi, Ibn ʿArabi.* Cambridge, MA: Harvard University Press, 1964.

Nassar, ʿIsmat. *Al-Abʿad al-Tanwiriyya li-l-Falsafa al-Rushdiyya fi al-Fikr al-ʿArabi al-Hadith.* Al-Fayyum: Dar al-ʿIlm bi-l-Fayyum, 2000.

Nassar, Nasif. *Al-Fikr al-Waqiʿi ʿinda Ibn Khaldun: Tafsir Tahlili wa-Jadali li-Fikr Ibn Khaldun fi Bunyatihi wa-Maʿnah.* Beirut: Dar al-Taliʿa, 1981.

———. *Al-Isharat wa-l-Masalik: Min Iwan Ibn Rushd ila Rihab al-ʿIlmaniyya.* Beirut: Dar al-Taliʿa, 2011.

Nawawi, ʿAbd al-Khaliq al-. *Al-ʿAlaqat al-Dawliyya wa-l-Nuzum al-Qadaʾiyya fi al-Shariʿa al-Islamiyya.* Beirut: Dar al-Kitab al-ʿArabi, 1974.

Netton, Ian Richard. *Allah Transcendent: Studies in the Structure and Semiotics of Islamic Philosophy, Theology and Cosmology.* London: Routledge, 1989.

Nizam al-Mulk. *The Book of Government or Rules for Kings.* Translated by Hubert Darke. London: Routledge & Kegan, 1978.

Norris, H. T. "*Shuʿubiyyah* in Arabic Literature." In *ʿAbbasid Belles-Lettres*, edited by Julia Ashtiany, T. M. Johnstone, J. D. Latham, R. B. Serjeant, and G. Rex Smith, pp. 31–47. Cambridge, UK: Cambridge University Press, 1990.

Öcalan, Abdullah. "Öcalan'ın Nevruz Mesajı." CNNTürk.com news service, 21 March 2013. http://www.cnnturk.com/2013/guncel/03/21/ocalanin.nevruz.mesaji/701058.0/ (accessed 23 May 2016).

Onosander. *Strategikos.* In *Aeneas Tacticus, Asclepiodotus, Onosander,* translated by William A. Oldfather, pp. 368–527. Loeb Classical Library. London: William Heinemann, 1923.

Pangle, Thomas L., and Peter J. Ahrensdorf. *Justice Among Nations: On the Moral Basis of Power and Peace.* Lawrence: University of Kansas Press, 1999.

Parens, Joshua. *Metaphysics as Rhetoric: Alfarabi's Summary of Plato's "Laws."* Albany: State University of New York Press, 1995.

Pasha, Mustapha Kemal. "Ibn Khaldun and World Order." In *Innovation and Transformation in International Studies,* edited by Stephen Gill and James H. Mittelman, pp. 56–70. Cambridge, UK: Cambridge University Press, 1997.

Paul, Jürgen. *The State and the Military: The Samanid Case.* Bloomington: Indiana University Research Institute for Inner Asian Studies, 1994.

Pegg, Scott. *International Society and the De Facto State.* Brookfield: Ashgate, 1998.

Pekesen, Berna. "Expulsion and Emigration of the Muslims from the Balkans." *European History Online,* 7 March 2012. www.ieg-ego.eu/pekesenb-2011-en (accessed 22 May 2016).

Pellat, Charles. "Al-Djāḥiẓ." *Encyclopaedia of Islam, Second Edition.* http://referenceworks.brillonline.com/entries/encyclopaedia-of-islam-2/al-djahiz-SIM_1935?s.num=0&s.f.s2_parent=s.f.book.encyclopaedia-of-islam-2&s.q=Al-Dj%C4%81%E1%B8%A5i%E1%BA%93 (accessed 22 May 2016).

———. *The Life and Works of Jahiz: Translations of Selected Texts.* Translated by D. M. Hawke. Berkeley: University of California Press, 1969.

Peterman, Larry. "An Introduction to Dante's *De Monarchia*." *Interpretation*, vol. 3, nos. 2–3 (Winter 1973): 169–90.

Peters, Rudolph. *Islam and Colonialism: The Doctrine of Jihad in Modern History*. The Hague: Moulton Publishers, 1979.

Petersen, Erling Ladewig. *ʿAli and Muʿawiya in Early Arabic Tradition: Studies on the Genesis and Growth of Islamic Historical Writing until the End of the Ninth Century*. Copenhagen: Munksgaard, 1964.

Pew Global Attitudes Project. "Iraqi Vote Mirrors Desire for Democracy in the Muslim World." Pew Research Center, 3 February 2005. http://www.pewglobal.org/2005/02/03/iraqi-vote-mirrors-desire-for-democracy-in-muslim-world/ (accessed 21 May 2016).

———. "Global Opinion Trends 2002–2007: Sharp Decline in Support for Suicide Bombing in Muslim Countries." Pew Research Center, 24 July 2007. http://pewglobal.org/reports/pdf/257.pdf (accessed 21 May 2016).

———. "Pew Global Attitudes Project Spring 2011 Topline." Pew Research Center, 15 May 2011. http://www.pewglobal.org/2011/05/15/spring-2011-survey/ (accessed 23 May 2016).

Pines, Solomon. "The Societies Providing for the Bare Necessities of Life According to Ibn Khaldun and to the Philosophers." *Studia Islamica*, no. 34 (1971): 125–38.

Polk, William R. "Encounters with Ibn Khaldun." http://www.williampolk.com/assets/encounters-with-ibn-khaldun.pdf (accessed 22 May 2016).

Polyaenus. *Stratagems of War*. Translated and edited by Peter Krentz and Everett L. Wheeler. Chicago: Ares Publishers, 1994.

Pourshariati, Parvaneh. *Decline and Fall of the Sasanian Empire: The Sasanian-Parthian Confederacy and the Arab Conquest of Iran*. London & New York: I. B. Tauris, 2008.

Poushter, Jacob. "In Nations with Significant Muslim Populations, Much Disdain for ISIS." Pew Research Center *Fact Tank*, 17 November 2015. http://www.pewresearch.org/fact-tank/2015/11/17/in-nations-with-significant-muslim-populations-much-disdain-for-isis/ (accessed 23 May 2016).

Puig, Josep. "Materials on Averroes's Circle." *Journal of Near Eastern Studies*, vol. 51, no. 4 (October 1992): 241–60.

Qadi, Wadad al-. "The Earliest 'Nābita' and the Paradigmatic 'Nawābit.'" *Studia Islamica*, no. 78 (1993): 27–61.

———. "The Impact of the Qurʾan on the Epistolography of ʿAbd al-Hamid." In *Approaches to the Qurʾan*, edited by G. R. Hawting and Abdul-Kader A. Shareef, pp. 285–313. London: Routledge, 1993.

———. "The Religious Foundation of Late Umayyad Ideology and Practice." In *Saber religioso y poder politico en el Islam: actas del simposio internacional, Granada, 15–18 octubre 1991*, pp. 231–73. Madrid: Agencia Española de Cooperación Internacional, 1994.

Qaradawi, Yusuf. *Nahnu wa-l-Gharb: Asʾila Shaʾika wa-Ajwiba Hasima*. Cairo: Dar al-Tawziʿ wa-l-Nashr al-Islamiyya, 2006.

Qutb, Sayyid. *Maʿalim fi al-Tariq*. Beirut: Dar al-Shuruq, 1980.
Rabiʿ, Muhammad Mahmoud. *The Political Theory of Ibn Khaldun*. Leiden: E. J. Brill, 1967.
Rahman, Fazlur. *Prophecy in Islam: Philosophy and Orthodoxy*. London: George Allen & Unwin, 1958.
Rashed, Roshdi. "Al-Kindi's Commentary on Archimedes' 'The Measurement of the Circle.'" *Arabic Sciences and Philosophy*, vol. 3 (1993): 7–53.
Renatus, Flavius Vegetius. *Epitoma Rei Militaris*. Translated and edited by Leo F. Stelten. New York: Peter Lang, 1990.
Rida, Rashid. "Islam and the National Idea." In *Arab Nationalism: An Anthology*, edited by Sylvia G. Haim, pp. 75–77. Berkeley: University of California Press, 1962.
Rieff, Philip. *The Triumph of the Therapeutic: Uses of Faith after Freud*. New York: Harper Torchbooks, 1968.
Rosenthal, Erwin I. J. "Ibn Jaldun's Attitude to the Falasifa." *Al-Andalus*, vol. 20, no. 1 (1955): 75–85.
Rosenthal, Franz. *Ahmad b. at-Tayyib as-Sarakhsi*. New Haven: American Oriental Society, 1943.
——. Introduction to *Al-Muqaddima*, by Ibn Khaldun. New York: Pantheon Books, 1958.
Sabet, Amr G. E. "The Islamic Paradigm of Nations: Toward a Neo-Classical Approach." *Peace and Conflict Studies*, vol. 8, no. 2 (January 2001): 23–50.
Safi, Omid. *The Politics of Knowledge in Premodern Islam: Negotiating Ideology and Religious Inquiry*. Chapel Hill: The University of North Carolina Press, 2006.
Say, Seyfi. *İbn Haldûn'un Düşünce Sistemi ve Uluslararası İlişkiler Kuramı*. Istanbul: İlk Harf Yayınevi, 2011.
Scheuerman, William E. "Carl Schmitt and Hans Morgenthau: Realism and Beyond." In *Realism Reconsidered: The Legacy of Hans J. Morgenthau in International Relations*, edited by Michael C. Williams, pp. 62–92. Oxford: Oxford University Press, 2007.
Schmidt, Nathaniel. *Ibn Khaldun: Historian, Sociologist and Philosopher*. New York: Columbia University Press, 1930.
Shahbazi, Shapur. "Army: I. Pre-Islamic Iran." *Encyclopaedia Iranica*, edited by Ehsan Yarshater, pp. 489–99. New York: 1991.
Shaked, Shaul. "From Iran to Islam: Notes on Some Themes in Transmission." *Jerusalem Studies in Arabic and Islam*, vol. 4 (1984): 31–67.
Shaltut, Mahmud. *Al-Islam wa-l-ʿAlaqat al-Dawliyya (fi al-Silm wa-l-Harb)*. Cairo: Matbaʿat al-Azhar, 1951.
Shariʾati, Ali. *On the Sociology of Islam: Lectures by Ali Shariʾati*. Translated by Hamid Algar. Berkeley: Mizan Press, 1979.
Sharif, Maher al-. *Tatawwur Mafhum al-Jihad fi al-Fikr al-Islami*. Damascus: Al-Mada Publishing Company, 2008.

Shaybani, Muhammad al-. *The Islamic Law of Nations: Shaybani's Siyar*. Translated by Majid Khadduri. Baltimore, MD: Johns Hopkins Press, 1966.

Sizgorich, Thomas. *Violence and Belief in Late Antiquity: Militant Devotion in Christianity and Islam*. Philadelphia: University of Pennsylvania Press, 2009.

Sonn, Tamara. "Irregular Warfare and Terrorism in Islam: Asking the Right Questions." In *Cross, Crescent, and Sword: The Justification and Limitation of War in Western and Islamic Tradition*, edited by James Turner Johnson and John Kelsay, pp. 129–47. New York: Greenwood Press, 1990.

Soroush, Abdolkarim. "Livelihood and Virtue." *Kiyan*, vol. 5 (June-July 1995): 2–11. Translated by the Foreign Broadcast Information Service in FBIS-NES-95-241-S (15 December 1995): 19–31.

———. "Life and Virtue: The Relationship between Socioeconomic Development and Ethics." In *Reason, Freedom, and Democracy in Islam: Essential Writings of Abdolkarim Soroush*, translated and edited by Mahmoud Sadri and Ahmad Sadri, pp. 39–53. New York: Oxford University Press, 2000.

Speer, James P., II. "Hans Morgenthau and the World State." *World Politics*, vol. 20, no. 2 (January 1968): 207–27.

Stowasser, Barbara Freyer. *Religion and Political Development: Some Comparative Ideas of Ibn Khaldun and Machiavelli*. Washington, DC: Center for Contemporary Arab Studies–Georgetown University, 1983.

Strauss, Leo. *Persecution and the Art of Writing*. Chicago: The University of Chicago Press, 1988.

Syrier, Miya. "Ibn Khaldun and Islamic Mysticism." *Islamic Culture*, vol. 21, no. 3 (July 1947): 264–302.

Talbi, Mohamed. "Ibn Khaldūn." *Encyclopaedia of Islam, Second Edition*. http://referenceworks.brillonline.com/entries/encyclopaedia-of-islam-2/ibn-khaldun-COM_0330?s.num=0&s.f.s2_parent=s.f.book.encyclopaedia-of-islam-2&s.q=Ibn+Khaldun (accessed 21 May 2016).

Tarabishi, George. *Madhbahat al-Turath fi al-Thaqafa al-ʿArabiyya al-Muʿasira*. London: Dar al-Saqi, 1993.

———. *Wahdat al-ʿAql al-ʿArabi al-Islami: Naqd Naqd al-ʿAql al-ʿArabi*. Beirut: Dar al-Saqi, 2002.

Taylor, Richard C. "Remarks on Cogitatio in Averroes' *Commentarium Magnum in Aristotelis De Anima Libros*." In *Averroes and the Aristotelian Tradition: Sources, Constitution and Reception of the Philosophy of Ibn Rushd (1126–1198)*, edited by Jan A. Aertsen and Gerhard Endress, pp. 217–55. Leiden: E. J. Brill, 1999.

———. "The Agent Intellect as 'Form for Us' and Averroes' Critique of al-Fârâbi." *Proceedings of the Society for Medieval Logic and Metaphysics*, vol. 5 (2005): 18–32.

———. Introduction to *Long Commentary on the De Anima of Aristotle*, by Ibn Rushd. New Haven, CT: Yale University Press, 2009.

Telhami, Shibley, in conjunction with Zogby International. *2011 Annual Arab Public Opinion Survey*. October 2011. http://www.brookings.edu/research/reports/2011/11/21-arab-public-opinion-telhami (accessed 23 May 2016).

Tessler, Mark, and Eleanor Gao. "Gauging Arab Support for Democracy." *Journal of Democracy*, vol. 16, no. 3 (July 2005): 83–97.

Thomas, Lewis V. *A Study of Naima*. Edited by Norman Itzkowitz. New York: New York University Press, 1972.

Tor, Deborah. "Privatized Jihad and Public Order in the Pre-Seljuq Period: The Role of the Mutatawwiʿa." *Iranian Studies*, vol. 38, no. 4 (December 2005): 555–73.

Treatise on Strategy. In *Three Byzantine Military Treatises*, translated and edited by George T. Dennis, pp. 1–136. Washington, DC: Dumbarton Oaks Research Library and Collection, 1985.

Tunik, H. C. "Averroes *Quaestiones in Physica*." PhD dissertation, Radcliffe College, 1956.

Tyan, Emile. "Djihād." *Encyclopaedia of Islam, Second Edition*. http://referenceworks.brillonline.com/entries/encyclopaedia-of-islam-2/djihad-COM_0189?s.num=0&s.f.s2_parent=s.f.book.encyclopaedia-of-islam-2&s.q=Djih%C4%81d (accessed 22 May 2016).

ʿUlaybi, Farid al-. *Ruʾyat Ibn Rushd al-Siyasiyya*. Beirut: Markaz Dirasat al-Wahda al-ʿArabiyya, 2007.

Wagemakers, Joas. *A Quietist Jihadi: The Ideology and Influence of Abu Muhammad al-Maqdisi*. Cambridge, UK: Cambridge University Press, 2012.

Waltz, Kenneth N. *Theory of International Politics*. Boston: McGraw-Hill, 1979.

Walzer, Richard. *Greek Into Arabic: Essays on Islamic Philosophy*. Cambridge, MA: Harvard University Press, 1962.

———. "Aspects of Islamic Political Thought: Al-Farabi and Ibn Xaldun." *Oriens*, vol. 16 (31 December 1963): 40–60.

Wardi, ʿAli. *Mantiq Ibn Khaldun: Fi Dawʾ Hadaratihi wa-Shakhsiyyatihi*. London: Dar Kufan, 1994.

White, Hayden V. "Ibn Khaldun in World Philosophy of History." *Comparative Studies in Society and History*, vol. 2 (1959–1960): 110–25.

Wisnovsky, Robert. *Avicenna's Metaphysics in Context*. Ithaca, NY: Cornell University Press, 2003.

Wolfe, Alan. *The Transformation of American Religion: How We Actually Live Our Faith*. New York: Free Press, 2003.

Xenophon. *Cyropedia*. Translated by Walter Miller. Loeb Classical Library. Cambridge, MA: Harvard University Press, 1994.

———. *Memorabilia*. Translated by Amy L. Bonnette. Ithaca, NY: Cornell University Press, 1994.

Yavari, Neguin. "Mirrors for Princes or a Hall of Mirrors? Nizam al-Mulk's *Siyar al-Muluk* Reconsidered." *Al-Masaq*, vol. 20, no. 1 (March 2008): 47–69.

Yousefi, Najm al-Din. "Islam without Fuqahā': Ibn al-Muqaffaʿ and His Perso-Islamic Solution to the Caliphate's Crisis of Legitimacy (70–142 AH/690–760 CE)." *Iranian Studies*, vol. 50, no. 1 (2017): 9–44.

Zaman, Muhammad Qasim. *Religion and Politics under the Early ʿAbbasids: The Emergence of the Proto-Sunni Elite*. Leiden: E. J. Brill, 1997.

———. "The Caliphs, the 'Ulama', and the Law: Defining the Role and Function of the Caliph in the Early ʿAbbasid Period." In *The Formation of Islamic Law*, edited by Wael B. Hallaq, pp. 367–402. Aldershot, UK: Ashgate Variorum, 2004.

Zaqzuq, Mahmud Hamdi. "Mafhum al-Tanwir fi Fikr Ibn Rushd." In *Ibn Rushd wa-l-Tanwir*, edited by Mourad Wahba and Mona Abousenna, pp. 105–14. Cairo: Dar al-Thaqafa al-Jadida, 1997.

Zuhayli, Wahba al-. *Athar al-Harb fi al-Fiqh al-Islami: Dirasa Muqarina*. Damascus: Dar al-Fikr, 1962.

———. *Al-ʿAlaqat al-Dawliyya fi al-Islam: Muqarana bi-l-Qanun al-Dawli al-Hadith*. Beirut: Muʾassasat al-Risala, 1981.

———. "Islam and International Law." *International Review of the Red Cross*, vol. 87, no. 858 (June 2005): 269–83.

Index

'Abbas, Ihsan, 27–28, 33
'Abbasids, 6, 24, 25, 26, 28, 30, 32, 35, 53–54, 58, 99, 103, 134, 144n12
'Abd al-Hamid al-Katib, 32–34, 45, 48, 117, 118
'Abdallah ibn Marwan, 33
'Abd al-Rahman, Taha, 169n132
'Abd al-Wahid (caliph), 175n106
'Abduh, Muhammad, 133
Abkhazia, 127
Abou El Fadl, Khaled, 174n82
Abu Bakr, 8, 175n102
Abu Bishr Matta, 59
Abu Dharr, 27
Abu Hanifa, 84, 97, 144n6
Abu Ya'qub Yusuf (Almohad), 83
Abu Yusuf, 26, 144n6, 144n9
Abu Yusuf Ya'qub (Marinid), 175n106
Abu Zahra, Muhammad, 2–3, 7, 11, 144n9, 144n14
Active Intellect, 63–64, 66–67, 68, 86, 115–16, 135
Afghanistan, xiii, 16
Afwah al-Awdi, 32
Ahmad ibn Abi Du'ad, 36
Ahmad ibn Tulun, 99
Ahmed, Shahab, 132–33
AK Party, 20, 129–32
Al-Azmeh, Aziz, 143n26, 177n129
Albanians, 127

Al-Dawoody, Ahmed, 144n8
Alexander of Aphrodisias, 62
Alexander the Great, 30
Algeria, 18, 107, 125
'Ali ibn Abi Talib, 23, 28, 174n88, 176n126
Almohads, 83, 175n106
Alp Arslan, 54
Al-Qa'ida, 14, 15, 148n86
'Amiri, Abu al-Hasan, 176n126
Andalusia, 62, 70, 175n106
angels, 29, 63, 67
Ankara, 129
Antun, Farah, 133
Anushirwan, 40, 49, 55
Aquinas, Thomas, 18, 19
Arab uprisings (2010–2011), 18, 20, 126, 129
Arafat, W. N., 146n43
Ardashir, 30, 40, 153n46
aristocratic regime, 78
Aristotelianism, 59, 63, 65, 66, 68, 71, 87, 103, 114, 134
Aristotle, 30, 59, 62, 64, 66, 68, 69, 70, 73, 78, 84, 93, 102, 114, 115–16, 167n97, 170n21
arts, xviii, 27, 35, 36, 41, 42, 55, 74, 81, 90, 91, 97, 99, 100
'aṣabiyya, xxi, 90–96, 99, 108–13, 118, 119–20, 125, 138, 139, 170n14, 171n27, 171n36, 181n38; 'aṣabiyya

ʿaṣabiyya (continued)
  crisis, xxi, 125–29, 132, 133, 135, 136
asceticism, xviii, xx, 24, 28, 29, 30, 31, 34, 37, 38, 39, 55, 59, 60, 61, 90, 106, 107, 120, 151n23, 154n79, 159–60n9
al-Ashʿari, 25
Ashʿaris, 64, 67, 75, 76, 77, 83, 166n76
astronomy, 59
Atatürk, Mustafa Kemal, 126
Athenian Stranger, 91
Augustine, 18
authoritarian secular nationalism, 125–26, 131, 133
ʿAwn, ʿAbd al-Raʾuf, 158n136
Awzaʿi, 144n6, 144n9
Azariqa, 104

Bacon, Francis, 119
Badawi, ʿAbd al-Rahman, 170n21
Baghdad, 15, 24, 35, 36
Balkans-to-Bengal Complex, 133
Banu Hadhan, 109
Banu Qurayza, 9, 12, 146n43
Barmakids, 29, 175n106
Baroudi, Sami E., 146n38
Barrak, ʿAbd al-Malik, 11–13, 18
Basra, 27, 30, 35, 98
Baʿthism, 125, 133
Beirut, 129
Benard, Cheryl, xiii
Berbers, 71, 99, 100, 109
best regime, 57, 74, 78–82, 89; realizability of, 61, 82, 108, 117, 132
Bin Tamassak, Mustafa, 135–36
Bonner, Michael, 29
Bosnia, 16, 126, 127
Boston, 137
Bourguibism, 125
Britain, 19, 126
Bulaç, Ali, 130–31, 181n37

Bush, George W., xiii
Buti, Muhammad Saʿid, 11, 17–18, 147n56
Butterworth, Charles, 78, 80
Byzantines, 26, 28, 29, 35, 38–39, 51, 56, 58, 107; military literature, 45–46, 49–51, 53, 153–54n62

Cahit, Hüseyin, xviii
Cairo, 105
caliphate, 17, 20, 23–24, 25–27, 28–29, 30–31, 33, 35, 37, 40–41, 83, 106, 111–13, 128, 129, 175n102
Carr, E. H., 141n5
Caucasians, 103
causality, 62–63, 64, 66, 67–68, 69, 76, 86, 132, 136, 161n22
caution, 33, 45, 48, 50, 51, 53, 153–54n62
Central Asians, 103
certainty, xx, 24, 36, 56, 137; in Ibn Khaldun, 101, 103, 116, 117, 120; in Ibn Rushd, xx, 57, 69, 70, 74, 75, 83–84, 87, 116; in the *Mukhtasar Siyasat al-Hurub*, 25, 45, 46, 49, 52, 54
Chechnya, 16, 126–27
China, 39, 41
Christianity, 2, 3, 8–9, 18–19, 35, 38–39, 55–56, 58, 119
classical doctrine of jihad, 2–9, 144n6, 144n8, 144n9, 144n12, 145n29, 145n38, 147n71
Clausewitz, Carl von, 51, 101
codification (legal), 26, 31, 83, 153n46
commonalty (*ʿamma*), 32, 36–38, 43, 54–55, 73, 80, 85, 126, 132, 136
conjunction (*ittiṣāl*), 63–64, 115–16
consent, 63, 111, 113, 118, 124, 127
Constantinople, 54, 107
constructivism, 181n38
contingency (vs. necessity), 62–63, 65, 67, 76–77, 86, 160–61n19

Index

Cook, David, 120 (quoted)
Cooperson, Michael, 154n79
Cordoba, 85
courage, 39, 43, 48, 51, 53, 86, 98, 101, 102, 121
Cox, Robert W., 181n38
crafts, 38, 41, 90, 99
Crone, Particia, 24, 25–26, 79
Crusaders, 109
Cyprus, 107, 126

Damascus, 24, 29, 107, 129
Dante, 119
dār al-ʿahd (abode of treaty), 6, 7, 145n29
dār al-ḥarb (abode of war), 3, 11, 13, 144n12
dār al-Islām (abode of Islam), 3, 11, 129, 144n12
Davidson, Herbert, 68–69
Davutoğlu, Ahmet, 127, 129, 132
Dawwani, 25
democracy, xiv, xvii–xviii, xxi, 18, 124, 128, 134, 135–36, 138, 142n14, 179n18; as regime, 78, 81–82, 138; militant critiques, 16, 19–20, 129; and AK Party, 20, 129–32, 142n14
demonstration (burhān), 58, 59, 61, 69, 75, 78, 86, 101, 114, 116, 117, 136
dhimma, 5–6, 10, 12–13
dialectic (jadal), 36, 67, 75, 76, 78
dialectical theology (kalām), 36, 39, 59, 64, 67–68, 73, 75, 76, 77, 83, 86, 114–15, 116
Diogenes, 60
Diyarbakır, 127, 129
Donner, Fred M., 21, 150n2
Dumyati, Ibn al-Nahhas, 120

economics, 10, 90, 99, 126, 130, 135
egalitarianism, xvii, xx, 24, 31–32, 34–44, 56, 81, 135–36, 137–38, 155–56n106

Egypt, 2, 5, 10, 13, 18, 94, 99, 125, 127, 131, 134, 135, 136
elites (khāṣṣa), 32, 36–38, 39, 43–44, 80, 85, 125–26, 132, 133, 136
emanation, 61, 63, 64, 65–66, 67, 68, 134, 135, 161n21
envy, 36–37, 38, 39, 40, 43, 109, 110
Erdoğan, Recep Tayyip, 129, 131, 149n101
ethics, 7, 33–34, 36, 61, 74, 118, 146n51
ethnic diversity, 31, 32, 39–42, 43–44, 99
Europe, 15, 18, 24, 124, 125–26, 127, 134

Farabi, 57, 61, 65, 66, 67, 81, 82, 115–16, 130, 132, 167n97, 167n102, 170n14, 173n63, 176n109, 176n126; on the best regime, 78–80, 108; on vain philosophy, 73–74
Faraj, Muhammad, 13
Faruqi, Ismaʿil, 21 (quoted)
Fath ibn Khaqan, 36
Fazari, Abu Ishaq, 28–29
ferocity, 96, 98, 100–101, 137
Fierro, Maribel, 83
Fleischer, Cornell, 178n3
fortune, 52, 55, 103–04, 106, 125
founders, 79–80
France, 126
freedom, 78, 81, 131, 135, 136, 138; of religion, 3, 8, 10

Galston, Miriam, 74 (quoted), 167n102
Gaza, 129
Gezi Park, 131–32
Ghannoushi, Rashid, xix
Ghazali, 64–65, 67, 71, 76, 105, 130, 134, 136, 163n39, 172–73n63
Ghunaimi, Mohammad T., 2, 144n6, 144n12, 146n43
Gibb, Hamilton, 25–26, 89

Gilpin, Robert, xvi, xvii (quoted)
glory, 27, 29, 43, 46, 96
Greece, 34, 35, 38, 58; military, 33, 34, 44–45, 47, 48; philosophy, 39, 41, 57, 59, 85–86, 170n14; statecraft, 25, 30; *see also:* Byzantines
Griffel, Frank, 163n39
Gutas, Dimitri, 35, 59, 61, 71, 87, 143n25

Hadith (Prophetic Tradition), 3, 8–9, 10, 36, 75–76, 102, 114; scholars of (traditionists), 28, 35, 36–37, 39, 42–43, 83
Hakam al-Mustansir, 175n106
Haldon, John, 45
Halevi, Judah, 72–73
Hallaq, Wael B., 150n2, 174n82
Hanafi, 6–7, 29, 53
happiness, 42, 61, 70, 78, 81, 82, 86, 116, 117, 167n97
Harran, 58
Harthami, 44
Harun al-Rashid, 29
Hasan al-Basri, 27–28, 29, 151n23
Hashemites, 125
Hashmi, Sohail, 145n35, 145n38, 146n51
Hassan, Margaret, 15
hedonism, xvii, 86–87, 90, 138
Hinds, Martin, 25–26
Hijaz, 98, 114
Hobbes, Thomas, xx, 119
honor, 41, 44, 78, 82, 156n106
human nature, xiv–xv, 41, 92, 109, 110, 118, 120, 136, 137
humanitarian intervention, 3, 8, 10

Ibn ʿArabi, 133, 136
Ibn al-Ashʿath, 28
Ibn Bajja, 79, 115, 174n88, 176n126
Ibn Hajar, 123 (quoted), 178n2

Ibn Hanbal, 26, 144n9
Ibn Jamaʿa, 25
Ibn Khaldun, xxi, 25, 26, 61, 87, 89–121, 131, 138, 139, 170n14, 171n44, 172n53, 175n102, 175n106, 175–76n109, 176n115, 176n118, 178n152, 178n154; on human nature, 92, 109, 110, 117, 118, 120; and Ibn Rushd, 87, 90, 93, 108, 114, 115–17, 119, 170n21; modern reception, xviii, 7, 133, 135, 136, 137, 143n26, 176–77n129, 181n38; on mysticism and the occult, 100, 103, 104, 173n69; Ottoman reception, xxi, 123–24, 178n3, 178–79n4; on philosophy, 61, 89, 108, 111–12, 114–17, 120–21, 124, 175n97, 176n121, 176–77n129; on the state, 91, 95, 97, 99–100, 106–07, 109–10, 111, 124, 170n12, 172n56, 181n38; on Sufism, 104–05, 116, 173n74, 173n79; *see also:* ʿaṣabiyya, certainty, realism
Ibn Manjli, Muhammad, 54, 120
Ibn al-Mubarak, ʿAbdallah, 29, 34
Ibn al-Muhallab, Yazid, 28
Ibn al-Muqaffaʿ, xx, 24, 26, 27, 30–32, 34, 35, 42, 83, 90, 114, 118, 138
Ibn al-Nadim, 28, 44, 59
Ibn Qutayba, 28, 42–44, 157n132, 157–58n134
Ibn Rushd, xx, xxi, 57–58, 61–62, 64–87, 90, 93, 114, 115–16, 119, 143n25, 163n39, 164n51, 170n21; on the best regime, 57, 74, 78–82, 108, 182n43; on democracy, 81–82, 138; and Ibn Sina, 58, 64–74, 76–77, 78, 86–87, 116, 132–36; on jihad, 84–86, 117, 168n122, 168n127; on metaphysics, 64–70, 74, 86–87, 116, 135, 163n44, 163n45; modern reception, 132–37,

169n132; on Sufism, 76, 162n38; see also: certainty, realism
Ibn Sina, xx, 58, 61–62, 78, 115, 165n65, 176n126, 182n43; Eastern philosophy, 70–74, 164n54; on metaphysics, 62–70, 73, 76–77, 86–87, 115–16, 134, 161n20, 161n21, 161n22, 164n51; modern reception, 132–36
Ibn Taymiyya, 43, 105–06, 130, 144n6, 174n82, 174n83
Ibn Tufayl, 70–71
Ibn al-Zubayr, 28, 107
idealism, xiv–xv, xvii, 3, 61, 74, 117, 137, 145n35, 160n9, 181n38; apolitical ascetic, xv, xx, 24, 28–29, 30, 31, 34, 55, 106, 107, 120, 130, 131, 137, 151n23; militant, xv, xix, xx, 17, 20, 24, 34, 55, 120, 137, 138, 151n23; modernist, xix, 7, 21
Illuminationism, 71, 132, 160n17
'Imara, Muhammad, 134
India, 30, 41, 44, 50, 51, 59, 175–76n109
Indonesia, 128, 180n25
İnönü, İsmet, 125–26
international law, 1–2, 4, 7, 18–19
intuition, 36, 45, 64, 105, 132
Iphicrates, 50
Iran, xvii, 39, 42, 45, 125, 131, 135, 156n106; see also: Persia, Sasanians
Iraq, xiii, 14, 16, 17, 98, 114, 127, 128, 130
'Iraqi, Muhammad 'Atif, 134
irascibility (*ghaḍab*), 30, 97, 110, 118
Isfahan, 160n17
ISIS, 17, 127, 128, 129, 132, 180n25
Isma'ilis, 54, 104
Istanbul, 129, 131
Ivry, Alfred, 68, 163n45
Izmir, 129

Jabiri, Muhammad 'Abid, 133–34, 135, 136, 171n27

Jackson, Sherman A., 2, 7–8, 174n82
Ja'd ibn Dirham, 12
Jahiz, xx, 24, 35–42, 43, 44, 60, 90, 99, 154n79
Jaysh ibn Khumarawayh, 99
Jerusalem, 129
Jews, 2, 8–9, 93–94, 146n43
jizya, 5, 8, 84
Jordan, 127, 128, 180n25
Jum'a, 'Ali, 18, 149n101
jurisprudence (*fiqh*), 13, 28, 31, 35, 80, 81, 83, 85, 86, 114, 120–21, 144n8
justice, xvii, 13, 17, 19, 47, 70, 77, 78, 107–13, 114, 118–19, 130, 145n35
just war, xix, 2–12, 18–19, 20–21, 23, 84–85, 89, 107, 110–11, 112, 144n8, 147n56, 175–76n109

Kaegi, Walter, 45
Kalın, İbrahim, 129, 132
Kalpakian, Jack, 181n38
Katip Çelebi, xxi, 123–25, 138, 178–79n4
Kedourie, Elie, 150n2
Kemalism, 125, 131
Kennedy, Hugh, 49
Keohane, Robert, xvi
Khadduri, Majid, 89
Khalid ibn al-Walid, 97
Khalidi, Tarif, 176n126
Khalilzad, Zalmay, xiii
Kharijis, 17, 23–24, 28, 33, 34, 51, 55, 76, 104, 118, 120, 128, 151n23
Khumarawayh ibn Ahmad, 99
Khurasan, 29, 30, 42, 61
Kindi, 57, 58–62, 159n5, 159–60n9, 160n12, 160n17
kingship, 54, 78, 91, 92, 93, 95, 110, 158n141
Kitab al-'Ibar, 96, 102, 175n106, 175–76n109

Kogan, Barry, 69
Kosovo, 126
Kraemer, Joel, 89
Kufa, 30, 42, 98
Kurds, 51, 109, 127

Lebanon, 3, 121, 136
Lerner, Ralph, 168n127
liberalism, xvii–xviii, xix, xxi, 1, 16, 18, 20, 129, 131–32, 136–38, 142n21; in international relations, xvi–xvii, 1, 3, 7, 18–19, 137, 181n38
lineage, 41, 44, 49, 93, 94, 170n21
luxury, 98, 103, 113

Mabruk, ʿAli, 135–36
Machiavelli, xv, xvi, xvii, xx, 14, 19, 119
Maghrib, 94, 100, 109
Mahdi, Muhsin, 61, 83, 91, 95, 116, 165n67, 170n12, 175n97, 176n126
Mahmassani, Sobhi, 3, 6, 145n24, 145n35
Maimonides, 72
Malik, 26, 29, 84
Malikshah, 54
Mamluks, 54, 123
Maʾmun (caliph), 25, 26, 34–35, 36, 37, 38, 41, 44, 58, 60
Mansur (caliph), 30, 32, 97
Maqdisi, Abu Muhammad, 14–17, 18, 19–20, 128, 129, 137, 138, 148n75
Marwan ibn Muhammad, 32, 33
maṣlaḥa (public interest), 5, 6–7, 14, 15, 17, 83, 84, 105–06, 108, 110, 113
Masʿud (Ghaznavid sultan), 175n106
Masʿudi, 34, 44, 114, 170n14, 174n88
Material Intellect, 68–69, 163n44
mathematics, 45, 49, 59, 60, 159n5

Maurice, Emperor, 45–46, 49, 51, 53
mawālī, 24, 27, 29, 32, 39, 40
Mawardi, 25, 26, 114, 130, 170n14
Mazdak, 54–55
Mecca, 10, 23, 146n51
Medina, 9, 11, 146n43
Menn, Stephen, 62, 161n19
metaphysics, 58, 60, 61, 116, 135; *see also:* Ibn Rushd, Ibn Sina
miḥna (al-Maʾmun's), 25–26, 27, 35, 36, 39, 42, 43, 60
militants (Islamic), xxi, 20–21, 127, 128, 134, 136–38, 147n71; on democracy, 16, 18, 19–20, 128–29; on jihad, xix, 1, 9–17
miracles, 70, 72, 110, 139, 175n102
Misbahi, Muhammad, 136, 137
modernists (Islamic), xiii, 17, 18, 20–21, 134, 136–37, 144n5, 144n8; on democracy, 18, 19–20; on jihad, xix, 1–9, 10–13, 17–18, 21, 143n2, 145n29, 147n56, 151n26
Morgenthau, Hans, xv, xx
Morocco, 7, 133, 136
Morris, James, 87, 173n79
Mottahedeh, Roy P., 155–56n106
Mourad, Suleiman Ali, 151n23
Muʿawiya ibn Abi Sufyan, 23, 24, 28, 98, 106–07, 130, 172n47, 174n88, 175n102, 176n115, 176n126
Mughals, 25, 125
Muhallab ibn Abi Sufra, 173n65
Muhammad, Prophet, 9, 10–11, 12, 23, 27, 43, 47, 49, 59, 83, 84, 87, 90, 96, 97, 102, 107, 113, 146n43, 175n102; Traditions (*Hadith*), 8, 10, 43, 47, 75–76, 86, 102
Mukhtasar Siyasat al-Hurub, xx, 44–54, 59, 90, 101, 103, 156n117, 158n136, 158n139, 171n37, 173n71; *see also:* certainty
mulk, 54, 91, 92–93, 95, 107–08, 110, 118

Mulla Sadra, 132
music, 173n63; war music, 86, 102, 105
Muslim Brotherhood, 20, 129
Mutanabbi, 92
Muʿtasim (caliph), 58
Mutawakkil (caliph), 39
Muʿtazilis, 36, 43, 64, 75, 76, 83, 118, 160n12
mysticism, xx, 70–73, 86, 100, 104, 116, 132–33, 134, 143n25, 164n54, 166n76
Mzoughi, Mohamed, 176–77n129

Nabatean Agriculture, 72
Nagorno-Karabakh, 126
Naima, 123 (quoted), 178n3
Nassar, Nasif, 121, 136
Nasser, Jamal ʿAbd al-, 146n45
Nasserism, 125, 133
Nawawi, ʿAbd al-Khaliq, 7, 9, 11, 144n14, 146n39
Neo-Ottomanism, 129, 130
Neoplatonism, 58, 61, 63, 116, 134
Nizam al-Mulk, 54–55

Öcalan, Abdullah, 127–28
occult, 54, 72, 103, 104, 120, 134, 173n69
Orosius, 119
Osman, 123
Ottomans, xxi, 25, 123, 125, 126, 129, 130, 133, 178n3

Pahlavis, 125
Pakistan, 128, 137, 180n25
Palestine, 15, 127, 129
Pasha, Mustapha Kemal, 181n38
Paul, Jürgen, 150n2
peace, xvi–xvii, 9, 18, 27, 38–39, 46, 53, 85, 117, 157n126; with non-Muslims, 2–3, 6–8, 10–11, 21, 53–54, 107, 144n9, 146n39, 147n56;
permanent, xv, xix, 1, 6, 11, 19, 21, 45, 53, 121, 137, 145n35
Persia, 11, 27, 29, 32, 34, 35, 38, 39, 43, 49, 59, 86, 99, 127, 134, 182n43; military, 33, 34, 44–45, 47, 48, 51, 157n132, 158n134; statecraft, 25–26, 30, 35, 40, 41, 43, 78–82, 100, 123, 108–09, 111, 114; *see also:* Sasanians, Iran
Peters, Rudolph, 143n2, 144n5
PKK, 127
Plato, 78, 81, 85–86, 91, 115, 117, 135
Plotinus, 116
Polyaenus, 50
Pourshariati, Parvaneh, 153n46
prestige, 43, 93–94, 113, 170n21
prophecy, 43, 64, 66–67, 70, 75–76, 87, 93, 111, 139, 175n102

Qadi, Wadad, 33, 154n75
Qadisiyya, 29
Qajars, 125
Qaradawi, Yusuf, 5, 8, 145–46n38, 146n40
Qarafi, Shihab al-Din, 105, 174n82
qiyās (analogical reasoning), 31, 83, 114, 120–21
Qurʾan, 2, 3, 8–9, 10, 12, 28, 34, 36, 40, 69, 84, 85, 96, 123, 144n8, 145n35, 164n51
Quraysh, 9, 113, 175n102
Qutb, Sayyid, 10–11, 13, 14, 16, 20, 146n45

Rahman, Fazlur, 64
Ramallah, 129
realism, xiv–xvii, 141n5; Ibn Khaldun's, xxi, 110, 113–14, 117, 118, 121, 143n26, 178n154, 181n38; Ibn Rushd's, xx, 58, 74, 85, 87, 134; in Islam, xiv, xix–xxi, 1, 24–25, 32, 33, 45, 55–56, 61, 74, 90, 125, 130–31, 137–39, 145n35,

realism *(continued)*
  146n38; neorealism, xv–xvii,
  181n38
rectification (legal), 31, 79–85, 104,
  114, 120–21, 168n122
rhetoric, 50, 59, 67, 75, 78, 79, 89,
  114
Rhodes, 107
Rieff, Philip, xvii
Rosenthal, Erwin I. J., 167n97,
  177n129
Rosenthal, Franz, 169n6, 171n36,
  173n79

Sabeans, 58, 59, 72–73, 134, 182n43
Sabet, Amr G. E., 181n38
Sadat, Anwar, 13, 18
Salah al-Din, 109
Salim Abu al-ʿAlaʾ, 30, 32
Sarajevo, 129
Sasanians, 39, 40, 45, 53, 55, 56,
  153n46, 157n128
Say, Seyfi, 181n38
science, xv–xvi, xviii, 35, 55, 64,
  90–91, 97, 107, 120, 124, 135, 138;
  faith in, xvi, xx, 45–46, 56, 104,
  116, 138, 159–60n9; of history,
  18, 90; natural, 59, 60, 66, 76,
  159–60n9; philosophical, 66–67,
  71–72, 73–74, 76, 78, 87, 114, 120,
  124, 176n121; religious, 114–15,
  116, 124, 176n121; of war, 49,
  51–54, 101, 105, 120; Western, 125,
  133
seafaring, 90–91, 98, 107, 172n47
Seljuqs, 54, 55
Senegal, 128, 180n25
September 11 attacks, xiii, 14, 15,
  137
Shafiʿi, 6, 144n6, 144n9, 145n29
shākiriyya, 44, 156n120
Shaltut, Mahmud, 2, 3, 11,
  145–46n38, 146n43

Shariʾati, Ali, 135
Shatibi, Abu Ishaq, 105, 174n82
Shaybani, 29, 53, 144n6, 144n9
shuʿūbiyya, 39–42, 43, 99,
  155–56n106
sieges, 45–46, 48, 50, 53, 107,
  158n134
Sirafi, Abu Saʿid, 59
Sizgorich, Thomas, 151n23
slavery, 5, 12, 19, 145n24
Socrates, 57, 59, 60–61, 69
Somaliland, 127
Soroush, Abdolkarim, xvii–xviii, 20,
  132, 138, 142n15, 142n21
South Ossetia, 127
Spain, 118
state, defined, 23–24, 150n2; in Katip
  Çelebi, 123–25; *see also:* Ibn Khaldun
Stoics, 64
Strauss, Leo, 72–73, 74
Sufism, xiii, xviii, 54, 71, 76, 104–05,
  116, 124, 132–33, 134, 162n38,
  166n76, 173n74, 173n79, 177n136
Sufyan al-Thawri, 27, 28, 29, 30
Suhrawardi, 71, 133, 134
Sykes-Picot, 126, 127, 129
Syria, 3, 11, 17, 18, 50, 127, 128, 133

Talbi, Mohamed, xxi (quoted), 121
  (quoted)
Tanrıöver, Hamdullah Suphi,
  xviii–xix
taxation, 5, 31, 84
Taylor, Richard C., 163n44
Thrasymachus, 61
Thucydides, xv, xvi, xx
thumos, 170n14
Transoxiana, 107
Tulunids, 99
Tunisia, xix, 125, 135
Turkey, xviii–ix, 20, 125–26, 127–28,
  129–32, 142n14, 149n101, 179n16,
  179n17, 180n25, 181n37

Turks, 39, 40, 41, 51, 59, 99, 103, 109, 127
Turtushi, Abu Bakr, 101, 120, 172n59
Tusi, Nasir al-Din, 66, 161n22
tyranny, xvii, 3, 10, 12, 18, 82, 95–96, 106, 113, 120, 125, 136

'ulamā', xxi, 26–27, 28, 29, 31, 42, 53, 81, 82–83, 105–06, 113, 120–21, 130, 166n76, 178n152
'Umar ibn al-Khattab, 48, 97–98, 104, 107, 172n47
'Umar ibn 'Abd al-'Aziz, 118
Umayyads, 24, 25, 30, 32, 33, 53, 175n102, 175n106
United States of America, xiii, xv, xvi, xvii, xx, 2, 15, 16, 129, 130, 137
urbanism, 54, 90, 91, 96, 97–98, 99, 106–07, 126, 131
urbanity, 30, 42, 100

'Uthman (caliph), 23

vain philosophy, 74, 82, 117
Veysi, 178n3
Vitoria, Francisco de, 18–19

Wagemakers, Joas, 148n75
Waltz, Kenneth, xvi
weeds (*nābita, nawābit*), 36, 39–40, 42, 154n75
West Bank, 129
wijdān, 102, 105, 173n79
Wisnovsky, Robert, 161n19, 161n22

Yavari, Neguin, 158n141

Zaman, Muhammad Qasim, 26–27
Zaqzuq, Mahmud Hamdi, 134–35
Zarqawi, Abu Mus'ab, 14, 15–16
Zoroastrianism, 56, 153n46
Zuhayli, Wahba, 3, 4, 7, 9, 11, 144n9, 145n35, 146n43, 151n26

www.ingramcontent.com/pod-product-compliance
Ingram Content Group UK Ltd.
Pitfield, Milton Keynes, MK11 3LW, UK
UKHW041918140426
5217IPUK00013B/205